KING of the ROAD by Andrew Ritchie

·AN ILLUSTRATED HISTORY OF CYCLING·

WILDWOOD HOUSE LONDON

TEN SPEED PRESS BERKELEY

First published 1975
© 1975 by Andrew Ritchie
Wildwood House Ltd, 1 Wardour Street, London W1V 3HE
ISBN hardback 0 7045 0108 2
      paperback 0 7045 0109 0

Ten Speed Press, Box 4310, Berkeley, California 94704
ISBN hardback   0-913668-42-7
      paperback   0-913668-41-9

Designed by Richard Adams and George Snow

Acknowledgments are due to the following for permission to quote from works which they publish: Oxford University Press for *Lark Rise to Candleford* by Flora Thompson and Calder & Boyars for *Energy and Equity* by Ivan Illich.

Condition of sale
This book is sold subject to the condition that it shall not, by way of trade or otherwise, be lent, re-sold, hired out, or otherwise circulated without the publisher's prior consent, in any form of binding or cover other than that in which it is published and without a similar condition including this condition being imposed on the subsequent purchaser.

Computer typeset in Great Britain by Input Typesetting Ltd.,
4 Valentine Place, London SE1.

CONTENTS

List of Illustrations	**7**
Introduction	**11**
Chapter One Bicycle Archaeology	**15**
Chapter Two Amateur Mechanics	**29**
Chapter Three Velocipedomania	**53**
Chapter Four The Cult of the Ordinary	**79**
Chapter Five Tricycling and 'Sociable' Cycling	**101**
Chapter Six The Search for Safety	**121**
Chapter Seven Women's Liberation	**145**
Chapter Eight A Fact of Everyday Life	**165**
Notes	**182**
Books about Cycling	**185**
Index	**189**

In effecting those vast onward strides in every branch of mechanical industry which have been made in England since the dawning of the present century, it is easy to discover the fact that the impetus has been derived not alone from the action of the few, but the combined influence of the many. I venture to say that there is scarcely an invention of an engineering nature in practical use at present which owes its existence to any one man. It is possible that the idea of a contrivance for accomplishing a certain purpose may have been the production of one fertile brain, but in its realization, in the perfecting of details, in the surmounting of practical difficulties, in short in the working out of the scheme, ninety-nine times in the hundred, the inventor is indebted to others for suggestions, and even more tangible assistance... (An extract from a paper read by Mr Joseph Newton before the London Association of Foreman Engineers on November 4th, 1865, and published in *The English Mechanic,* December 1st, 1865.)

Acknowledgments

I have searched for material in the libraries of the British Museum, the Science Museum and various photo libraries in London, and everyone has been very helpful. The Coventry City Library let me read the books in the Bartleet Collection. Mr Warner, the Secretary of the Cyclists' Touring Club, gave me access to the Club's collection, and Mr Brian Young lent me books from his collection. *Cycling* let me look through their photographs; Mr Gerhold showed me the old photographs in the Olney Collection which he owns, and Mr Harrod lent me the glass plates from the same collection to make prints from.

Richard and Sally Greenhill showed me their beautiful photos of China, and Stuart Wilson at Oxford showed me his man-powered machines.

Tony Brock spent hours getting some of the pictures as good as they are, and copying older photographs, and taught me a lot about photographic processing. Richard Adams, who designed the book, took a lot of trouble explaining about layout and pasting-up.

Above all, Derek Roberts and Dave Twitchett of the Southern Veteran-Cycle Club gave me books, photos and information, and helped me to understand some of the complexities of the subject, and the necessity for historical accuracy. They also read the manuscript and made many valuable suggestions.

Any research in a subject as complicated as the history of cycling has mistakes and gaps. I'd be very glad to hear from anyone who has any criticisms of the book, or additional information, photographs, or documentary material, and will answer any letters. (Please write to me care of Wildwood House.)

LIST OF ILLUSTRATIONS

Racing bicyclist with his machine (Hulton Picture Library) 8
Johnson's Pedestrian Hobby-horse; from Ackermann's **Repository of Arts,** February 1819 (Science Museum) 14
Richard's velocipede; from 'Velox', **Velocipedes,** 1869 16
Céléripèdes, from J. F. Bottomley-Firth's **The Velocipede: Its Past, Present and Its Future,** 1869 (British Museum) 16
A rustic vélocifère-rider; from 'Velox', **Velocipedes,** 1869 17
Richard's velocipede; from Hooper's **Rational Recreations,** 1774 (British Museum) 17
Baron von Drais in the Luxembourg Gardens (Hulton Picture Library) 18
Draisienne-riders, about 1818 (Hulton Picture Library) 19
Johnson, the First Rider on the Pedestrian Hobby-horse; published by Ackermann, May 1st, 1819 (Science Museum) 20
'A new Irish Jaunting Car'; from J. F. Bottomley-Firth, op. cit. 20
Johnson's riding-school, about 1819 (Smithsonian Institute) 21
'The Hobby Horse Dealer', 1819 (British Museum) 22
'The Parson's Hobby', 1819 (British Museum) 23
'Anti-Dandy Infantry Triumphant', 1819 (British Museum) 23
'Hobbies, or Attitude is Everything', 1819 (British Museum) 24
'R-1 Hobby!!!', 1819 (British Museum) 25
'The Female Race', 1819 (British Museum) 26
'Drais' Improved Velocipede'; from **Mechanics' Magazine,** September 29th, 1832 (British Museum) 27
The 'Aellopodes'; from the **Mirror of Literature, Amusement and Instruction,** March 23rd, 1839 (British Museum) 28
Gompertz's velocipede; from 'Velox', **Velocipedes,** 1869 30
'Smythe's British Facilitator'; from the **Imperial Magazine,** 1819 (British Museum) 31
Pedomotive carriage; from **Mechanics' Magazine,** April 17th, 1824 (British Museum) 32
'Mr Merryweather's Pedomotive Carriage'; from **Mechanics' Magazine,** May 18th, 1839 (British Museum) 33
'Mr Baddeley's Manumotive Exercising Carriage'; from **Mechanics' Magazine,** April 13th, 1839 (British Museum) 33
'Mr Williams's Locomotive Carriage'; from **Mechanics' Magazine,** April 1843 (British Museum) 34
'Frank's Mechanical Horse'; from **Mechanics' Magazine,** November 13th, 1841 (British Museum) 34
McCall's copy of Macmillan's velocipede (Science Museum) 35
Willard Sawyer on one of his velocipedes (Dover Museum) 38
Willard Sawyer's catalogue, 1858 (Science Museum) 39
Oiling instructions (Dover Museum) 39
Sawyer's racing velocipede (Science Museum) 41
Henry Hodgson on his Sawyer velocipede (Derek Roberts) 42
'The Old Park Skiff Velocipede'; from **English Mechanic,** May 28th, 1869 (Science Museum) 43
J. Ward's velocipede (Science Museum) 44
Ladies' tricycle velocipede (Science Museum) 45
'The Latest Style of American Velocipede'; from **English Mechanic,** June 11th, 1869 (Science Museum) 46
'The Celeremane'; from **English Mechanic,** September 17th, 1869 (Science Museum) 47
Novel plan for a velocipede; from **English Mechanic,** May 7th, 1869 (Science Museum) 48
Hemming's Unicycle; from **Cyclist and Wheel World Annual,** 1882 49
The velocipedist in the country, French caricature (Edward Goldsmith) 51
Lady on a bicycle; from **Le Vélocipède Illustré,** November 14th, 1869 (British Museum) 51
Lewis Carroll's brother, taken by Lewis Carroll (From the Dodgson Family Collection in the Guildford Muniment Room) 52
Ernest Michaux; from H. O. Duncan's **The World on Wheels,** 1928 (British Museum) 54
Velocipedomania in Paris; from **Girl of the Period**

Miscellany, May 1869 (British Museum) 55
The riding-school of the Compagnie Parisienne; from L'Illustration, June 12th, 1869 (British Museum) 57
James Moore and André Castera with one of the Paris-Rouen race bicycles; from H. O. Duncan op. cit. 59
The American velocipede; from Harper's Weekly, December 19th, 1868 (British Museum) 60
MacDonald's Adjustable Bicycle; from English Mechanic, May 14th, 1869 (Science Museum) 61
Scene in a velocipede riding-school, New York City; from Harper's Weekly, February 13th, 1869 (British Museum) 63
'Hanlon's Improved Velocipede'; from English Mechanic, September 4th, 1868 (Science Museum) 64
'The Velocipede Mania'; from Harper's Weekly, May 1st, 1869 (British Museum) 65
'The "New World" Pleasure Velocipede'; from English Mechanic, June 25th, 1869 (Science Museum) 67
'Very Considerate'; from Will-o'-the-Wisp, May 8th, 1869 (British Museum) 68
Hedges' velocipede, 1869 (Science Museum) 69
Toll gate joke; from Fun, August 14th, 1869 (British Museum) 70
Rotten Row; from Fun, April 10th, 1869 (British Museum) 71
Cover of 'Velox', Velocipedes (Dave Twitchett) 72
The first English bicycle advertisement; from English Mechanic, February 19th, 1869 (Science Museum) 73
'The Bicycle Galop' (Dave Twitchett) 74
Prince Leopold on a boneshaker, 1870 (Hulton Picture Library) 75
The Phantom bicycle, 1870 (Author's collection) 76
A large-wheeled boneshaker (Hulton Picture Library) 77
W. H. J. Grout, bicycle-maker (Author's collection) 78
Two Ordinary-riders on the road, about 1885 (Olney Collection) 81
The 'Ariel' bicycle (Author's collection) 82
American bicycle pioneers (Smithsonian Institute) 83
More American pioneers (Smithsonian Institute) 84
Cover of Bicycle Riding: Its Theory and Practice, 1878 (Dave Twitchett) 85
Cover of Charles Spencer's The Modern Bicycle, 1876 (Dave Twitchett) 85
Bicycle race from Bath to London, 1874 (Hulton Picture Library) 86
City Bicycle School advertisement, 1878 (Author's collection) 86
Bicycle race in Paris; from L'Illustration, September 25th, 1875 (British Museum) 87
A 'meet' of cycling clubs, about 1886 (Hulton Picture Library) 88
Keen's bicycle works at Thames Ditton, about 1885 (Olney Collection) 88
The photographer photographed, about 1885 (Olney Collection) 91
A club in the Upper Richmond Road, about 1885 (Olney Collection) 91
Mounting an Ordinary, 1885 (Olney Collection) 92-3
Bicycle racing; from The Pleasures, Objects and Advantages of Cycling, 1887 94
Going downhill on an Ordinary; from The Pleasures, Objects and Advantages of Cycling, 1887 95
'The delightful freedom and comfort of balance'; from The Pleasures, Objects and Advantages of Cycling, 1887 96
The dangers of bicycling. Bown advertisement, 1882 (Author's collection) 97
Humber advertisement, about 1883 (Dave Twitchett) 97
Mr Pierce's monocycle; from Cyclist and Wheel World Annual, 1882 99
The Needham Safety Tricycle; from English Mechanic, August 13th, 1869 (Science Museum) 100
American boneshaker tricycle; from English Mechanic, June 4th 1869 (Science Museum) 101
James Starley on a Salvo, 1878 (Derek Roberts) 102
Jackson's velocipede; from English Mechanic, February 4th, 1870 (Science Museum) 102
Singer tricycle of 1879 (Science Museum) 103
Starley's Coventry Lever Tricycle (Science Museum) 105
An advertisement for Royal Salvo tricycles, 1884 (Author's collection) 106
'Chacun à son goût'; from Wheel World, 1885 (British Museum) 107
'En route to the lake'; from Wheel World, 1885 (British Museum) 107
An advertisement for W. H. J. Grout's Arrow tricycles; from Cyclist and Wheel World Annual, 1882 (Author's collection) 108
The New Inn, Ham Common, Surrey, early eighteen-eighties (Olney Collection) 109
Tandem tricycle, early eighteen-eighties (Olney Collection) 109
Sociable tricycle, early eighteen-eighties (Olney Collection) 110
Tricyclists, about 1882 (Frank Whitt) 111
Carrier tricycle, mid-eighteen-eighties (Author's collection) 112
'The wretch rides like the very demon'; from Wheel World, 1885 (British Museum) 112
Carrier tricycle, mid-eighteen-eighties (Author's collection) 113
Humber advertisement, about 1885 (Dave Twitchett) 113
The Premier Tandem Dwarf Safety Roadster, 1887 (Author's collection) 114
'Quadrant' tricycle advertisement, 1884 (Author's collection) 114
Rudge advertisement, 1889 (Author's collection) 115
The Premier Racer, about 1890 (Author's collection) 116
The 'Rover' tandem bicycle, 1885 (Author's collection) 117
F. T. Bidlake in 1896 (Author's collection) 117
Wayside tricycling photo, about 1887 (Olney Collection) 119
Rivals, the 'Rover' and the 'Kangaroo'; from Wheel World, November 1885 (British Museum) 120
Thomas Wiseman's 'safety' bicycle; from English Mechanic, July 16th, 1869 (Science Museum) 122
Shearing's bicycle; from English Mechanic, July 30th, 1869 (Science Museum) 122
Lawson's 'safety' bicycle of 1876 (Science Museum) 123

Shergold's 'safety' bicycle of 1878 (Science Museum) 124
Lawson's 'Bicyclette', patented in 1879 (Science Museum) 125
Singer 'Xtraordinary' bicycle, 1878 (Science Museum) 125
'Facile' 'safety' bicycle advertisement; from **Cyclist,** June 4th, 1884 (Dave Twitchett) 126
'Kangaroo' bicycle (Science Museum) 127
American 'Star' bicycle, patented in 1885 (Science Museum) 128
B.S.A. 'safety' bicycle, 1884 (Author's collection) 129
First Humber 'safety' bicycle, 1884 (Science Museum) 129
'Rover' 'safety' bicycle, second design, 1885 (Author's collection) 130
'Rover' 'safety' bicycle, first design, 1884 (Author's collection) 130
'A quiet spin'; from **Wheel World,** 1886 (British Museum) 131
The Biggar Cycling Club, Lanarkshire, about 1890 (Brian Lambie, Biggar Museum) 132
The Angel Inn, Ditton, Surrey, about 1892 (Author's collection) 133
Military cycling, the 26th Middlesex Regiment's bicycle corps in the early eighteen-nineties (Author's collection) 133
Members of the Catford Cycling Club, 1887; from **The First Fifty Years of the Catford Cycling Club,** 1939 134-5
Cover of **A Wheel to Moscow and Back,** by Robert L. Jefferson (Dave Twitchett) 136
Rabbits & Sons Cycling Club in the early eighteen-nineties (Cyclists' Touring Club) 137
St Helens Cycling Club, Lancashire; from **Cycle and Motor World,** January 20th, 1897 (Science Museum) 138
The Old Salisbury Arms, Barnet; from **Cycling World Illustrated,** June 17th, 1896 (Science Museum) 138
Record-breaking publicity; from **The Wheeler,** July 4th, 1894 (Dave Twitchett) 139
The Anchor, Ripley, in 1896 (Author's collection) 140
Cycling in Hyde Park, 1895 (Hulton Picture Library) 141
Cyclists and a C.T.C. danger-board; from the Badminton **Cycling,** 1896 (Author's collection) 142
Professional pacing triplet; from **Cycling World Illustrated,** April 8th, 1896 (Science Museum) 143
No stiffness here; Elliman's advertisement from the late eighteen-nineties (Hulton Picture Library) 144
A Pilentum, or Lady's Accelerator, 1819 (Science Museum) 146
French woman rider, late eighteen-sixties (Hulton Picture Library) 147
A women's race at Bordeaux; from **Le Monde Illustré,** November 21st, 1868 (British Museum) 148
'Les Baigneuses' — a caricature of about 1869 (Derek Roberts) 149
'Oh! then this is what we may expect to see this season'; from **Punch,** May 15th, 1869 (British Museum) 150
Samuel Thomas's side-saddle boneshaker, 1870 (Science Museum) 150
James Starley's ladies' 'Ariel', 1872 (Science Museum) 151
Wheeling on Riverside Drive, Manhattan, 1886 (Smithsonian Institute) 152
A 'Lady-front' tandem tricycle, 1887 (Author's collection) 153
'He stoops to conquer'; a drawing by George Moore from **Wheel World,** 1884, (Dave Twitchett) 153
Lady tricyclist; from **Wheel World,** 1885 (British Museum) 154
A very early ladies' bicycle, early eighteen-nineties (Derek Roberts) 155
Health suggestions; from **Lady Cyclist,** 1895 (Author's collection) 156
Miss Reynolds of Brighton, about 1893 (Derek Roberts) 157
Rational dress, mid-eighteen-nineties (Author's collection) 158
At the mercy of his wife; from the Badminton **Cycling,** 1896 (Author's collection) 159
Women's rights', from the Badminton **Cycling,** 1869 (Author's collection) 159
Rudge-Whitworth advertisement, 1895 (Author's collection) 160
Fashionable ladies in Battersea Park, 1895 (Hulton Picture Library) 161
High society, with bicycles, in Hyde Park, 1895 (Hulton Picture Library) 163
'Give me health and a day'; from **Cycling,** June 10th, 1920 (Author's collection) 164
Mlle Dutrieux, professional woman cyclist, late nineties (British Museum) 166
Bicycling belle, about 1895 (Hulton Picture Library) 166
Cycling on the Epping Road in April 1914 (Hulton Picture Library) 167
Cycling in a busy street, in the mid-eighteen-nineties (Olney Collection) 167
Cycling couple, about 1910 (Science Museum) 168
North London C.C. touring party; from **Cycle and Motor World,** June 9th, 1897 (Science Museum) 168
A bicycle outing of the I.L.P., 1906 (Hulton Picture Library) 168
Women's liberation in the nineteen-thirties (Hulton Picture Library) 169
Dursley Pedersen bicycle, 1902 (Science Museum) 170
Advertisement for bamboo bicycle, 1895 (Author's collection) 171
Edwardian tandem, with a trailer (Cyclists' Touring Club) 172
Triplet with sidecar, 1948 (Hulton Picture Library) 172
Tommy Simpson (John Carter) 173
Alf Engers (Mal Rees) 173
The inside of a small bicycle-manufacturer's workshop, taken in East Anglia some time in the eighteen-nineties (John Malseed) 174
Cycling in Wisley Woods, Surrey, 1915 175
Cycling on Sunday morning, 1911 (Hulton Picture Library) 175
Bicycle transportation in China in the nineteen-seventies (Richard and Sally Greenhill) 176
A bicycle bush ambulance designed by the Intermediate Technology Development Group 178
The Pedicar, 1973 (James Pickerell – Camera Press) 179
Bicycles versus a car (Francis Goodman) 180-81

INTRODUCTION

This book is a celebration of the amazing potential of human muscle-power, which is now, in the nineteen-seventies, relegated in the developed world to a very low place among acceptable sources of energy. Other societies and other cultures have always understood its value and exploited it to the best of their ability. And in our own society, the ingenious and functional use of his own muscle-power was looked upon until very recently as one of a man's most important assets. But it has been pushed into the shade by machinery.

This book is an attempt to show how and why bicycles and tricycles developed in the past, and how they affected people in their day-to-day lives. And I also make a few suggestions about how and why they ought to be used much more at the moment, and why they will almost certainly *have* to be used a lot more in the future.

One of the main themes running through the book is the search for an alternative, and the finding of it. Horseless carriage, velocipede, bicycle and tricycle inventors and devotees have always been aware of the peculiar fascination of man-powered machines. They shared a conviction that their pet machines were potentially more convenient, independent and economical than almost any other kind of transport, and they realized that it was possible to travel short distances more quickly and long distances more enjoyably on them. Man-powered machine users have always felt pleased at being able to travel at almost no cost, and indulged a good-humoured superiority over people trapped by the expense of horses and cars, and by the timetables of coaches and trains.

In the earliest days of hobby-horses and four-wheeled velocipedes, the people who designed them and used them invariably saw their machines as an alternative to the railways and stage-coaches which they very often could not afford to use, and which anyway did not come very close to the towns and villages where they lived. The lack of versatility of institutionalized transport systems, and their expense, meant that people stayed at home most of the time. But it encouraged some of them to experiment with their own private vehicles. Later on, the possibility of making a killing in a promising market provoked inventors and investors to a flurry of commercial activity. A demand was voiced, and suitable vehicles were produced.

By the early nineteen-hundreds it had become possible for almost everyone who wanted to own a bicycle or a tricycle, except perhaps the very poorest. There were hundreds of different designs and makes to choose from, which were developed in a twenty-year period of incredible industrial activity. A complete personalized, private, door-to-door short-range transport system was in operation. A major social revolution was taking place.

The railways had killed the coaching businesses and closed down England's excellent turnpike system, throwing coach-makers and drivers, innkeepers, blacksmiths, provisioners, roadmenders and servants out of work. By the end of the eighteen-seventies cyclists in England were venturing out into the countryside in increasing numbers, and bringing back custom to sleepy country inns. Record-breakers and tourists proved that it was possible to travel long distances on a bicycle, though terrible conditions were often encountered. By the eighteen-eighties they had taken over the country roads and they had them practically to themselves until well after the turn of the century. By the late eighteen-nineties, after the boom of about 1895–8, the bicycle was used on a massive scale.

Bicycle technology laid the foundations for the development of motorcycles, cars and aeroplanes. In the bicycle factories of the eighteen-eighties and 'nineties assembly-line mass-production was intensively applied to the building of a high-quality product. Gradually, motorized bicycles and noisy cars became competitors, filling the quiet cyclists' air with dust and fumes, and making them angry. Some of them were killed by cars on the roads, and a battle began which is still being fought. But it was not until after the Second World War that cyclists began to be quite literally driven off the roads, and even then they were there in vast numbers to fight back.

In the developed world, post-war affluence led to the car explosion of the nineteen-fifties and 'sixties, and the use of the bicycle slumped abysmally. In the United States, a mobility-hungry and automobile-obsessed nation scoffed at the bicycle as a child's toy. But in the Third World, and to poor workers everywhere, it went on being as useful and vital as ever.

Now, in the nineteen-seventies, the internal-combustion engine looks as if it might be on its last legs, life gets more and more expensive and complex, and the bicycle is booming all over the world, nowhere more spectacularly than in the United States. Its future looks very bright. For cyclists the old pride of independence is still alive and well as they contemplate the coming transportation revolution, and the possibility that, at long last, governments may recognize the value of the bicycle, and appreciate its sanity and humanity.

There are strong threads of both individualism and socialism running through the story of the bicycle.

It was designed and tested by strong-willed individualists, and the industry was established by ambitious, talented mechanics. Later, uncompromising speculators moved into the expanding bicycle trade, some of them becoming millionaires almost overnight. The people who worked in their factories were an industrial proletariat who worked long hours for little money, and were increasingly exploited as the industry grew larger, and more impersonal. Rival firms competed with each other on a scale that had not before been equalled in manufacturing for the consumer.

But, ironically, as it grew in popularity and availability, the bicycle broadened people's outlook. It enabled them to escape from their houses into the countryside and to discover people and places they had never known before. It encouraged women in particular to demonstrate that they too had the right to go out and enjoy themselves as men did, and thereby liberate themselves from the narrowing confines of the family and domestic chores. It allowed workers trapped all the week in unhealthy factories to get exercise and pleasure at week-ends. It saved time and money for millions. And all this for an outlay of a few pounds or francs or dollars.

At the same time, cyclists were initially criticized, ridiculed and even assaulted. Respectable citizens thought them vulgar, noisy and disruptive. Their common interests — legal protection, the improvement of neglected roads, the publishing of road maps and the exchange of ideas and information in newspapers and magazines — led to the growth of a spirit of community, and the formation of a huge network of clubs which sprang up in almost every town. A kind of freemasonry of the wheel was spoken about, the bare bones of which still exist. Cyclists still talk to each other when they meet on the road.

Hobby-horses, velocipedes, boneshakers, bicycles and tricycles are all *kind* machines. They do not enclose people, alienate them, kill them or maim them. They help them to keep healthy and strong. They do not consume vast amounts of productive energy, and they do not cause environmental disruption and destruction. Ivan Illich has said:

> Bicycles let people move with greater speed without taking up significant amounts of scarce space, energy or time. They can spend fewer hours on each mile and still travel more miles in a year. They can get the benefit of technological breakthroughs without putting undue claims on the schedules, energy or space of others. They become masters of their own movements without blocking those of their fellows. Their new tool creates only those demands which it can also satisfy. Every increase in motorized speed creates new demands on space and time. The use of the bicycle is self-limiting. It allows people to create a new relationship between their life-space and their life-time, between their territory and the pulse of their being, without destroying their inherited balance. The advantages of modern, self-powered traffic are obvious, and ignored.[1]

A bicycle respects the human body because it has been designed to harness the body's energy, and must be intimately related to it. It is ergonomically highly efficient. The development of the bicycle is a long love-affair between the human body and mechanical ingenuity, a long search for a more perfect relationship. Riding a good racing bike demands sensitivity, strength, relaxation, balance, determination, judgment and a feeling for the condition of the body under differing environmental conditions. You cannot fight against a bike; you must learn how to live with it and understand its strengths and weaknesses.

The full technical and social story of bicycles and tricycles is so huge that it is impossible to tell it all in a book of this size. Besides, there are still a great many facts to be established and there is a great deal of research to be done. The bicycle reaches into many corners of life; the literature of cycling is surprisingly extensive. I have read many books and magazines and looked at many pictures, but inevitably, there is a lot more that I did not read, and many more people I should have talked to. One cannot do everything at once.

The book concentrates on England and France, partly because bicycles were invented and were first used in those countries and partly because that is where it was written, but I have not ignored America. The outlines of the bicycle's development are nevertheless true whatever country is being talked about.

I was inspired to write the book by riding a bike in the bright sun and mountains of California, and coaxed it into existence in the damp grey light of a London winter.

ANDREW RITCHIE July 1974

14 King of the Road

CHAPTER 1
BICYCLE ARCHAEOLOGY

It is very hard to say when the bicycle's ancestors, the first man-powered mechanical vehicles, appeared. There are illustrations in old books of huge four-wheeled machines which were supposed to have been driven by men, and one such was engraved by Albrecht Dürer in 1520. But they were used either in various kinds of festivities or as war machines, and were regarded as skilful tricks rather than as practical or recreational vehicles. And we do not have very much information about how they were driven.

How far you go back into the archaeology of technology to find the roots of the bicycle depends really on your definition of a man-powered vehicle. You could call a Roman battering-ram on wheels one of the links in the chain, but its purpose was not travel, and it was not much good for getting to the next village.

My search among the bicycle's ancestors goes back to the more recent point where wheeled machines began to be made and talked about and ridden which were designed with the sole purpose of carrying a person by his own muscle-power, and which were continuously driven over considerable distances by the legs or arms (and sometimes both) of energetic travellers. It is at this point that the connection between these early experiments and a bicycle of today becomes clear enough to make it worthwhile studying, and the beginnings of a consistently developing pattern of ideas can be seen emerging.

Of course, there can be no absolute proof that there were no bicycles in Renaissance Florence, and the Florentines were certainly cunning enough to have made one if the idea had occurred to them. A newly discovered drawing by Leonardo da Vinci apparently shows a bicycle-like machine, which it will be fascinating to examine when a new edition of his work is published soon.

The real search begins in the middle of the seventeenth century, when there were a few coach-makers who designed and built mechanical carriages, although they were only used by the rich and

Denis Johnson's Pedestrian Hobby-horse: a somewhat idealized figure in an arcadian English landscape. In reality, the hobby-horse demanded more sweat than this, and the smart dress would have been quite impractical.

16 King of the Road

Dr Elie Richard's velocipede was a man-powered imitation of a small horse-drawn carriage. It was steered by the man sitting under the canopy, while the servant behind bounced inefficiently up and down on the cranked rear axle.

Céléripèdes of about 1800; drawn in 1869.

privileged and were as rare as kings' crowns.

The famous German inventor Jean Hautsch of Nuremberg (1595-1670) was one of them, and he sold a carriage to Prince Charles Gustav of Sweden for a princely sum. A traveller who visited Nuremberg in 1663 describes how he saw a Hautsch carriage which had been ordered by the King of Denmark, which

> goes backwards and forwards and turns round without the help of horses, and goes 3,000 paces in an hour, propelled only by handles which are turned by two children who are inside the carriage, making the back wheels go round, and a person inside holds a lever which turns the front of the carriage where the two little wheels which steer it are attached.[1]

Another inventor, a Parisian called Jean Théson, was honoured on 4th February, 1645 by the Queen of France, who awarded him a thirty-year pension for having invented 'a small four-wheeled carriage which has no horses, and is driven solely by two seated men'. And there are other accounts of similar carriages being built by French and German inventors, who seem to have been more interested at this stage than the English. But these early machines were not very versatile, and were as heavy and slow as giant tortoises. They seem to have been considered only as curiosities. Long journeys were not contemplated; the makers hung about the royal courts hoping for preferential treatment. The important thing is to take note of the fact that they existed, and that the idea of man-powered travel was in the air.

The end of the seventeenth century saw a further evolution. Mechanical carriages got lighter and smaller. The most important development even as early as this was the realization that some kind of pedalling action, using the strength of the legs and the weight of the body, was far more efficient than any arrangement of hand-cranks could ever be. The arms have never stood much chance in competition with the legs.

In 1696, a M. Ozanam published a book called *Recréations Mathématiques et Physiques*, in which he describes and illustrates a number of horseless carriages. Among them was one invented by Dr Elie Richard, of La Rochelle: 'A kind of carriage or chair has been seen in Paris for several years. A servant riding on the back drives it by pressing alternately with each leg on two pieces of wood which are connected to two little wheels hidden in the back, set between the two driving wheels.'[2] Quite efficient on the flat, Dr Richard's carriage was impossible uphill, and downhill was as dangerous as many later velocipedes; he and his assistant escaped serious injury when they crashed into a high wall after losing control on a steep hill.

Nearly a hundred years later, in 1774, almost the same carriage crops up again in William Hooper's *Rational Recreations*, a book which describes all kinds of ingenious inventions. Not much mechanical progress has been made in the century that has elapsed. Hooper praises the machine for affording 'a salutary recreation in a garden or a park', but he comes to the conclusion that 'in a rough or deep road it must be attended with more pain than pleasure'.[3] He also suggests that it would be much more efficient to have only one passenger, who would do the driving and the steering at the same time.

There are several other machines recorded in the eighteenth century, and in 1761 a Mr Ovenden emerges as mysteriously as his predecessors. Mr Ovenden built himself an undemocratic horseless carriage, which like Dr Richard's, was driven from the back by a servant while his 'gentleman' passenger sat in front and did the restful job of steering it. The *Universal Magazine* of 1761 makes it clear that this was not the first such machine in England, describing it as

> doubtless the best that has hitherto been invented, as it is capable of travelling with ease six miles an hour, and by a particular exertion of the footman, might travel nine or ten miles an hour on a good road, and even go up a considerable hill where there is a

sound bottom. But this carriage is in general only calculated for the exercise of gentlemen in parks or gardens for which it answers extremely well.

Whether the 'gentlemen' changed places with the footmen to get their exercise is not made at all clear. Perhaps, on occasion, two 'gentlemen' might even drive it together.

The *Public Advertiser* of November 20th, 1769 tells of another inventor, Mr Patence, who 'late on Friday night ran his newly invented Phaeton, which moves without Horses, from the Bottom of Salisbury Court, Fleet Street, to the End of Southampton Street in the Strand, and back, amidst a vast Croud of Spectators, who had received information of his Design'.[5]

Across the Channel, M. Blanchard, a Parisian inventor of mechanical carriages and balloons, publicized his creations energetically and appears to have had more confidence in their ability to excite and impress. On 24th July, 1779, reported the *Journal de Paris*, M. Blanchard demonstrated his mechanical carriage in the Place de Louis XV, watched by a huge crowd of people, among whom were several Academicians. He made several circuits of the square and then drove it to Versailles, doubtless in the hope of catching the eye of the nobility.[6]

In 1783 Blanchard went to America and twice gave demonstrations in Philadelphia, on 20th June and then on 26th August. Here too, he may have met a more famous inventor, Benjamin Franklin, for much later, in 1805, back in France, he writes boastingly from Montpellier:

> I am at present constructing one of my horseless carriages. I once drove Doctor Franklin from Paris to Versailles in 1 hour 45 minutes in a similar kind of machine, and I have had the honour of taking the Queen and certain Ladies for rides in the Park at Versailles, and I also drove my carriage up the ramp in front of the Opéra at Versailles which is impossible even for the best horses.[7]

The time that it takes him to go from Paris to Versailles is obviously very important to Blanchard, for that is the standard by which people will be able to judge the success of his trip. It was only when he and his successors could show that they could beat a coach or a horse that other people began to take them seriously and their efforts began to be rewarded with a little praise.

At the end of the eighteenth century, during the French Revolution, another branch of the ancestral family of the bicycle makes its first appearance. A child's toy becomes a fashionable fad and then develops into a serious experimental vehicle.

Children had for a long time ridden on hobby-horses, poles with a horse's head on one end and sometimes a wheel on the other. More lifelike toys were made; a whole horse's body was put on four wheels, so the children could ride on its back. In either 1790 or 1791 a well-known eccentric Parisian gentleman, a M. de Sivrac, appeared in the gardens of the Palais Royal mounted zanily on his own adult version of the toy. Sitting on the animal's back, hanging on to its mane, he surprised even the sophisticated *habitués* of the Palais Royal, and set a fashion.

Whether or not de Sivrac was the one and only original *vélocifère*-rider is not known, but it has come to be associated with his strange performance. These *vélocifères* or *célérifères*, as they were called, had the bodies of either horses or lions, and other elegant gentlemen followed de Sivrac into the Palais Royal, where they caught the eyes of the whores who sat in the shade of the trees or paraded under the arcades. For them, evidently, style was more important than speed, and the slightly indecent, irresponsible impression they left among more restrained people encouraged a bohemian image that was to stay with velocipede-riders for many years.

Other *vélocifère*-riders were more interested in winning cash than spending it, as the Parisian newspaper *Le Siècle* makes clear in 1802:

A rustic *vélocifère*-rider ten miles from home.

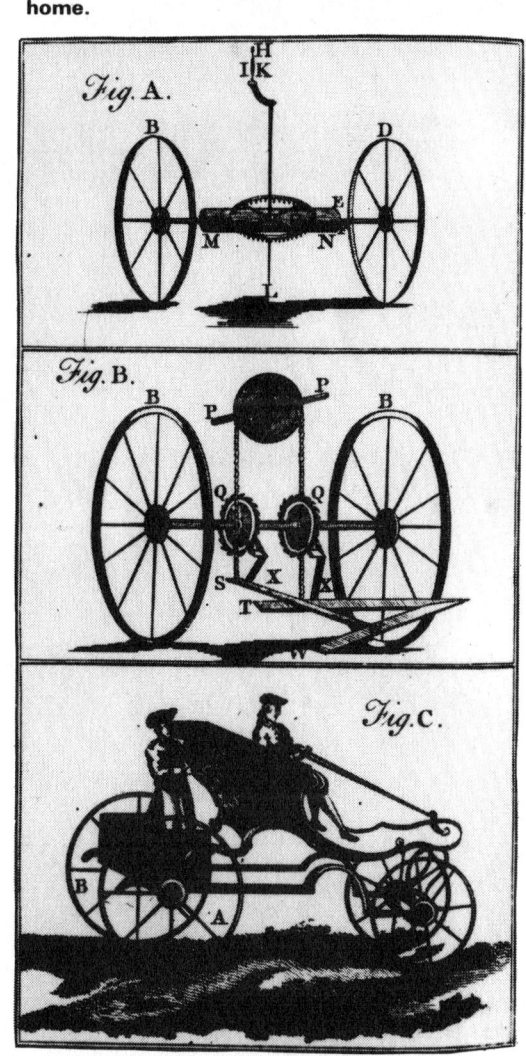

'A machine of this kind will afford a salutary recreation in a garden, or park, or on any plain ground, but in a rough or deep road must be attended with more pain than pleasure.' William Hooper's illustration of Richard's velocipede, 1774.

18 King of the Road

Baron von Drais in the Luxembourg Gardens in Paris, 1818. 'If the numerous spectators were not satisfied with the result, the curious were well repaid by the number of pretty women in their most brilliant dresses.'

The Hanover Pavilion was the rendezvous of the ardent lovers of this pastime. Outside a well-known café in the Boulevard des Italiens, a number of races were organized to the rue Royale and the Champs-Elysées. However, the most important races were offered to the young aristocrats of the time, and betting was lively.[8]

These were, I suppose, the first 'bicycle' races. It was hardly surprising that the *vélocifère*-riders were laughed at. It was a ridiculous sport. The machine could not be steered or stopped and the rider, grasping the horse's or lion's head, ended up either covered in mud and dust, or came a cropper on the uneven *pavé*. Later, the *vélocifère* was redesigned and seems then to have been called the *céléripède*. This was a much-improved version that could be steered and had big wheels, a more practical vehicle which was the father of the *Draisienne*.

The Baron Karl von Drais of Karlsruhe, a German agricultural engineer and inventor, and Master of the Woods and Forests of the Grand Duke of Baden, made yet another horseless carriage to be driven by two people together. But it was, he decided, too complicated, heavy and expensive. So he worked on an improved version of the *vélocifère*.

He eliminated the ridiculous animals' heads and bodies, lightened the wheels and framework and made the front wheel pivot on the frame so that it could be steered round corners. The result was that the child's toy was transformed into a serious road vehicle. The Baron took it very seriously.

Whether or not he himself gave his own name to his invention is not known for sure, but it became known as the *Draisienne* in Paris, and the name has stuck.

German newspapers of 1817 were the first to take notice of it, and the Baron was soon afterwards in Paris, where he was to gain considerable social notoriety. On February 17th, 1818 he was granted a five-year French patent through Louis-Joseph Dineur, a patent agent, of 47 Quai de l'Horloge, Paris, and in April he was ready to sell his invention to the world.

Taking it to the Luxembourg Gardens, he paraded in front of a large crowd who had paid for the privilege of seeing him. *La Petite Chronique de Paris* reported his act and was not very polite about him:

> This machine can never be of an real utility as it can only be used in a garden or park or a well-kept road ... The velocipede is only of use for children to play with ... If the numerous spectators were not satisfied with the result, the curious were well repaid by the number of pretty women in their most brilliant dresses ...[9]

Later in the month, the Baron tried again, and this time news of the event reached as far as Liverpool. The *Liverpool Mercury* was more sympathetic to him:

> An immense concourse of spectators assembled yesterday afternoon at Luxembourg to witness the experiments with the Draisiennes ... The crowd was so great that the experiments were but imperfectly made. The machine however, went quicker than a man at full speed and the riders did not appear fatigued ... The Draisiennes appear to be convenient for the country and for short journeys on good roads.[10]

His most convincing demonstration was given that summer in Germany on the open road, proving that his vehicle was not just a toy for pottering round the gardens of noblemen's houses:

> Baron von Drais travelled last summer, previously to his last improvement, from Mannheim to the Swiss relay-house, and back again, a distance of four hours journey by the posts, in one short hour, and he has lately, with the improved machine, ascended the steep hill from Gernsbach to Baden, which generally requires two hours, in about one hour, and convinced a number of scientific amateurs assembled on the occasion of the great swiftness of this very interesting species of carriage.[11]

Parisian satirists were quick to exploit Drais's pretensions. One caricature is entitled 'Velocipedraniavaporiana, a very astonishing contraption invented in Germany which could replace carriages, *vélocifères*, *célérifères* and *accélérifères* when all horses are dead'. Another makes fun of the inventor 'who has taken out a patent for a speedy vehicle which does 14 miles in 15 days'.

But people in general were interested in and amused by the *Draisienne*. The Baron sold quite a few. Posters were plastered over the walls of Paris advertising races, and at Monceaux they were hired out by the hour. At the end of 1818 *La Petite Chronique de Paris* was forced to eat its words:

> We shall see if this plot against our horses will meet with better success than the attempts in the Luxembourg Gardens. We must admit that at the moment it seems to be having some success, as throughout the summer of 1818, velocipedes were the main attraction at the fêtes at Sceaux, Belleville and Montfermeil on the outskirts of the city.[12]

A Frenchman with the memorable and unpronounceable name of

An engraving of *Draisienne*-riders, about 1818.

Johnson, the First Rider on the Pedestrian Hobby-horse; published by Ackermann, May 1st, 1819.

'A new Irish Jaunting Car': these hobby-horses, copied with a certain amount of poetic licence from earlier caricatures, were drawn from J. F. Bottomley-Firth's *The Velocipede*, published in 1869.

Joseph-Nicéphore Niepce has been claimed as a rival to the Baron von Drais. It was Niepce, it has been suggested, who was the real inventor of the *Draisienne*; Drais came along and improved it later. Lack of strong supporting evidence, however, leaves Niepce's case a weak one.

Niepce is best known as a pioneer of photography. A rich bourgeois of independent means from Burgundy, he experimented from 1813 onwards with primitive photographic plates, and in 1822 succeeded in producing what is now generally regarded as the first definitive photograph. When he died, some old velocipedes were found in his loft, and he was certainly interested in them and may early in his life have made some improvements in them, but it is French chauvinism more than anything else, it seems, which has been responsible for the attempt to oust the Baron from his niche in history.

Niepce's claims are based on three letters which his brother Claude wrote to him from London which were published in the *Moniteur de la Photographie* in 1868. The two brothers appear to have been contemplating setting up some kind of business deal, but there is nothing in the letters which can be read as proof that Nicéphore Niepce was either inventing or manufacturing velocipedes.

The first letter is dated Hammersmith, November 19th, 1818:
Dear brother, thank you very much for the information which was in your letter about the new machine, the velocipede, which you have already been using, and which I didn't know anything about at all. It seems to me, after what you've told me, that it could be really useful, in this country especially, where there are so many well maintained roads. It seems that with effort and a good road, you could go very fast, although you would look rather funny on it. I should think that someone with long legs like Isodore [Nicéphore's son] might go very fast, since you make use of your legs to propel you forward and the longer your paces, the better you would get along without tiring yourself. I'm anxious to hear some other details about this new machine; I'm sure if you wanted to, you could succeed in perfecting it.

The second is sent just over a month later, on December 21st:
I'm very pleased that you were interested to hear what I had to say to you about velocipedes, though you interpreted it in your own way. I agree with you that we could really make a big thing of it, and I agree too that this kind of exercise must be very enjoyable. Congratulations on the success which you've achieved — it's really surprising that the invention hasn't yet arrived in this country.

The last, and perhaps most interesting, is written by Claude on August 24th, 1819, by which time England's hobby-horse had been produced and was already making the sceptical laugh:
It seems that you're always out riding your velocipede from all the things you've written. I enjoy the exercise very much too, but I haven't wanted to get one, especially as I'm a foreigner here, because a machine like this encourages the English to scoff a little bit, and also because it would really be too much of an expense on top of my other commitments. I'd rather wait until a bit later.[13]

The hobby-horse which Claude says 'encourages the English to scoff a little bit' first appeared in London in the spring of 1819. Probably there had been one or two *Draisiennes* brought over from Germany before this but, if so, nobody had taken much notice. The entrepreneur who patented and propagated his own version of the *Draisienne* was Denis Johnson, a coach-maker, of 75 Long Acre, in Covent Garden, and he was also the first rider.

Johnson had wisely taken out a patent for his design on June 21st, 1818, very shortly after Drais had started putting his own invention on show in Paris. Perhaps Johnson arrived at his design independently, but it is much more likely that he read about what was happening in Paris, perhaps even went over there, and decided that he could make his own version of the *Draisienne* quite easily. His patent application describes his invention as

> a pedestrian curricle or velocipede, a machine for the purpose of diminishing the labour and fatigue of persons in walking, and enabling them at the same time to use greater speed ... The dimensions of this machine must depend upon the height and weight of the person who is to use it, as well as the materials of which it may be formed, consequently no specific directions can be given about them, further than saying that the lighter and more free from friction the whole can be made, and the larger the diameter of the wheels, the better and more expeditious the machine will be ...[14]

Johnson's hobby-horse or dandy-horse, as it was soon christened and has been called ever since, was more upright than the *Draisienne*, but in most other respects was an improvement on it, especially as useless weight was ruthlessly pared away. Its construction was more refined. The backbone, with its padded saddle dipping down in the middle, made it possible to use bigger wheels and thus to cover more ground with each stride, and the steering and the arm-rest made travelling more controlled and relaxing. The framework which supported the wheels was of light metal, while the wooden wheels themselves were bound with iron and were strong and light. It weighed about fifty pounds, which was not too much of a burden to ride along a flat road, but must have been very tiring to push up every hill.

How many Johnson made is impossible to say. That he did rather well for himself as a hobby-horse-manufacturer is given away by one journalist who added up the cost of the raw materials: 'The first cost of

Denis Johnson's riding-school in London, where well-bred young men learned to ride, in 1819.

22 King of the Road

the machine to the patentee is not more than forty or fifty shillings; but the price to the public is from eight to ten pounds'.[15] There was also a ladies' model available, and a de luxe model, hand-painted to order. As it gained in popularity, Johnson opened a riding-school in Soho where he taught people to ride, and rented out hobby-horses to those who could not afford to buy them.

It was initially greeted with a guarded optimism. 'It is a most simple, cheap and light machine,' says Ackermann's *Repository of Arts*,

> and is likely to become useful and generally employed in England, as well as in Germany and France. By medical men on the Continent it is esteemed a discovery of much importance, as it affords the best exercise for the benefit of health. The swiftness with which a person well-practised can travel is almost beyond belief; 8, 9, even 10 miles may be passed over within the hour, on good and level ground.[16]

In the crowded streets of London, this kind of speed was seen as a danger, and hobby-horses were forbidden. A stage-coach of the period could do about ten miles an hour on the open road, but such a speed was unthinkable in a city. 'The crowded state of the metropolis does not admit of this novel mode of exercise, and it has been put down by the Magistrates of Police.' The prohibition may not have been rigidly enforced, especially since so many of the riders were influential people, but, under Mr Taylor's Paving Act, at least one conviction was made.

Races were held and wagers made. One rider beat a four-horse coach to Brighton by half an hour, and another military gentleman made a bet to go from Bury St Edmunds to London by the side of a coach. In 1869, an old hobby-horser reminisced in the *English*

'The Hobby Horse Dealer', a caricature of 1819.

'The Parson's Hobby' and 'Anti-Dandy Infantry Triumphant' were two more scathing attacks on the hobby-horse.

Mechanic about how he used to race the four-horse Paddington stage-coach, varying this sport sometimes with a 'go-ahead competition with Medhurst's road locomotive', presumably a steam-driven coach.[17] Even the old hobby-horse, it is clear, could be a challenge to more conventional ways of travelling when it was ridden by the right person.

The speed of the fastest vehicle of the period, the coach, was the standard that had to be equalled or beaten, and when the coaches *were* beaten, that was no mean achievement:

> Clergymen used the new machine to visit their parishioners, and to travel between scattered congregations. Postmen with their letter bags sailing in the wind, rode the dandy-horse; young swells of the period used it, not only for exercise but for the purpose of making calls; and, strangest, if not saddest spectacle of all, old men who had hitherto borne blameless characters for sedateness and respectability were to be seen careering along on the dandy-horse. Sometimes the so-called horse was elegantly painted or gilt, and some apprehension appears to have prevailed that the natural breed of the genuine animal would suffer from

24 King of the Road

Caricaturists jokingly predicted that country roads would be swarming with aristocratic hobby-horses.

this daring competition.[18]

The hobby-horse was not entirely monopolized by the dandies. If it could beat a coach, it was obviously more than a plaything for the rich and foppish. It was a serious machine for narrowing the distances between two places.

The most passionate and committed advocate of the hobby-horse I have come across is a man who signs himself 'Speedy-Pace', who writes a long letter to the *Gentleman's Magazine* in 1819, pleading the cause of the velocipede, a new invention which, he says, 'though now simply considered as a toy, has a real philosophical character'.

'Speedy-Pace' himself also turns out to have a real philosophical character, appealing to his readers to devote 'dispassionate, serious attention' to the subject of the velocipede:

With our heavy population, velocipede carriages may hereafter be substituted, worked by two or more men, through which light weights may be speedily conveyed, and the quantity of arable soil now diverted to the keep of animals, as well as the employment of the poor, admit of considerable augmentation ...

That it must be of eminent use to Tradesmen, who go out to work at distances in the country, is self-evident.

To gentlemen's servants who go on messages and errands it must be equally useful. In short, in every profession, where locomotion and gain of time is requisite, it must be supremely beneficial.

But, under every view, circumstances may occur which will render the knowledge and practice of the velocipede an affair of high moment, especially in families which cannot afford to keep horses. In many parts of England, medical aid is not to be

'Oh dear! Oh dear! I cannot go on at this rate, my Constitution will not stand it; I find I shall never be able to push it home, cries the Prince Regent in this caricature. Two hobby-horses are imagined here, which look as though they might be pedalled with the hands, and yet the first practical pedal-driven velocipedes did not appear for almost another fifty years.

procured under a distance of nine miles. Now a new trade will be thus gained to the poor, if, in every village, a man be used to the practice of this ingenious piece of mechanism; and under circumstances [sic] numerous lives be saved in various sudden attacks of disease.[19]

The satirists did not share 'Speedy-Pace's' radical insight and optimism. For them of course the opportunities offered by this latest craze were irresistible. The sight of rich and influential young aristocrats hurtling along in the London parks and on the open road was the inspiration for a whole series of brilliantly sarcastic comments on the finances of the ruling class, the sexual habits of the monarchy and the death of the horse. Cruikshank and Gillray squeezed every satirical drop out of the hobby-horse that they could, and then turned to something new. If the hobby-horse was banned from the streets of London, at least people could have a good laugh when they went past the print-maker's shop, and ogle at the rich and famous riding in the parks.

The caricatures are almost all preoccupied with the famous and aristocratic, for there is not much money in making fun of the poor. Lords and ladies are shown at their most disreputable and ridiculous, scooting away on their 'hobbies' and frequently ending on their heads in the dust; a team of hobby-horse-riders replaces horses pulling a smart lady's carriage, the hunting set chases after its fox on hobby-horses, fat lords carry their mistresses across country in compromising positions, and the rich on their hobby-horses, people worth £10,000 a year, are mocked for making miserly economies. The hobby-horse dealer stands at his stable door assessing the merits of his new animals, and in a country village angry tradesmen smash up the hobby-horses which are taking their business away from them. It was a beautiful opportunity; no one can blame the caricaturists for seizing it with relish.

Ordinary people were not made fun of, but they rode hobby-horses too, when they could get hold of second-hand ones. As the rich tired of their craze and discarded their velocipedes, labourers and children could pick them up for a pound or two. The caricatures were profitable for a year or so, and then they were stale. But the hobby-horses did not disappear, and they were not killed by the mockery that was levelled at them in print. The hobby-horse disappeared from fashion, but it remained very much alive for the small number of mechanically minded people scattered around the country who were interested in man-powered vehicles.

The impracticalities of the hobby-horse were of course severe; it bounced, and shook, and rattled and broke. But these drawbacks were not seen as being insurmountable. Given ideal conditions, a smooth, flat road, a strong, young, uninhibited rider and a fine day, it was possible to get around town or from village to village much more quickly than on foot, which was its most important advantage. But the disadvantages of incredibly bad roads, bad weather and steep hills were very serious.

There also seems to have been a real danger of muscular strain from the extraordinary action of the legs that was required to keep it moving, and it was attacked in various medical journals. All in all, this ironical account of its vices and virtues, written in 1869, is not so very far from the truth:

> Where they were driven along smooth paths and roads, a considerable amount of healthy exercise might be got out of them; and if a man had no fear of sprains or ruptures; if he had unlimited credit with his tailor; and if he did not object to use as much shoe-leather as would suffice for the most extensive family, no doubt he could enjoy the dandy-horse. But the numerous evils attendant upon its use, and the comparatively small increase of speed which resulted from the increased expenditure of power, no doubt accelerated its downfall.[20]

Baron Drais took no notice of the ridicule of the French and English satirists. He continued to use his velocipede on the estates of his employer the Duke of Baden, and went on trying to improve it and sell it. His confidence is evidence enough that it really was practically useful to him. Other riders in France also put it to the test: 'A demonstration was given today, in the Place Royal, of the travelling machine called the Draisienne. A turner from Beaune, Monsieur Lagrange, came from that

Although it is very improbable that women did ever ride such hobby-horses, the idea of it was full of satirical possibilities.

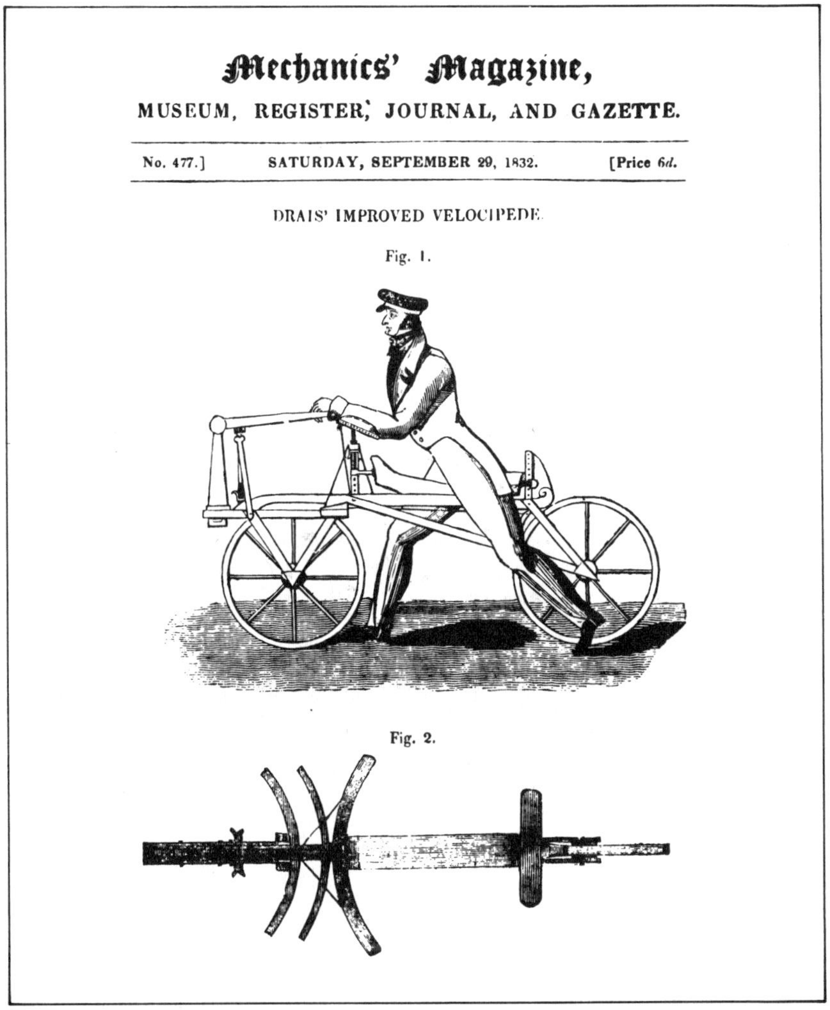

Mechanics' Magazine,
MUSEUM, REGISTER, JOURNAL, AND GAZETTE.

No. 477.]   SATURDAY, SEPTEMBER 29, 1832.   [Price 6d.

DRAIS' IMPROVED VELOCIPEDE.

Fig. 1.

Fig. 2.

'Drais' Improved Velocipede', 1832: 'Since his arrival in England, he has been endeavouring to revive the use of the velocipede.'

town to Dijon in two and a half hours. Today he once again showed how quick this steed is, which eats neither hay nor oats.'[21] Beaune is thirty-seven kilometres from Dijon, which would give M. Lagrange an average speed of about fifteen kilometres an hour, a good speed for a galloping horse.

In 1832, long after the English hobby-horse craze had slackened, the Baron was in England. The *Mechanics' Magazine* of September 29th, 1832 published a drawing of 'Drais' Improved Velocipede', and a rather haughty article about it: 'Since his arrival in England, he has been endeavouring to revive the use of the velocipede, and insists that it must have been owing to some error in the construction of our English edition of the invention, or great inexpertness in the management of it, that it fell into such general discredit among us.'[22] He insists on its viability. It will, he says, travel uphill as fast as someone can walk, on the level dry road it will go as fast as a galloping horse and downhill as fast as a horse at full speed.

But by this time, the English mechanics and engineers were absorbed by the new railways which had begun to be built, and the steam-carriages which spluttered heavily and noisily along the country roads. There was a huge growth of interest in the systematic application of power to drive many different kinds of machines and vehicles, and velocipede inventors looked to the principle of the steam-engine for their inspiration. No wonder that they took little notice of Baron Drais.

His machine had had its day; it did not apply new scientific principles. What was needed was a machine which would make use of new ideas and new technology, and which a man could ride without such fantastic and crippling exertion.

The Mirror
OF
LITERATURE, AMUSEMENT, AND INSTRUCTION.

No. 941.]   SATURDAY, MARCH 23, 1839.   [Price 2d.

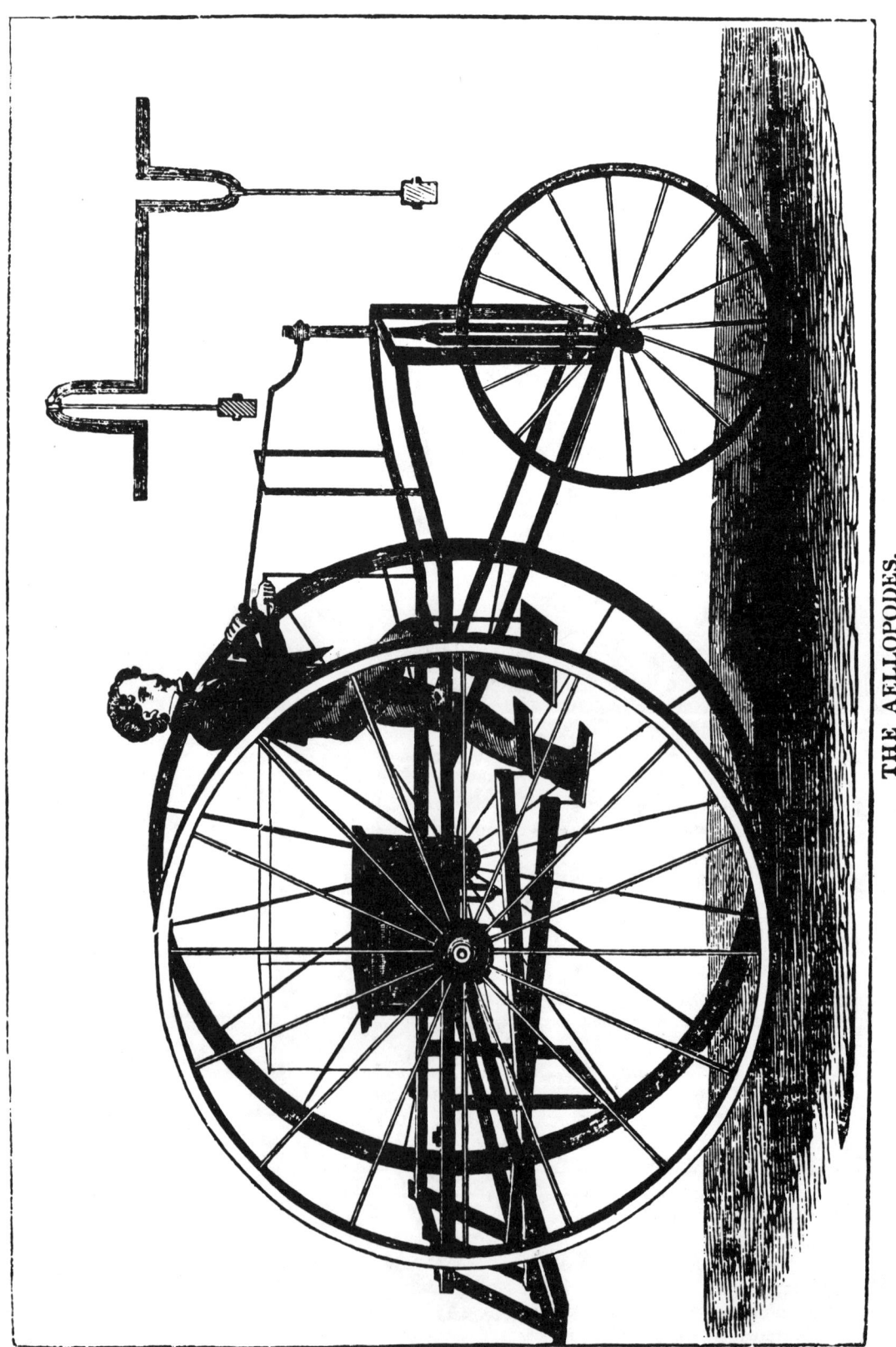

THE AELLOPODES.

CHAPTER 2
AMATEUR MECHANICS

After the hobby-horse

The hobby-horse won fashionable notoriety in England and France for a short period, but at the same time there were other less-publicized experiments going on. The one essential and undeniable drawback of the hobby-horse was of course that it could not be driven in the true sense of the word — it was not at all efficient in converting human energy into motion. It was relatively light, it had only two wheels, and it could be held upright through the force of its own momentum; that much was a discovery. But the strength of a man's legs was completely misapplied; they were jarred and jolted and sometimes damaged. Its critics could justifiably quip that the average person might just as well walk.

The idea of independent mobility, however, was widely discussed, and inventors were given new inspiration. Louis Gompertz made a clumsy but significant attempt in 1821 to fit the hobby-horse with a continuous drive by attaching a mechanism to the front wheel which was worked by the arms and supplemented the normal striding of the rider. But, in general, experimenters turned away from two-wheeled machines, and until the late eighteen-sixties there was very little interest at all in them — with one famous and unprecedented exception.

For reasons which are hard to understand, until the eighteen-sixties very little attention was paid to the development of the principle of the two-wheeled velocipede. Instead, inventors concentrated on three- and four-wheeled velocipedes, exploring the possibilities of the familiar cranked axle driven by treadles.

Very little has been written about man-powered travel between the eighteen-twenties and eighteen-sixties. The generally accepted idea of the period is a patronizing one, that there were a few crazy people messing about with clumsy and ungainly and, of course, impractical machines, but that the proper place for these freaks is in a museum of

Mr Revis' 'Aellopodes', illustrated in an artisan's weekly magazine in 1839, typifies better than almost any other machine the energetic and confident imagination of the early velocipede-builders. It was driven by two men, who made use of the whole weight of their bodies in turning the huge back wheels.

Louis Gompertz's velocipede, made in 1821, was the earliest attempt to fit a continuous mechanical drive to the hobby-horse.

Victorian follies.

But it is a mistake to patronize these early inventors, many of whom were talented and imaginative craftsmen. They were working within and trying to extend the possibilities of the contemporary level of technological development, and they were very much aware of the profound social implications that the invention of a successful velocipede would have. 'The proudest triumph of mechanics will be the completion of a machine or carriage for travelling without horses or other animals to drag it,' says the *Monthly Magazine* on November 1st, 1819, at the same time regretting 'the slow progress of the invention in question, which is pregnant with so many social, luxurious and economical advantages'. The article continues: 'That the perfection of such machines is important, is evident from the consideration, that horses consume half the product of the soil, and that our population are encouraged to emigrate, at a time when there are yet four acres to every soul, or ten times as much as necessary ...'[1]

Louis Gompertz had a similar lofty view of the importance of velocipedes. Mankind would reap great advantages from them, he argued, 'being converted from one of the slowest animals in creation, to one of great continued speed from his own salubrious exertions; the ridicule then with which they have been assailed by some of the idle and the caricaturists must yield to the advantages which they will bestow on the world'.[2]

That some of the early mechanics' creations were strange and looked incredible is undeniable, but they were serious experimental inventions, not whims. To their contemporaries they must have seemed quite astonishing.

The foundations of cycling were laid down during this period. The sudden and extraordinary success of the two-wheeled 'boneshaker' velocipede, when it was introduced commercially in the eighteen-sixties, was made possible by the amount of interest in velocipedes that had already been generated, and by the bases of a technology that had been gradually developed and extended.

This forty-five-year period, from about 1820 to 1865, was one of intense activity in every kind of technology. Ideas bounced backwards and forwards from one mechanical field to another, artisans' and mechanics' magazines and journals disseminated information, and a new kind of technical worker began to emerge. Capital investment made industrial expansion possible, and a collective fervour for invention, improvement and progress seized hold of many people.

In a time of expanding empire and spreading national affluence, the idea grew that every material object was perfectible, including the humble velocipede. The search for this perfection was pursued with great energy, and fame and fortune might await the happy discoverers of the perfect solution. For an inventor, theorizing was less important than practical experiments; a credible machine had to demonstrate its value.

'A velocipede on a new construction is said to be building by an artist of this city,' reported the *Hereford Journal* on May 12th, 1819. 'It is to have beams or bodies on springs, and four wheels, which will ensure its safety. It is to quarter on the roads like other carriages, and, with four impellers, it is supposed that it will proceed with astonishing rapidity, but its peculiar recommendation is to be, the conveyance of two ladies and two impellers, at the rate of six miles the hour.'[3]

In Liverpool, B. Smythe, a surveyor, invented a 'British Facilitator or Travelling Car', which is a remarkable machine with two speeds, the first on record, one for going uphill and one for going down. Mr Smythe admits that going up steep hills will be extremely difficult, but, he argues, 'for this additional labour, the traveller is amply repaid in his descent, since he may then sit at ease, doing nothing more than guiding the machine'.[4] Thus it seems to have had some kind of a freewheel as well as two speeds.

Dr Edmund Cartwright, the famous inventor of the power loom and a wool-combing machine, among many other machines, experimented with velocipedes in London and Dover until he died in 1823. He 'often astonished the natives of London by working and steering his carriage through the streets. He expressed himself with great confidence, that this child of his old age would come into general use, and that carriages of every kind would in a few years travel the roads without the aid of horses.'[5]

In Chard, Somerset, a carpenter from a village called Buckland demonstrated another carriage 'which will travel without horses', and in Plymouth a Mr Rogers, a coach-maker, built himself a velocipede, 'which in the course of the next ten days, will be launched to travel to London in three hours less time than the mail!'[6]

Inventors were not concentrated in London or the northern cities, but were scattered all over the country. The *Mechanics' Magazine*, which was started in 1823, was full of the inventive energy of the time. Its motto was 'Knowledge is Power' and the issue of April 17th, 1824 has a confident proclamation on its front page: 'Genius is the gift of the Deity; it discovers itself without effort, and is unknown to the possessor.' Underneath the quotation is a detailed drawing of a Pedomotive Carriage designed by 'K.W. a Welshman':

Gentlemen — Having seen in your valuable Magazine for February 21st, a plan of a carriage of slender construction which may be propelled on the road without the assistance of horses, I take the

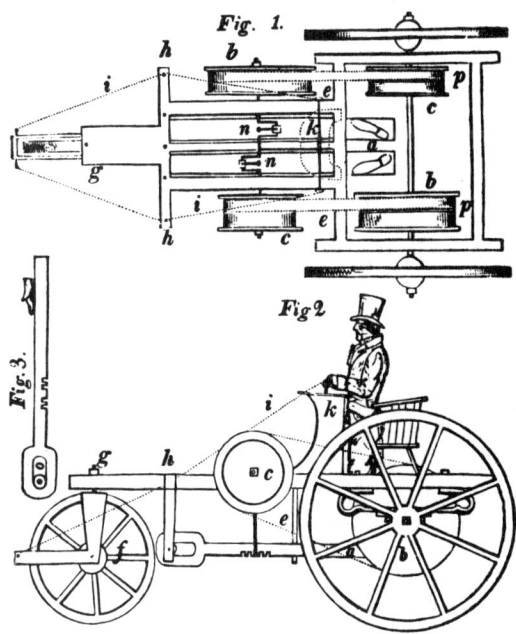

'The British Facilitator or Travelling Car. Invented by B. Smythe, Surveyor, Liverpool'. 1819.

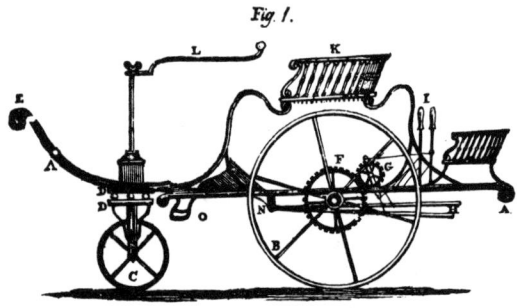

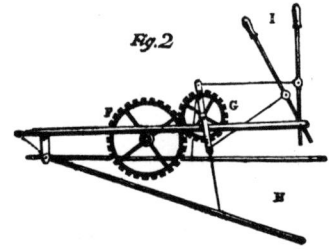

A pedomotive carriage of 1824, which carried three people and was driven from the back seat. It appears to have had a braking or a gearing system operated by the two levers.

liberty of sending you a plan of a machine for the same purpose, invented by myself, which was exhibited in Manchester, to the entire satisfaction of a number of clever mechanics; but not having been in the habit of acting as showman, I found my expenses greater than my receipts, and was forced to give it up for a bad job.

This machine went with ease eight miles an hour, carrying two persons besides the one who conducted it. [7]

Six years elapsed before another writer asks the magazine for details of K.W.'s machine:

The pedomotive carriage of your ingenious Welsh correspondent seems to require rather too much labour for it to become very general, but might become very useful if contrived for one person only. As I am anxious to have such a carriage constructed for my own use, perhaps you would be kind enough to procure K.W.'s address for me. [8]

This inventor was optimistic enough, but the Editor of the *Mechanics' Magazine*, surprisingly, expresses his distrust of such mechanical contrivances in no uncertain terms:

Going for a short distance at the rate of 8 miles an hour is a very different thing from travelling for a continuance at the same speed. We do hold it to be impossible for an individual to travel faster in the long run, in a machine propelled by his own personal strength, than he would do by employing his limbs in the usual and natural way. Man is a locomotive machine of Nature's own making, and not to be improved by the addition of any cranks or wheels of mortal invention. The velocipedes which were in vogue several years ago had as fair a trial as invention ever had; and they were universally abandoned, simply because it was found there was nothing to be gained by them. [9]

Sentiments like this were rare at the time, when confidence was more common, and a reader soon takes the Editor to task for his conservatism:

Sir — You say man is a locomotive machine of Nature's own making, and not to be improved by the addition of any cranks or wheels of mortal invention. Now sir, I once skated a mile in four minutes, which is a rate of velocity far exceeding anything ever accomplished by the naked foot; and on untying my velocipedes, I found they were made not by Dame Nature, but by Giles Handsaw of Ironmonger Lane, London. What saith thy philosophy to this, good Mr Editor?

Yours, doubtingly, A Fenman [10]

Another reader writes grumbling that 'one of the most promising inventions of this inventive age, the velocipede, or pedestrian curricle [i.e. the hobby-horse] has been consigned to the neglect of an obsolete trifle', and he wants to know why:

... the means of locomotion in question possesses the qualifications of celerity, lightness, elegance, compactness, durability and ease of propulsion ... This invention provides individuals with a means of conveyance independent of the casualties and preparations inseparable from the use of vehicles in general ... The end of knowledge is practical improvement, in adding to the facilities, comforts, and resources, and consequently to the moral amelioration of the human species. [11]

The velocipede's time had come. Reports come in thick and fast from all over England, France and America. Its utility is now almost beyond question. A better solution has to be discovered. But there are problems, not just with the machinery, but also with the roads.

In Paris in 1830, a high-up official in the Post Office, a M. Dreuze, succeeded in persuading the authorities to give three- or four-wheeled velocipedes to rural postmen, to speed up deliveries:

The summer, a very dry one, passed away very pleasantly and without a hitch; the carriers were charmed with their steeds, and the simple country folk were enchanted with the regularity with which their letters reached them, and Monsieur Dreuze himself might be seen morning after morning in his snug department in the Hôtel des Postes rubbing his hands over the good reports of his machines and the picture of general contentment spread out before him. But alas! the unfortunate velocipedes which had conquered the prejudice of the country, and soothed their once rebellious riders into complacency, were destined to engage in a struggle with Dame Nature herself, and to be beaten in the contest. The winter which succeeded the charming summer was a severe one. Snow fell in quantities, and froze on the ground. The velocipedes turned out as usual, but with a prudence characteristic of intelligent beings, refused to progress. It is true their wheels rotated rapidly on the slippery surface, but not a yard would they progress. Their unfortunate riders, by this time accustomed to the luxury of riding, were compelled to leave their unruly steeds behind them, and, slinging the bags on their shoulders, trudge off on foot.[12]

'Aellopodes', a huge and wonderful tricycle, typifies better than any other velocipede, I think, the energetic and confident imagination of the early velocipede-builders. While trains were running on tracks and steam-driven locomotives taking to the roads, Mr Revis, a well-known Cambridge inventor, was to show the world that men can do without any steam except their own! 'Aellopodes' was illustrated and described in 1839, in the *Mirror of Literature, Amusement and Instruction*.[13]

Mr Revis showed 'Aellopodes' in London, and it was driven by some of the students at Cambridge University. He claimed that a speed of between twenty and thirty miles an hour was possible. Was it? With its six-foot back wheels, and the weight of two heavy men bearing down on the treadles, this might have been achieved on a good flat road, but would have been impossible on the rough surfaces of any turnpike.

Mr Revis, like Baron Drais and M. Dreuze before him, had great faith in his invention. He offered it to the heads of the Post Office in London, confident that, even at fifteen miles an hour, it could beat the mail-coaches, but by 1839 the railways were a more viable proposition. His offer was refused.

William Baddeley, a London inventor, rode on 'Aellopodes', and while he was 'bound to confess that it affords a species of gymnastic exercise that is highly beneficial and agreeable', he did not think that treadles and the whole weight of the human body was the best system that could be devised for a velocipede. He drew a sketch of his own idea, called it a Manumotive Exercising Carriage, and sent it to the *Mechanics' Magazine*, where it appeared on April 13th, 1839. Mr Baddeley pedals with his hands and steers with his feet. He argues that:

> the power applied to cranks by the hand is more continuous and uniform than can possibly be obtained by treddles; the action, too, as a gymnastic exercise, is much more advantageous, opening the chest and giving tone and elasticity to muscles not sufficiently called into action by ordinary occupations, while the daily act of walking sufficiently employs the muscles of the lower extremities.[14]

It is strange that he did not put two and two together, and conclude that the legs too could supply a continuous and uniform power to cranks.

But in another letter to the *Mechanics' Magazine*, in which he describes Mr Richard Merryweather's Pedomotive Carriage, William Baddeley obviously feels that a treadle-driven velocipede deserves a second, closer look:

> The present machine, like its predecessor, can be propelled by one traveller, at a rate of from six to eight miles an hour, if on good level roads; but on rough roads, or ascending hills, the labour becomes excessive. Two persons appear to be the most advantageous load for this machine, a moderate degree of

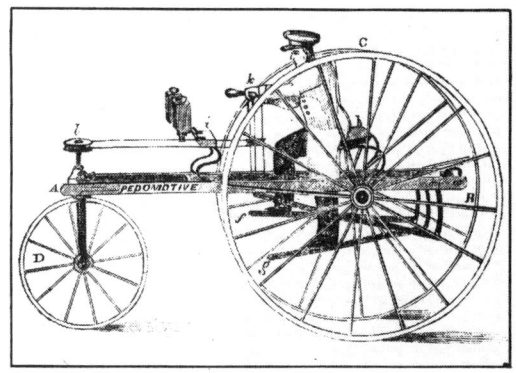

Like 'Aellopedes', Mr Merryweather's Pedomotive Carriage of 1839 was driven by a man standing up. The main problem of the amateur mechanics seems to have been the enormous size and weight of their vehicles.

'Mr Baddeley's Manumotive Exercising Carriage', 1839: 'The power applied to cranks by the hand,' he argues, 'is more continuous and uniform than can possibly be obtained by treddles ...

Mr Williams's passenger-propelled locomotive carriage. Mr Williams, of Holywell, a surgeon, tested this carriage, which went at ten miles an hour. He thought it particularly suitable for young people and invalids. The man at the front is strapped into clogs and is standing on a cranked driving-axle, as well as steering with his arms, while the man at the back turns a driving wheel with his hands and also steers with his feet. The purpose of the revolving umbrella is not quire clear, but the continuous rotary action of the rear drive is an interesting innovation.

'Frank's Mechanical Horse': 'Being a traveller, of course, I require some assistance in transferring me from one town to another, and finding, to my cost, that a horse of flesh and blood needed the needful to keep him ajogging, 13 months ago I constructed a horse, composed of stout wood, tough iron, and bold brass ... I find that it is as easy to propel myself and 1 cwt of luggage at 6 miles an hour as it is to walk 3 in the same time, and when fortunate enough to get my luggage forwarded, why, I can spin along at a speed that a crack trotter would find his task set to keep up with me.'

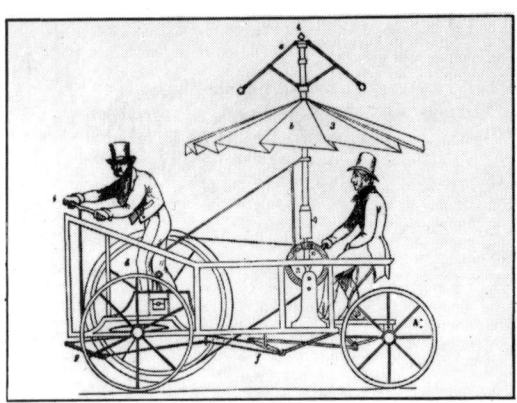

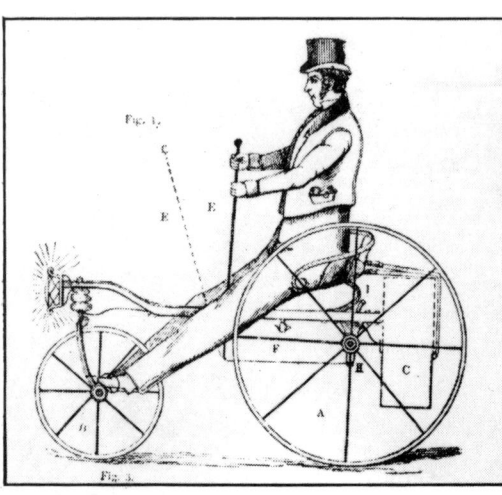

exertion on their part being sufficient to ensure a very respectable speed, say from ten to twelve miles an hour. Under very favourable circumstances, on a level road, one mile has been accomplished in three minutes, being a speed equal to twenty miles an hour! But such a rate of travelling is quite out of the question for all practical purposes ... [15]

He is an enthusiastic, but sceptical, observer and experimenter, with a limited vision:

Mechanical men will have their hobby, and we occasionally meet with some one of these numerous contrivances for aiding and extending the locomotive powers of man, wending their solitary way through unfrequented roads, as if the owners were more than half ashamed of their production or of its performance ...

I have stated before that, as an amusing and agreeable gymnastic exercise, these machines have a limited range of usefulness, but to imagine they can ever be made extensively or usefully subservient to the purposes of trade or commerce in any shape, is a chimera altogether unworthy of this mechanical age. [16]

The technology to make a decisively efficient velocipede was not yet developed. Each one of these machines is hand-made and a product of the imagination of its inventor. There is a common pool of ideas, but as yet no agreement even on the fundamentals. Experiments are under way, discussion is energetic, but they are expensive to build, and there is always something lacking in the solutions. Should velocipedes be driven by hand or foot? Should the driving-wheels be worked by cranks and treadles, or by a continuous rotary action? And then, how should they be steered and stopped, and how could the drive be made variable so that it would be easier for the rider to adjust his effort to the lie of the land?

Mr Williams, the designer of the fantastic Passenger-propelled Locomotive Carriage, writes to the *Mechanics' Magazine* on June 24th, 1843, and apologizes for the fact that he is only 'an empiric in mechanics, who can boast no more than an ardent love for it'. Nevertheless, he goes on with great foresight to support the idea of the 'continued rotary motion produced by the weight of the body as the only true principle' for efficiency, and shows a very expert awareness of the need for some kind of differential to enable a four-wheeled rear-driven velocipede to take a corner without putting too much strain on the driving-axle. The problem here is simply that in turning a corner, one wheel on the driving-axle prescribes a larger circle than the other, causing skidding and instability, and so there needs to be a break in the middle of the axle.

So, in spite of all the activity, a really successful and practical velocipede evaded the early amateur mechanics. 'In several of the past volumes of your valuable Magazine,' writes one reader, 'you have given sketches and descriptions of various forms and contrivances for manumotive machines, still it is rare to see such a machine in use, and few who have them continue to use them long. The inferences from this statement are, that there is a continued desire in the public mind to have such machines, and also that there is something wanting to render them successfully useful.' [17]

What was 'wanting' of course, was a technology equal to solving the problems in hand, a technology that could only emerge through the experiments that were then being carried on. It would be hard to find more powerful evidence of a social need preceding a successful invention than the letter of this disgruntled reader of the *Mechanics' Magazine*.

Kirkpatrick Macmillan 1813-78

Through the pages of the *Mechanics' Magazine* inventors and riders

A copy of Kirkpatrick Macmillan's velocipede made in about 1860 by Thomas McCall, a joiner and wheelwright of Kilmarnock, who was born and brought up near where Macmillan lived. He sold the velocipedes he made for £7 each.

who would otherwise never have been heard of, and whose ideas and velocipedes we should never have known about, become a part of cycling history. But one inventor, a Scotsman called Kirkpatrick Macmillan, did not write long letters or publish drawings advertising himself, and left very little information about himself behind, except two copies of his velocipede.

Macmillan, a blacksmith from a village called Courthill, near Dumfries, in Scotland, invented and used a velocipede which at that time and place was a very extraordinary machine. Produced, as far as is known, in isolation, it stands out like a prophecy. From the perspective of 130 years, its simplicity and efficiency can be seen to distinguish it from the other recorded experiments of the period; the essential 'rightness' of its design separates it from the other complicated contemporary experiments.

While other inventors were arguing about the relative merits of 'pedomotives' and 'manumotives', and indeed, one or two of them were asking publicly whether it was worth going ahead at all with man-powered machines, Macmillan seems to have gone right to the heart of the problem. And he lived and worked, not in one of the centres of industrial and mechanical activity, where he might have been inspired by other people's experiments, but in rural Scotland, seventy miles from the nearest large city, Glasgow. Even if he had been the most compulsive reader of the *Mechanics' Magazine*, he would have found nothing there to help him design a two-wheeled velocipede.

Macmillan's machine was developed between about 1839 and 1842, when he was employed in the blacksmith's shop on the Drumlanrig Estate of the Duke of Buccleuch, near Courthill. A man from Dumfries called Mr Charteris brought a hobby-horse to the workshop, and both Macmillan and his assistant, John Findlater, made copies of it for themselves and rode them on the estate and in Courthill.

Macmillan was a curious and inventive craftsman, who made and repaired all kinds of farm machinery, and had a reputation as a man who would try his hand at any kind of mechanical task. His son, John Macmillan, reported that his father could 'make wooden pumps, play the harmonium, pull out teeth, and was well known at parties in the district for his grand whistling and fiddling'. He was also a talented veterinarian, and worked on improvements to the horse-drawn plough. Kirkpatrick re-designed the hobby-horse, providing it with a continuous drive to the back wheel, using principles which he had probably seen used in other kinds of machinery. His original velocipede does not survive, but two copies exist and they have been assumed to be similar enough to give a fairly accurate picture of what it was like.

It had two wheels running in line, and was steered by the front wheel and driven by two 'pedals' attached by connecting rods to crank-arms on the back wheel. The frame was wooden, and the wheels also, reinforced with iron-band tyres for strength. It weighed about sixty pounds.

Macmillan's is the first surviving two-wheeled machine which a man could drive forward without having to touch the ground with his feet, creating enough momentum to stay upright, and it is thus the earliest 'bicycle'.

Superficially it does still look a bit like a hobby-horse. It had to be pawed along the ground with the feet at first, since the dead-centre effect of the simple crank mechanism made it very hard to get under way. Macmillan made himself some spiked shoes to make this easier. But it is mechanically much more sophisticated than a hobby-horse. As well as connecting the back wheel to cranks and pedals, and thus converting a backwards-and-forwards movement of the legs into a circular motion in the wheel, he also applied the principle of variable gearing by making it possible to alter the throw of the cranks on his machine, and discovered the fact that a front wheel set between forks which have a slight forward rake has an inherent stability. In Thomas McCall's copy, made some time in the eighteen-sixties, the length of the horizontal connecting rods, and thus the gear, could be altered.

The real snag in the design appears to be the position of the pedals, which are so close to the front wheel that it is hard to see how they would not get tangled up with the wheel every time the handlebars were turned. Perhaps Macmillan used his spiked shoes to heave himself round sharp corners.

In spite of all the difficulties, Macmillan often rode the velocipede in and around Courthill, and from Courthill to Dumfries. He was often seen on the country roads, and thus earned a reputation as an eccentric.

To prove its viability, and perhaps because he could not afford to make the journey any other way, Macmillan set out on the evening of June 6th, 1842 to ride the 140 miles to Glasgow and back, a venture which would have seemed foolhardy to people used to travelling slowly and reliably on horseback. Stopping at Old Cumnock for the night, he went on into Glasgow the next day, and was involved in an accident in the Gorbals, on the outskirts of the city. He caused such excitement in the crowded streets that he knocked over a child and was summoned to the Gorbals, South Side, Police Court the next day, and fined five shillings. A report of the incident was printed in the *Glasgow Argus* on June 9th:

> On Wednesday a gentleman, who stated he came from Thornhill in Dumfries, was placed at the Gorbals public bar, charged with riding along the pavement on a velocipede to the obstruction of the passage, and with having, by so doing, thrown over a child. It appeared from his statement that he had on the day previous come all the way from Old Cumnock, a distance of 40 miles, bestriding the velocipede, and that he performed the journey in the space of five hours. On reaching the Barony of Gorbals he had gone upon the pavement, and was soon surrounded by a large crowd, attracted by the novelty of the machine. The child who

was thrown down had not sustained any injury, and under the circumstances the offender was fined only 5 shillings. The velocipede employed in this instance was very ingeniously constructed – it moved on wheels, turned with the hand by means of a crank; but to make it 'progress' appeared to require more labour than will be compensated for by the increase of speed. This invention will not supersede the railway.[18]

The reporter may have misunderstood the construction of the velocipede, but, according to one account, not actually proven, the magistrate who fined him was so interested in the machine that he paid the five-shilling fine himself and asked Macmillan to give a special demonstration for his benefit.

It may seem a little surprising that news of the first bicycle and the exploits of its inventor did not reach further afield and appear in the *Mechanics' Magazine* or some similar journal. But it is nevertheless understandable. Dumfries was a small rural town and far from London, from which information about mechanical matters was largely disseminated, and most of the machines which appeared in print did so because their inventors sent their ideas and designs to London. There were, sadly for us perhaps, no reporters out in the field, and there were almost certainly dozens of velocipedes which were never publicized in any way. It was not until the later eighteen-sixties that anybody with the slightest pretensions to being an inventor of velocipedes rushed to the Patent Office to get his idea registered, and for Macmillan a patent would have been an expensive business.

Macmillan, in fact, does not seem to have been much interested in advertising his invention. He probably saw it as a hobby. He was not interested in production or profit and he did not realize the profound implications of what he had done. He was an unassuming person. His father, Robert Macmillan, who died in 1854, had also been a blacksmith, and Kirkpatrick, who had received a large body of traditional knowledge, was an experimenter and improver, but a craftsman not an entrepreneur.

But I do not think it would be right to assume that he was, therefore, completely isolated from the mechanical and industrial activities in the rest of the country, and learned nothing from them. He had three brothers in Glasgow, two of whom were teachers, and the third a clerk, from whom he could have learned a great deal. On the estate where he worked, too, he may possibly have talked with experienced, mechanically minded members of the upper classes. He was certainly not an illiterate peasant.

Macmillan's velocipede did make enough impact in the area around Dumfries for quite a number of other craftsmen to be interested in copying it. Perhaps they had already experimented themselves. He did not object to this, in fact, he seems rather to have encouraged it. Gavin Dalzell, a cooper from Lesmahagow, which lies between Courthill and Glasgow, made a copy in about 1846, which still survives. And a Mr Thomas McCall, a joiner and wheelwright in Kilmarnock, built several in the eighteen-sixties, one of which is now in the Science Museum, London.

A letter about McCall appeared in the *English Mechanic* on May 14th, 1869, entitled 'The Kilmarnock Velocipede':

> Sir – I enclose a photograph of a velocipede which meets with great approval here. I have tried it, and find it very light and easy of motion. The maker, Mr T. McCall, Langlands Street, Kilmarnock, has raced and beaten some of the ordinary two-wheeled velocipedes [i.e. boneshakers] in Glasgow.
>
> Mechanical Hawk

Less than a month later, 'Mechanical Hawk' writes again, noting that McCall has improved his velocipede, and sending another photograph:

> It has, as my brother readers will perceive, a far better steering handle, being fitted with brake and gun-metal bearings; the connecting rods are also made alterable to a long or short leg. It is

Willard Sawyer, velocipede-manufacturer, riding on one of his own machines, probably the one which was exhibited at the Great Exhibition of 1851 and which is now in the Science Museum, London. This may be the oldest surviving photograph of a cyclist.

a remarkably safe velocipede, being so low and easily mounted. The speed is from 8 to 12 miles an hour, though I have gone downhill at what I should think a much greater speed. The price, through improved fittings, has risen to £7. The machine weighs about 58 pounds.[19]

McCall, it is apparent, has changed and improved on Macmillan's original design, and it is in fact very difficult to know just what this *did* look like. Was it essentially a less sophisticated version of the McCall machine, or was it something altogether different? Although there can be no doubt from the evidence that Kirkpatrick Macmillan was a velocipede-maker, it does seem extremely hazardous to attribute to him with any certainty the precise design of those copies that have survived. Given the haze of mystery which surrounds this little-documented and much-mythologized figure, it does seem that the *Glasgow Argus* reporter's statement that the velocipede was 'turned with the hand by means of a crank' should be given a little more serious consideration than it has been given up to now.

Kirkpatrick Macmillan died in 1878. It is interesting to speculate about what would have happened if he had developed and refined his ideas himself, and succeeded in perfecting a rear-driven bicycle by about 1860. There would have been no subsequent boneshaker, no 'Ordinary', and Macmillan himself might have become a very rich man. But it did not happen like that. In the eighteen-forties and 'fifties the chains so essential for a rear-driven bicycle were not yet developed, and there were many lessons still to be learnt.

Macmillan's velocipede, although in some senses prophetic, was, with its weight and its cumbersome pedalling action, very much a product of its time. And so was Macmillan himself; an inventive and precocious innovator and experimenter, yet securely anchored to the world of the traditional craftsman, and to the rural society in which he lived.

Willard Sawyer, Velocipede Manufacturer

Willard Sawyer is a man of a different kind. Sawyer, a carpenter by trade, abandoned the activities traditionally associated with carpentry, and used his carpenter's skills and his interest in velocipedes to launch himself into a new kind of business enterprise. He was, I believe, the first truly professional maker of man-powered vehicles, in the sense that he specialized in them alone, and marketed and sold them himself. A hobby-horse could be made by almost any craftsman in metal or wood, but to build successful velocipedes in large numbers as Sawyer did demanded specialist knowledge and methods of production. He began as a craftsman and became an engineer, entrepreneur and factory-owner, selling his products to royalty and the aristocracy. His career began in a traditional technology, and as it progressed he invented new techniques of construction and motion.

By 1858, Sawyer is described as 'a manufacturer of velocipedes', and three of his surviving catalogues, one issued in about 1858, the others in 1863 and 1868, leave no doubt at all about his ambitions and his pride in his new profession: 'Willard Sawyer, Original Inventor and Registered Improver,' one proclaims, 'Manufacturer by Special Command to His Majesty the Emperor of Russia, and Chief Manufacturer for the Crystal Palace, Sydenham, of the celebrated Velocipede, Hand-Propeller and Double-Action Self-Locomotives.' Crowning this bold assertion is the royal coat-of-arms, the ultimate status symbol of the self-made man, and the proud boast, 'Under Royal and Imperial Patronage'.

Sawyer's confident advertising continues:

W. S. having, after 20 years of careful study and personal labour succeeded in bringing these Carriages to a perfection of ease, rapidity, lightness, and durability — combined with cheapness — defying all competition, ventures to draw public attention to some of the most prominent features and merits of his Invention, and to announce the very distinguished patronage and encouragement it has received.[20]

Sawyer occupies a special place in his period. At a time when all the other velocipedes to be seen on the roads of Britain were experimental, and there was almost no one sharp enough to appreciate their commercial potential, Sawyer succeeds in developing a whole range of workable, everyday velocipedes, and builds himself a sizeable reputation as a specialist in the field.

His career was based on the south-east coast of England in Dover, and then Deal, Kent. In local directories for 1838 and 1839, he is listed as a carpenter living in Chapel Street, Dover, and his interest in velocipedes must have begun soon after this, for by 1845 there were quite a number of them to be seen in and around Dover. But his first real success was probably at the Great Exhibition of 1851, where there were three velocipedes on show, one of them Sawyer's.

Sawyer rode from Dover to London and back on this occasion, a feat typical of his drive and energy. The Great Exhibition was the grand show-case of Victorian ingenuity and expertise, and the rich and powerful and inquisitive came from all over the world to see it. His velocipede, Sawyer himself says, 'was received with a very flattering distinction', and it was undoubtedly the exposure which his machines received on this occasion which laid the foundations of his success and his subsequent flirtations with the monarchy and the aristocracy.

The man with the bushy beard and the flat-topped peaked cap riding on a velocipede in the illustration on page 38 is almost certainly Willard Sawyer himself, and since the date of the picture is between about

The front page of a catalogue issued by Willard Sawyer in 1858.

A card probably given by Sawyer to buyers of his velocipedes gives an interesting glimpse of the days before mass-produced lubricating-oil was available.

1850 and 1860, it may be the very machine that he rode up to London to the Exhibition. Certainly it is one of his very best creations, and is identical in every respect to the one which is now owned by the Science Museum, London, one of the few Sawyer vehicles which survives.

The Science Museum's Sawyer is a racing velocipede made some time between 1850 and 1860. It is driven by the front wheels, and is built as lightly and as sparely as possible; the clearances are very fine, and the wooden-spoked wheels almost as fragile as they could be. Sawyer is not searching around for a workable solution when he builds this; he has already discovered an efficient system, and his intention is to perfect it as far as possible. How it stood up to the rough roads and cobbled streets of the time, or whether it was actually raced, we do not know. But it is a superb example of the sophisticated level of Sawyer's technology and his superb craftsmanship.

After the Great Exhibition, recognition was not slow in coming to Sawyer. He sent a velocipede to the American Exhibition in 1854, and at the new Crystal Palace, in Sydenham, his machines were 'in great request there by Visitors of all classes for driving on [sic] the Grounds'. In the summer of 1857 the young Prince of Wales visited Dover with his tutor and went to see Sawyer's manufactury. 'Having enquired concerning the principles of construction and use of the Velocipede with evident interest, W. S. had the privilege of building a Carriage expressly for His Royal Highness's acceptance.'[21]

The velocipede in question was illustrated and described in the *Illustrated London News* in 1858, and the free advertising brought Sawyer a lot of work. He made velocipedes for the Emperor of Russia, for the Prince Imperial of France, for the Crown Prince of Hanover, for various viscounts, earls and marquises, and for anyone else who could afford one. He sold machines in India, Australia, all over Europe and in California.

By 1860 he is at the height of his career. He has no rival, and his velocipedes are used all over the world. There are not as yet any two-wheeled boneshaker velocipedes, and Sawyer's light and practical vehicles must have given a strong impetus to the enthusiasts who were interested in developing man-powered travel. As they became more widely known in the eighteen-fifties and 'sixties, it must have been obvious that there was no longer any future in the heavy and complicated velocipedes of twenty years before, like 'Aellopodes'.

Willard Sawyer knew how to diversify; he was a businessman who wanted to sell his velocipedes to everybody. The catalogues of 1858, 1863 and 1868 are a mine of rich information about the people who used them. So anxious is Sawyer to sell his different models that he depicts almost an entire society seated on his vehicles, at work and at play:

> Of self-propulsion by the Velocipede etc, as developed at W. S.'s establishment, it may be said generally, that it equals walking in the healthfulness of the exercise afforded, and ordinary riding as to comfort and convenience; while it surpasses the one in speed, as much as it does the other for independence, and both in regard to economy.
>
> W. S.'s Registered Velocipede is manufactured under his own constant and immediate supervision, and, as to its more delicate parts, chiefly by his own hands; of well-seasoned material, and first-class workmanship; and of every size and variety, adapted for ladies and gentlemen, adult and juvenile. The SOCIABLE, made to carry any number up to 6, is peculiarly adapted for Excursionists – every passenger enjoying an agreeable seat, and sharing in the work of propulsion – thus realizing all the conversational charms and activity of pedestrianism, without its fatigue, and with the advantage of velocity into the bargain.
>
> The RACER, especially constructed with a view to the highest point of speed consistent with safety, and to accommodate gentlemen inclined for sport; while the TOURIST and TRAVELLER is

Sawyer's racing velocipede is a superb example of the sophisticated level of his craftsmanship. The wrought-iron crankshaft, with its enormous throw and four bearings, is made from a single length of iron bar and is no mean engineering achievement.

42 King of the Road

Henry Hill Hodgson bought this velocipede from Sawyer in 1860 for £17 2s. 6d., and rode back to London from Dover on it in two days. It is driven by the front wheels, and steered by the back wheels with levers which Hodgson is holding. This is one of the oldest photographs of cycling to survive, and is a wonderful evocation of the confidence and adventurousness of an early tourist.

designed for persons of itinerant habits or avocations having more taste for freedom than ceremony.

The PROMENDADE and VISITING CARRIAGE is admirably fitted for military officers wishing to unite the pleasure of sight-seeing with the profit of exercise, and, at the same time to preserve their evening costume in suitable condition for indoor pursuits; Ministers requiring to communicate with a remote or widely-distributed flock; Lawyers having to attent [*sic*] upon Clients beyond the immediate vicinity of their offices; and Youths, seeking gymnastic diversion.

In the LADY'S CARRIAGE, W. S. has, by an expressly contrived double-perch, and other provisions for confining and protecting the dress etc, rendered the Velocipede available for the fair sex; and it can now be used with such perfect decorum and security, that only the most ante-diluvian prejudice can object to the ladies at once universally embracing the opportunity of a safe, easy, and exhilarating means of obtaining, more sufficiently than hitherto, changes of both air and scene.[22]

Satisfied customers write to Sawyer, and he publishes their letters as testimonials in his catalogues. The Honourable J. C. Skeffington says:

I cannot speak in terms too highly of the convenience and comfort of such a mode of travelling, when one can run off 60 miles in a day, and feel as little fatigued as if one had gone on foot a dozen. I hope for the good of the public they may become more generally used. I have travelled all over England in my carriage, worn out one set of wheels, and now, after some years' experience, I still maintain that nothing for pleasure, expedition, or healthy exercise, comes near a velocipede constructed on your excellent model.[23]

On another trip, he says, he started from London, went to Bath, Gloucester, Malvern, Worcester, Birmingham, Lichfield, Derby, Buxton, Sheffield, Grantham, Peterborough, Huntingdon, Cambridge and back to London – 526 miles in twenty days. And this was before the days of cycling!

Henry Hill Hodgson (1835-1918) bought a Sawyer velocipede in 1856, and rode it and a second one hard for the next nine years at least. He kept a diary of his rides, which once again attests to the versatility of velocipedes. He used it around London and for rides out into the country and noted the details of his travels. In September 1857 he rode from London to Salisbury and back, 130 miles each way, covering $62\frac{1}{2}$ miles on one day. 'March 31st, 1858, Brixton to Handcross, 8 hours, stopping time 1 hour, 30 miles distance, Wet with Strong S.E. wind,' or 'Brixton to Henfield, 14 hours, stopping time 5 hours, 40 miles distance, Very Hot and Dry.'[24]

In September 1860 he travelled the seventy miles from London to Dover and back to see Willard Sawyer, where it seems he may have taken possession of a new velocipede, for afterwards he wrote a letter of thanks which Sawyer used as a testimonial in one of his catalogues:

I left Rochester this morning at half-past eight, reaching my home about half-past four this afternoon ... The roads were very heavy today; notwithstanding this great drawback, I have got home very comfortable, and feel very little fatigue from the exertion. You have my most hearty testimony to the efficiency of your machine.[25]

Of all the accounts of Sawyer and his velocipedes, the most complete and fascinating is contained in a letter written by a Mr H. F. Wilcox, an enthusiastic and knowledgeable velocipedist, to the *English*

'From the resemblance which this vehicle bears when in motion to a boat or a skiff, on account of the rowing principle, I have called it the "Old Park Skiff Velocipede". I may state that I think this plan admirably adapted for ladies as well as gentlemen, and particularly if the machine is made with but one crank, for there is then no unnatural excitement of the feet, and the dress will remain undisturbed because both feet move together.'

44 King of the Road

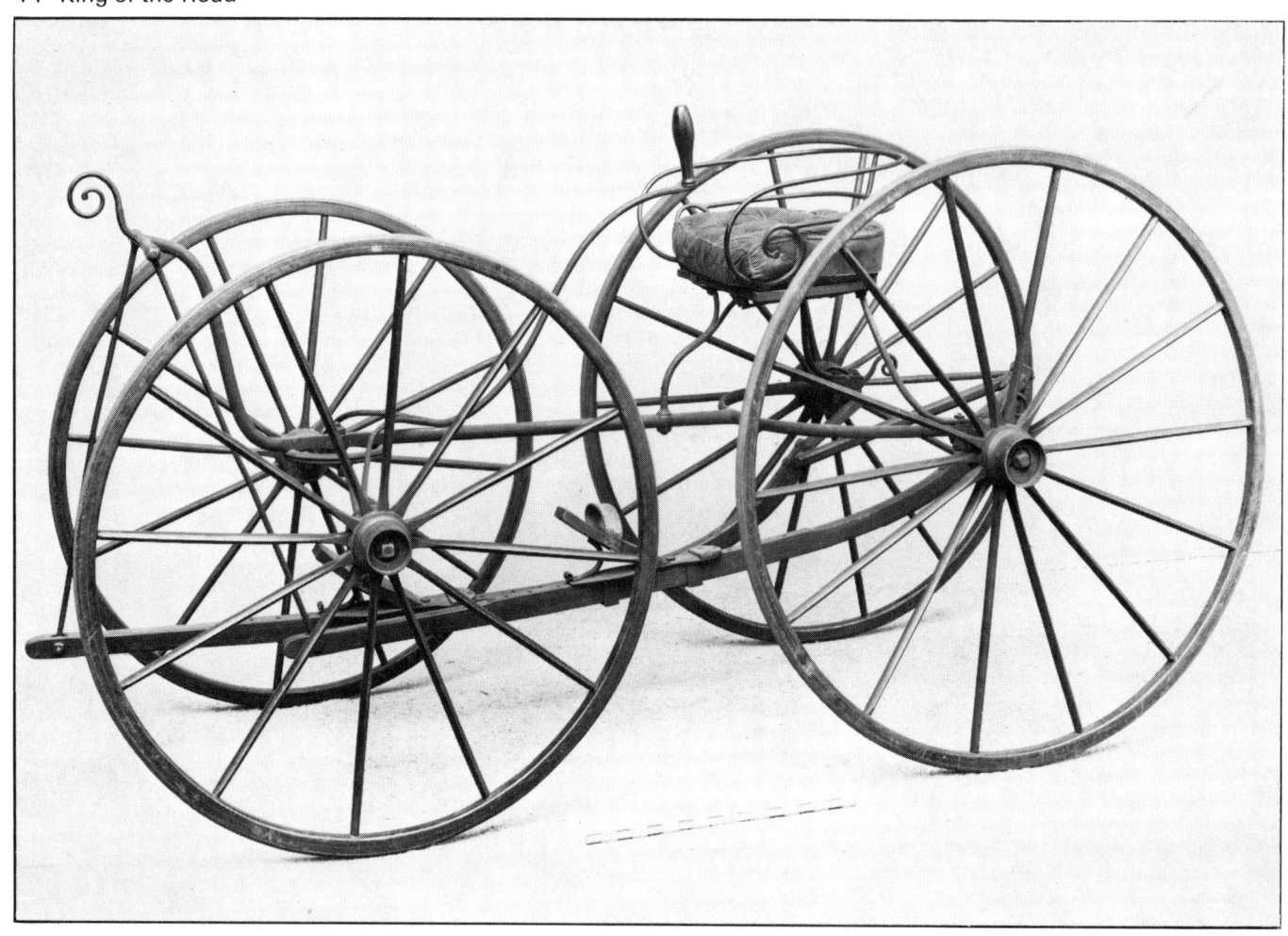

The substantial, solid velocipede built for Prince Albert, the Prince Consort, in 1851 by J. Ward, a coach-builder of Leicester Square. It is now in the Science Museum, London.

Mechanic and Mirror of Science, and published there on February 26th, 1869. It is such a colourful picture of life on the road in pre-bicycle days that it is worth quoting almost all of it:

Sir — As a regular subscriber and constant reader of your matchless little journal, I hope you will allow me some space to ventilate my ideas upon one or two subjects, and I shall be only too glad if some of those ideas prove useful to any of my brother readers.

I shall first say a word or two on the all-absorbing subject of the velocipede. In my humble opinion, the velocipede has arrived at as complete a state as can be attained, and the only thing necessary to make it a most useful agent to the human race, is perfection in the roads upon which it is to run. All the ideas and inventions during the next century will not improve our position if the roads still remain bad.

About two years ago I bought from Mr Sawyer, of Dover, a velocipede, than which I am of opinion nothing could be more perfect, and I am inclined to think that one of that gentleman's best machines cannot be beaten by any of the proposed schemes lately published in the columns of our journal.

I do not think that velocipedes are of much use for high speeds; for even on the best of our high roads the rattling and shaking of such slight machines is dreadful at the speed of anything over seven or eight miles an hour, and if driven constantly at this rate they cannot last long.

In my Sawyer I have climbed all the steepest hills in this neighbourhood except the celebrated Houghton Bank.

This ladies' tricycle velocipede was probably built some time between 1850 and 1860. It is similar in its basic conception to Sawyer's velocipedes, but little attempt seems to have been made to lighten its eighty-six pounds. The most interesting thing about it is that it is a purpose-built ladies' machine.

But in a long journey I consider it far wiser to walk up the worst of the hills, for I am sure a steep hill of 100 yards will take more out of a man than two miles of level road, at least I have always found it so.

I am not a good walker, and never care to travel more than six or seven miles at a stretch on Shank's mare, but I went from home to Durham, a distance of 16 miles, in my Sawyer, walking up the worst of the hills, and completed the distance in $2\frac{3}{4}$ hours, and I can positively affirm that when I got out of my carriage I felt no fatigue whatever except a slight weakness in my knee joints. The $2\frac{3}{4}$ hours included walking up the hills, and a stoppage I made to get some milk at a farm.

I do not believe I could have walked the distance except possibly in hard frost, and with a pleasant companion.

I think that with perfect roads there would be no limit to the speed a velocipede might be driven at. It would then merely be a question of diameter of driving wheels.

On level flagstones, the exertion required to drive my Sawyer seemed, if possible, nil; there I conclude that on a perfectly level road, as smooth as a well-worn flagstone, the diameter of my wheels, which was 3'1" might be doubled or trebled without altering the cranks, and a man might then drive himself at any speed up to 25 or 30 mph, provided there was no wind opposing him, and that he had sufficient width of road for safe steering. The steering of 4-wheeled velocipedes at high speeds requires the greatest attention.

With all due respect to our numerous contributors of 'ideas' in

'**The Latest Style of American Velocipede**': 'The rider sits astride of a saddle-bar in the centre of an hexagonal frame from which uprights rise, connected at the top by an adjustable neckyoke ... The ease with which, withdrawing the feet from the stirrup, he can reach the ground, throw off the saddle-bar, and walk within his light machine uphill, then, adjusting it, can slip on again and resume his journey, or perform his evolutions on rough or obstructive portions of the road, seem features that ought to seccure for this machine a favourable reception, to say nothing of its superior capabilities for healthful exercise and invigorating movement.'

the shape of newly-invented velocipedes, I must say that I think nothing is to be gained by departing from the old direct-acting crank and treadles as in Mr Sawyer's carriages.

Moreover, I think 'legomotives' will always beat 'armotives' hollow, if not in speed, in distance certainly, for I think there can be no question but that the enduring strength of the legs is immeasurably greater than that of the arms.

With regard to the two-wheeled velocipedes used by the French and Americans, I think there are one or two great objections to these. First, the constant anxiety there must be on the mind in endeavouring to keep an upright position; and, secondly, the inability to sit quietly and rest upon the machine when it is at rest, owing to the same tendency to fall over. Then again, I cannot think the seat on the saddle can be very comfortable to maintain for any length of time, and there must be great danger of creating "raws" upon the inner sides of the legs. Nevertheless, I should like to see and try one of these machines.

Sawyer was still selling his machines in 1867, and they were thus used extensively all over England for a long period, as long as thirty years. Interestingly enough, in 1869, Mr Wilcox, living sixteen miles from Durham, had not yet seen the novel two-wheeled boneshaker velocipede, which had been used in France for about four years by then, and was becoming very popular in London.

The boneshaker was a new and startling development which caught the public imagination, but people were not entirely prepared for it, and some treated it with suspicion. The career of Willard Sawyer and the enthusiasm of Mr Wilcox for his machines shows that there was a large following for the safe and stable, but relatively slow, four-wheeler, and its devotees would not so easily abandon it in favour of the slick little boneshaker, which you could so easily fall off, and on which you could not carry very much baggage.

Sawyer's velocipedes were as finely made as the first boneshakers, but they were heavier and more expensive; a good Sawyer cost between £15 and £40, and although there were cheaper models and second-hand ones available, even these would not have been very easy for a person of limited means to afford. So the boneshaker quickly provided competition for the four-wheeled velocipede.

More amateur mechanics

On Friday, March 31st, 1865 the first number of a new weekly magazine appeared. It cost a penny a week and was called the *English Mechanic, a Record of Mechanical Invention, Scientific and Industrial Progress, Applied Chemistry, Arts, Manufactures, Engineering, Building etc*, and is an encyclopedia of Victorian inventions, and the manifesto of confident, inquisitive and talented mechanics. Its editors explained its intentions to their readers:

> With the appearance of this, the first number of the English Mechanic, vanishes the oft-repeated reproach that ... no journal devoted to the nurture and advancement of science and art has yet been published in a spirit and at a price sufficient to recommend it to the sympathy and support of the multitude — to the brain and pocket of the 'bone and sinew' of the land, our great 'workers'. No man who earns his bread as a mechanic or labourer in any department of the great field of 'labour' need for the future be without his record, ay, or a corner in the same, for the making known of his ideas or schemes ... There are thousands of working men who would dearly like to have under their hand at the fireplace an epitome of the progress in the Arts and Sciences from week to week ...

And the workers did write; hundreds of letters on all kinds of mechanical subjects. The pages of the *English Mechanic* are full of velocipedes. Between 1865 and 1872, there are hundreds of illustrations and descriptions of projected and finished machines. Some are sane and some are crazy. The old heavy four-wheeled velocipedes jostle with much lighter versions, American designs are reported, one system is weighed against another and, in 1867, the new little French boneshaker puts in its appearance — the first real bicycle, driven by cranks and pedals directly attached to the hub of the front wheel. Velocipedes had penetrated much further into the public consciousness since the eighteen-twenties and 'thirties, when they were mentioned but rarely and ridden only occasionally.

'We have before us some half dozen sets of drawings, from our amateur friends, of this useful vehicle, the velocipede,' says an early issue, 'which seems to come more into vogue the greater the distance working men have to travel between their homes and their jobs, carrying their tools with them in many cases.'[26] Time after time, the amateur mechanics write giving details of their latest adventures, how many miles they covered, how long it took. There is no longer any doubt about the feasibility of the velocipede; what is now crucial is the best design, and who can do the longest distance in the shortest time. The spirit of the race is already there.

On March 16th, 1866, a wheelwright says: 'Two or three persons can propel our velocipede at the rate of 10 or 12 miles an hour with ease. Two of us have run 19 miles in 1 hour 45 minutes with but slight exertion,' and another more ambitious traveller describes his velocipede and his pride in his achievement:

> As a sample of its capabilities, I may say that two persons have propelled themselves with it 42 miles a day for two days without their being overfatigued by the exertion.
>
> Journeys have frequently been made of 34, 24, 20, 18 and 16 miles in a day, and distances of 12 miles out and 12 back between tea and supper. 1 mile in $3\frac{1}{2}$ minutes has been done by

'The Celeremane': where a steam locomotive has pistons to drive its wheels, this velocipede has men. 'The action of the men is thus similar to that of rowing,' says the *English Mechanic* on September 17th, 1869, 'and we believe that there is no way in which a man can prolong his muscular energy for any prolonged period to greater advantage ... The Celeremane is intended expressly for quick running, and thus every part has been made as light as possible. The whole machine weighs only $2\frac{1}{2}$ cwt. (280 pounds).'

48 King of the Road

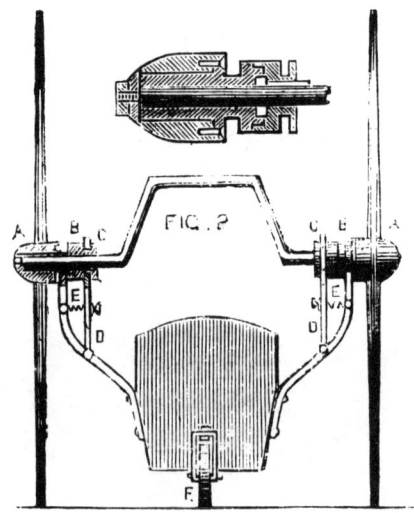

From *English Mechanic*, May 7th, 1869.

two persons, showing that a considerable portion of a journey can be accomplished at 16 miles an hour when the roads are favourable.

Velocipede-riders were tough and enterprising. Mr Meldrum took a holiday in Scotland in 1866, and was very happy with the money that he saved on the trip; but a velocipeding holiday was certainly not for the weak or lily-livered:

> Sir – I manufactured a velocipede to carry three persons when I was in Scotland. It was made in a fortnight. I enjoyed the pleasure of driving it for a month, when I broke it up, not a regular smash, in going down a very steep intricate road between the Spital of Glenshee and Braemar. It gave way in one of the main points, and I sold it to the country blacksmith for old iron. However, you have no idea how much labour and money it saved in that time. The distance we travelled with it would have cost us for riding at the rate of 14 shillings per day for 19 days.[27]

Again and again, writers to the *English Mechanic* talk about the convenience and the cheapness of using a velocipede, whether they are setting out to make long journeys or, like a man from Hull, who signs himself 'Experience', carrying potatoes from his garden on one side of town to his house on the other.

And, as a Mr J. Hastings points out, the velocipede is also extremely educational:

> I am much pleased to find the velocipede question again occupying a place in your columns. I look upon the velocipede not only as a useful machine for locomotion, but as a valuable educator of the mind. Any intelligent man giving earnest attention to the construction and working of a velocipede must necessarily study the beautiful laws of nature relating to force, motion, friction and gravity, and these will be far more pleasantly brought before his notice than could be done by the most popular authors or lecturers. I have never done much with the velocipede myself, but I have felt a deep interest in the correspondence in your pages.
>
> I have been especially interested in the experiments of Mr Goddard, residing at Staleybridge, near Manchester. He has constructed many a velocipede, and performed long journeys on them at the rate of 70 miles a day. In the course of his excursions he has twice performed the journey from Staleybridge to London and back, 188 miles. His first journey was to see the Great Exhibition of 1862 ...[28]

Mr Goddard is an interesting man, full of initiative: he educates his mind by building a velocipede, which he then rides to London to improve his mind still further at the Great Exhibition. With such energy, it is not surprising that the amateur mechanics were on the brink of a revolutionary breakthrough in velocipede design.

In the pages of the *English Mechanic* there is very little agreement, except that the matter must be pursued, and the perfect velocipede discovered. Some machines are designed for three or four people, some for only one; some are driven by the feet, others by hand and some by both; some have four wheels, others only one. One writer pleads the necessity of a variable-gear system, another still supports the idea of the hobby-horse. The formation of a velocipede club is suggested and widely supported, and a competition with prizes is considered as an inducement to the quick invention of the perfect solution. Some of the velocipedes discussed have been tested and tried and proved reliable, others are just hypothetical improvements. Into the midst of the controversy over treadle-driven machines comes the two-wheeled French velocipede, causing even more argument and confusion.

But there is one point about which there is almost no disagreement, and that is that the velocipede is good for the health, and that it might have a very profound effect on the social life and habits of people all over the country, if it should be widely used.

Hemming's Unicycle, or the Flying Yankee Velocipede: 'Richard C. Hemming, of New Haven, Conn., invented the machine herewith represented, two years ago, but has only recently brought it onto the market, and applied it to practical purposes...Mr Hemming says that this machine can be manufactured for 50 dollars, of a weight of only 30 pounds, and that it can be driven on the roads with but little exertion at the rate of 2 or even 25 miles an hour.'

The middle years of the nineteenth century were a time of intense innovation and activity. Many of the fundamental problems of mechanics and physics were worked out and applied, first in an experimental, and then in a commercial way. Steam-power was perfected, and the railways grew so quickly in the eighteen-forties that they completely ousted the stage-coach as they narrowed the distance between cities. In 1835 there was not a railway out of London; by 1847, the railway fever was at its height — nearly 4,000 miles were being used, and the construction of another 11,500 miles was authorized.

The mechanization of industry was also taking place, and mass-production methods developing. London and the industrial cities of the north of England were expanding rapidly as labourers moved into them to find work.

It was also a time of intense social change, one of the most significant aspects of which was the emergence of a growing new class of labourer, the mechanic or industrial artisan, the man for whom the *English Mechanic* was intended. He would become the factory worker of the latter part of the century. For the most part, he performed a routine, boring and often brutal function. Where he could be replaced by a machine, he often was.

But he was also hired to operate the machinery which put others out of work, and a new kind of mechanically minded urban proletarian was created who knew about machinery and had access to it. He learnt to use power tools, lathes and drills, and sometimes had the opportunity to climb up the social ladder. At the same time, he kept his knowledge of the old traditional skills, of the blacksmith, wheelwright, carpenter, locksmith, gunsmith and clockmaker, which he had most likely learned from his father.

If he had not been educated, he made the workshop or factory into his school, and there were many Improvement Societies where he could learn outside the factory gates in such free time as his rigorously organized work allowed him. It was in this kind of environment that mechanics became the pioneers of the bicycle industry.

The artisans and inventors who send their ideas to the *Mechanics' Magazine* and the *English Mechanic* during the eighteen-forties, 'fifties and 'sixties reject traditional solutions, and direct their attention to solving sophisticated problems. They are engineers and designers, and they might well be called the founders of the science of ergonomics, since they were wrestling with the efficient harnessing of the energy of the human body.

It is entirely typical of the radical spirit of their time that it should be their own mobility that concerned them. Victorians were great travellers. The railway was speedy, but for ordinary people it was also expensive. One writer talks angrily of the need for working men to co-operate to fight against the 'abuse and extortion' of the financial demands of 'over-gorged, and overgrasping railway directors' and suggests the formation of a co-operative club to advance the cause of the velocipede. 'The velocipede is, in England, a much neglected and useful machine,' he says, 'and besides being the best means of road travelling, because it is absolutely under the control of its user, both in practice and expense, also excels as a means of recreation and enjoyment ...'[29]

To an enterprising working man, then as now, a machine which would be cheap to make or buy and easy to store, and which would give free service every day, was obviously a very attractive proposition. Some people who were interested in getting about could not even afford to experiment: 'I am but a country labourer, and therefore cannot enter into any lengthy argument respecting velocipede construction. I only sent the sketch illustrated in the *English Mechanic* for the opinion of my fellow readers. I have not the means get a machine made ...'[30]

It was in the backyards and workshops of the amateur mechanics that the foundations of bicycle manufacturing were established. The bicycle was not invented by any one man, but was the product of a long development and of a community of experimenters. English makers were inspired by the more advanced French bicycle-designers in the eighteen-sixties. They were not at first businessmen, but their curiosity does seem to have grown, in a different sense, out of a keen sense of where their own interests lay.

> The mechanic's frame is his wealth, it is his capital, his all. Break down his health, or his strength, and you take from him the means whereby he himself lives, and by which alone, perhaps, he supports a family ... Consider how unfortunately it happens that the mechanic, more than most other men, is of necessity, from the nature of his occupation, often placed in situations where a greater degree of care is required for the purpose of preserving health than is necessary for individuals of other classes. Some men are perpetually exposed to the fumes of molten metals, which are well known to be poisonous; others again are liable to injury from the positions in which they are obliged to work, and from the want of sufficient exercise. But worst of all are the homes to which they return after the day's toil.
>
> Now, if a mechanic has all these trials to contend with in the course of his manhood, of what great importance to him is good air and exercise, combined with wholesome food, in his early youth.[31]

Mobility without the expense of a train ticket or oats for the horse meant more freedom and independence; it meant in fact a better life. And if the velocipede gave good exercise, it meant better health too.

The velocipedist was not at all welcomed in country districts at first. This is a French caricature of about 1870.

A woman rides a velocipede, her lamp blazing, her banner of progress blowing out behind her. She is a symbol both of mechanical advancement and the emancipation of her own sex. *Le Vélocipède Illustré*, **in which the picture first appeared, was the first periodical in the world devoted to the subject.**

50 King of the Road

52 King of the Road

CHAPTER 3
VELOCIPEDOMANIA

In France

> The two-wheeled velocipede is the animal which is to supersede everything else. It costs but little to produce, and still less to keep. It does not eat cart loads of hay, and does not wax fat and kick. It is easy to handle. It never rears up. It won't bite. It needs no check or rein or halter, or any unnatural restraint. It is little and light, let alone it will lean lovingly against the nearest support. It never flies off at a tangent unless badly managed, and under no circumstances will it shy at anything ...[1]

Cycling began in the late eighteen-sixties. Then, they talked about 'velocipedes' and 'velocipeding', and only during the last two years of the decade did the words 'bicycle' and 'bicycling' come into circulation. 'Bicycle' was used to distinguish a two-wheeled velocipede from all the other different kinds. 'It has been remarked that the word "bicycle" is an innovation, and that some genuine English word should be used,' remarked Alfred Howard, an early cycling writer, in 1874, 'but no other name has been suggested. "Bicycling" is now part of the English language; we all understand what it means, we are all familiar with it, and we all use it.'

The surge of interest in man-powered machines in the eighteen-fifties and early 'sixties was as nothing compared to the fever that was to follow. What had before 1865 been an enthusiast's fad indulged by a small number of technically-minded people became almost overnight a massive craze, a huge social phenomenon in France, the United States and England.

An invention was launched commercially by a French manufacturer which very quickly stimulated a new industry, a new sport and a new recreation for thousands of people. A new style of travelling became popular, and a new dimension was added to people's experience of the world.

Charles Dodgson, better known as Lewis Carroll, the writer, took this picture of his brother Wilfred Dodgson on a velocipede in about 1870.

Embryonic 'bicycles' with pedals fitted to the front wheel were certainly evolved in several different places in the eighteen-fifties and 'sixties. In the 'fifties a German called Philipp Fischer built a wooden one, and about ten years later another German, Karl Kech, fitted cranks and pedals to the front wheel of an old *Draisienne*. There were almost certainly others which do not now survive; inventors were inspired by the hobby-horse idea, which showed them how it was possible to balance on two wheels, and they quite easily adapted it. But, as with most of the other early velocipedes, these 'bicycles' were one-off affairs; they were not produced commercially, and had no more than a local influence.

In 1801, it is claimed by some Russian sources, the first two-wheeled velocipede with pedals, a large front wheel and a small back one, was built in Russia by the serf and master-craftsman E. M. Artamonov. On it he is supposed to have ridden from Verkhotur'ye, near Perm, to St Petersburg. A photograph of this machine does exist, but the date is incredibly early and although it is impossible to pass any serious judgment on it without much more research, it does seem most unlikely that such an advanced bicycle could have been constructed at that time.

'Who invented the bicycle?' people often ask. The answer is, no one 'invented' it. It was the product of persistent curiosity and continual experimentation. It evolved gradually. Mechanical ideas were being energetically explored in France and England. Each mechanic built on the work that others had done before him.

What matters most is not who was the person who first *thought* of an idea, but who it was who most energetically, effectively and successfully extended and developed it. The search for the 'inventor' of the bicycle always leads a little further back into history.

But at certain times evolution is speeded up, and change happens more and more quickly, as one good idea is piled upon others.

There is no doubt that two men, Pierre Michaux and his son Ernest, were the first people to manufacture and sell a two-wheeled velocipede that was good enough to be a commercial success. They designed, developed and improved the velocipede that became the bicycle, and they achieved a really historic breakthrough in mechanical design.

It quickly became so popular to '*vélociper*' in Paris that it was widely and sometimes rudely spoken of as a mania. From Paris the successful machine soon sailed the Atlantic to the east coast of the United States, where the mania broke out in a new peak of frenzy, and it finally caught on in England, where it was disparagingly labelled the 'fast' adjunct to a 'fast' age, and the staid upper classes looked down on it with the utmost disdain. In fact, the velocipede was greeted in England with much more reserve than in excitable Paris, though that did not stop it from having the most far-reaching consequences there.

Pierre Michaux (1813-83) was a Parisian manufacturer of perambulators, invalid carriages and three-wheeled velocipedes. His workshops were near the Champs-Elysées. He had two young sons, Ernest and Henri, who were his assistants. In March 1861, according to one story of Michaux's early days, a hat-maker, M. Brunel, of the rue de Verneuil, brought a broken *Draisienne* to the workshops to be repaired. It was probably not the first that Michaux had seen. Ernest tried it out on the Avenue Montaigne, outside the shop, discussed it with his father, and, between them it seems, they hit on the idea of fitting cranks and pedals to the front wheel, as other observant mechanics had done.

Michaux et Compagnie carried out experiments and made modifications. The 'bicycle' was always in the workshops, and Ernest rode it, gradually acquiring a sense of its possibilities as he learned to master it. Friends commented as the idea gestated. It was not hard for Michaux to build his velocipede since he already possessed many of the techniques that were required. Wheels and framework were at first wooden, and the other parts were iron, and quite easy for a craftsman

Ernest Michaux with one of the Michaux Company's later velocipedes. From a photo taken in the late eighteen-sixties.

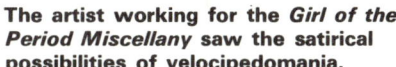

The artist working for the *Girl of the Period Miscellany* saw the satirical possibilities of velocipedomania.

to put together. It was not new techniques which at first made his breakthrough possible, but an original application of old ones.

But events become a little more difficult to elucidate, and personal conflicts blur historical accuracy. The neat story told so far is challenged by an employee of Pierre Michaux, who claimed that it was he, and not his boss, who had in fact 'invented' the first bicycle.

In about 1863 Pierre Lallement, from Pont-a-Mousson, near Nancy, came to Paris and worked for a few months for Michaux. Lallement was a coach-builder, and had been carrying out some experiments of his own with velocipedes, one of which he rode in the streets of Paris soon after arriving there.

What exactly happened while Lallement was working for Michaux is hard to say, but it is possible that he contributed a considerable amount of his own experience and a number of his own ideas at this crucial stage. Later, a heated dispute arose between the two pioneers. Michaux, of course, as the owner of a successful business, was more likely to get the credit for ideas than one of his workers. But Lallement, in his turn, had more to gain from exaggerating his own importance in the early years. The truth seems to be that both men were working on improving the basic design of the velocipede at the time, that they were in fact co-workers, and that later each tried to exclude the other.

Lallement was unlucky. Although a pioneer in a field with great potential, and though he was for a year or so right at the centre of very significant developments of the bicycle, he afterwards showed an unfortunate knack of being in the wrong pace at the wrong time. He might easily have been a major figure, but instead he is a minor one.

Perhaps thinking of the wide-open markets and the business energy across the Atlantic, and perhaps annoyed by Michaux's lack of recognition of him, Lallement left France in 1863 or 1864, and went to Ausonia, Connecticut. On November 20th, 1866 he and J. Carroll, of New Haven, Connecticut took out a patent for a two-wheeled velocipede, the first American bicycle patent.

Their efforts were not immediately rewarded with success. Had he waited two more short years in the United States, Lallement would probably have made his fortune. But, hearing of the growing success of Michaux et Compagnie in Paris, he left Ausonia, arriving back in France just in time to see the International Exhibition of 1867, where Michaux's velocipedes, now just at the high point of their development, were astonishing the Parisian public, and beginning to set a trend.

Lallement did not hesitate. He re-established himself in Paris, calling his company the Ancienne Compagnie Vélocipèdienne, a strange title for a brand new venture. It was of course intended as a direct challenge to Michaux, to show that he, Lallement, was the oldest man in the business, the original creator of the velocipede. Lallement's ambition seems to have been for overnight success, and he felt that he had to prove that he was better than Michaux.

The fierce competition between Michaux and Lallement was indicative of a change of style in the velocipede world and in manufacturing in general. Where money and reputation were at stake, generosity tended to be forgotten. From this point onwards the history of the bicycle is full of fierce rivalry and animated competition. The birth of the bicycle coincided with the death of the amateur mechanic; to be a bicycle-manufacturer a man had to possess more than one of the old craft skills; he had to be a worker in wood and metal, as well as a wheelwright and a painter. The boundaries between the traditional specialist crafts were breaking down under the impact of new technologies. A market was created, advertising began, patenting was necessary for the protection of an idea, and capital was crucial for the success of an enterprise.

Ideas were no longer flung willingly into the open for everybody's consumption, but began to be jealously guarded. Competition gave a tremendous impetus to design and to technical improvements. New ideas were compulsively explored. By the early eighteen-seventies the bicycle-manufacturer had become a specialist and a professional, and the amateur could not hope to compete any longer.

From 1867 onwards a lot of money could be made from bicycles in the right place and at the right time. And the right places were London, Coventry, Wolverhampton, Paris, New York and the Boston area.

The manufacturers were almost all riders at first. They had to be. Without practical experience they could not hope to understand the needs of the public, or the difficulties of improving their inventions. Each new experiment needed to be rigorously assessed and tested on the road, as riders and manufacturers struggled to find solutions to the many difficult practical problems of riding new machines.

Races were a vital testing-ground for new ideas, for the machine that could go farthest and fastest would obviously gain respect, and the winning machine in a well-publicized race could set a fashion that might last several years.

The year 1867 was the first really big one for the velocipede and for Pierre Michaux. At the time of the Paris Exhibition his machine was introduced to the public for the first time, and the public loved it. Business expanded and thrived through 1867 and 1868, and Michaux was unable to keep pace with the demand for the new craze. The price

The riding-school of the Compagnie Parisienne, Paris, in about 1869.

was high, from 350 francs for the plainest to 500 francs for the de luxe model, while some that were exported to England fetched as much as £25.

Other makers went into business to supply the unsatisfied demand: Lallement, Olivier Frères, Tribout and Meyer in Paris, Jules Truffault in Tours and Rousseau in Marseilles. The very best advertisement of all for their businesses was that velocipedes appeared in increasing numbers in the streets of Paris and other cities, and newspapers picked up on anything to do with them as sure to interest their avid readers.

In 1861 Michaux et Compagnie had made two experimental velocipedes, in 1863, 142 and by 1865 more than 400. By 1868 Pierre Michaux, then fifty-three years old, had opened a new factory where he employed about 300 workers, who worked as hard as they could to produce about five velocipedes a day. He earned a reputation for the very high quality of his machines: 'His velocipedes are really models of perfection,' wrote the Paris correspondent of a London magazine *The Orchestra*, 'but they cost as much as a horse ...'

Michaux et Compagnie was a spectacularly successful business, the acknowledged leader in the trade. Beside the new factory an indoor training-school was erected where free lessons were given to people who bought velocipedes, and machines hired out to those who could not afford to buy them. Riders circled round and round, the beginners hesitantly, while the more skilful did tricks, pedalled with one foot only, stood on their saddles and performed like acrobats in the circus. After five or six lessons riders were sent out to brave the hazards of the streets.

'Velocipedes have become a rage. Everybody talks of them,' wrote one visitor in 1869. 'Athletes and gymnasts lead the way, and now you see them in the hands of the old, young, serious and gay.' 'Paris is in a perfect state of frenzy with respect to its new toy,' wrote another English visitor.

It is interesting how quickly the new velocipede caught the public imagination. Suddenly it was front-page news and everybody was aware of its presence. Foreigners seem to have seen it as just another manifestation of French whimsy. 'Paris is just now afflicted with a serious nuisance,' said *Once a Week* on March 21st, 1868:

> velocipedes, machines like the ghosts of departed spiders, on which horrible boys and detestable men career about the streets and boulevards. But Paris has been afflicted with these machines for a long time past. What with macadam and asphalt, the roads are so smooth that the velocipedes have a chance in the French metropolis which is denied them in London, and they roll swiftly along, to the discomfiture of foot passengers, who are startled by their noiseless sudden approach, and to the affright of horses unaccustomed to this strange species of biped. The Parisians scarcely know whether to scowl or to laugh at this new rage, which has now lasted in Paris for about a year.

Another reporter, writing in May 1869 for the *Girl of the Period Miscellany* has a similar story to tell:

> Velocipedes have become quite a social institution in Paris, and velocipeding as necessary an accomplishment as dancing or riding. The veloceman, as he styles himself, is to be seen in all his glory careering at full speed through the shady avenues of the Bois de Boulogne or skimming like some gigantic dragonfly over the level surface of the roads intersecting the Champs-Elysées. The converging avenues of the Arc de l'Etoile are amongst his favourite hunting grounds; there he disports himself continually, to the terror of the aged and short-winded ... What will be the end of the present Velocipedomania is difficult to predict, but according to all appearances, it seems fair to suppose that the machine is very far from having reached its furthest stage of development ...

What the sceptical popular press saw as a trivial fashion and hoped would be a nine-day wonder, and made fun of in numerous satirical drawings, was in reality taken very seriously by riders and makers.

The first velocipeding clubs were founded in Paris to advance the cause, and what was probably the first cycling paper in the world, *Le Vélocipède Illustré*, appeared. Velocipedes took their place as the most popular attraction at festivities in and around Paris and advertisements for manufacturers, fêtes and riding-schools were pasted on walls all over the city.

The authorities did not like the velocipede at all. Old and respectable people demanded that it should be outlawed, and an official pronouncement banished it from the streets, forcing riders into the parks. 'Velocipedists are imbeciles on wheels!' the newspaper *Le Gaulois* told its readers on February 17th, 1869. One of them replied that he was a velocipedist; did that mean that he was an imbecile? 'Sir,' responded *Le Gaulois,* pushing its luck a bit, 'you are not an imbecile because you buy *Le Gaulois,* but a person who is intelligent enough when he walks or when he goes by coach becomes quite ridiculous when he climbs up on a velocipede.'

But in spite of the mild persecution, people persisted in riding their velocipedes to work and the riding-schools were full of learners. The craze cut across all class barriers; aristocrats and artisans showed equal enthusiasm, though of course they rode in different places.

The velocipede featured as the star of a number of music-hall acts, and private displays of riding and acrobatics were given indoors by a few not over-reputable ladies.

And of course, there were races. The first recorded track-race was held on May 31st, 1868, at Saint-Cloud, outside Paris, over a distance of 1,200 metres, and was won by James Moore, an Englishman then living in France. Moore was a friend of Ernest Michaux and had earlier been taught to ride by him. Soon such races were a great success:

> The racing ground is all marked out with flags, and there is certain to be a large cluster of banners flying at the starting place, near to which, in some reserved enclosure, scores of velocipedists are exercising their docile steeds. A certain number of them wear jockey caps and jackets of various coloured silks, and all appear to have their legs encased in high leather boots. The moment of starting arrives, and the competitiors are duly drawn up abreast ... The fair sex mount on chairs and wave their little hands and flourish their pocket handkerchiefs and laugh and almost scream with delight as at the grounding of the starter's flag, their favourites dart off, working their legs up and down ... After the lapse of a few minutes, distant shouts and cheers announce their return, and the crowd opens to allow the passage of the victor, drenched in perspiration, who passes the winning post amidst the cheers and laughter of the crowd.[2]

The first road race in the world was held on November 9th, 1869, between Paris and Rouen, a distance of 123 kilometres. It was a remarkable race, for there were 323 entries and about 100 starters, among whom were at least four women riders, who in France were allowed to compete against men, and were willing to do so. All kinds of

James Moore and André Castera, first and second in the first-ever long-distance bicycle-race, Paris–Rouen, 1869, with one of the machines which won all the leading places.

Pickering's American velocipede in action in New York City. The brake is applied by the rider pressing downwards on the saddle.

machines were entered, monocycles, bicycles, tricycles and quadricycles, and the result, another victory for James Moore, who arrived in Rouen in only ten and three quarter hours, an average speed of about twelve kilometres an hour, was also a victory for the two-wheeled velocipede over all its rivals. All the leading places were won by them in fact.

International racing soon began. English newspapers boasted of the English victories in France, and soon after the big race two French champions, one of whom was Ernest Michaux, were giving the English a beating on a track at the Crystal Palace, Sydenham.

Racing emphasized the need for lighter and better machines. Manufacturers competed with each other to improve the wheels and bearings of their velocipedes, and James Moore's success in the Paris-Rouen race was achieved on a machine which had ball-bearings fitted to the front wheel, the first time they had ever been used on a bicycle according to some accounts. On 7th and 9th August, 1869, at Sorgues, near Lyons, a M. Thévenon won all the prizes in local races on a velocipede with strips of rubber nailed on to the rims of the wheels.

The beaten competitors appealed, demanding that he be disqualified. But the judges upheld his victories.

Richard Lesclide, the founder and Editor of *Le Vélocipède Illustré*, and the man behind the organization of the Paris-Rouen race, published a small and now very rare book called *Manuel du Vélocipède* in 1869. He is confident and proud of the machine which he is helping to propagate. The velocipede is a sign of the times, he says:

> Of course, a train goes much faster, but has a mechanical, violent, unintelligent kind of speed. The speed of the velocipede is related to each individual person; it has a reasonable speed which can be varied according to whim; personal transportation replaces collective transportation and muscle-power takes the place of steam ... This wooden and steel horse fills a gap in modern life, it is an answer not only to its needs, but also to its aspirations ... It's quite certainly here to stay.

But his confidence was soon to be destroyed. The visions of progress and expansion and the undoubted supremacy of the French velocipede trade collapsed. The Franco-Prussian War of 1870-71 ruined the adolescent industry and paralyzed it for at least the next five years. Machines were given over to the manufacture of guns and bullets and the economy slumped. The English industry, based in London, Coventry and Wolverhampton, made solid and systematic progress and took the initiative away from the French.

Pierre Michaux finished his life tragically, though the exact facts of his later career have still to be established. Between about 1867 and 1869 he had gradually sold out his share in the Compagnie Parisienne to Olivier Frères, with whom he was in partnership. Probably in 1869, he finally sold them the sole interest. It was an early age to retire. Michaux apparently regretted what he had done, and started out in business again under his own name, a move which was plainly a breach of contract. Olivier Frères sued him for 100,000 francs and won. He was completely ruined, and died penniless in 1883 in the Hospice de Bicêtre in Paris, wearing the hospital uniform for the poor and insane.

This was a strange end for a man who had made a small fortune with such panache a few years before.

In The United States

> When the rumour first came across the water, a few years ago, of that wonderful and fascinating little two-wheeled machine, upon which one could go so gracefully annihilate time and space, the author of this little book was seized with his first attack of Velocipede fever.
>
> When, in the spring of 1868, we heard how popular this invention was becoming in France, we were again seized with the disease with renewed virulence. We could hardly delay for one from across the Atlantic, and embraced the first opportunity to learn the art of riding.[3]

If Paris was 'fast', so were New York and Boston. Invention boomed at the time; capitalism was expanding fast. The velocipede caught on so quickly there that, by the end of 1869, French and English makers were already looking with interest at the improvements that were pouring into the American patent office in Washington, and the *English Mechanic* was regularly publishing news of the developments on the other side of the Atlantic. Even as early as the beginning of 1868 a New York firm, Pickering & Davis, were exporting Pickering's Improved velocipede to Liverpool, where it was sold by the Liverpool firm of Samuel & Peace. Business enterprise spanned the Atlantic with surprising ease, a significant indication of the energy of the bicycle pioneers.

Goddard writes of America in March 1869 that in Washington 'the Patent powers are literally overwhelmed with applications for patents

MacDonald's Adjustable Bicycle attempted to overcome the steering problems of the boneshaker by mounting the back wheel in a circular framework. It can hardly have been very stable.

of different models of these articles. In a large room in the Patent Office, there are some 400 of these models awaiting investigation. Over 80 have already been examined and patents for them issued ... In one week 80 applications and caveats were received.'[4]

The velocipede was not an entirely novel idea in America. There had been a hobby-horse craze in 1819, soon after it was introduced in England. 'The excitable citizens went into an ecstasy of astonishment and delight, and the manufacturers found it impossible to meet the demand,' says Goddard. They were ridden in New York, in the then placid streets of downtown Manhattan, and then in Philadelphia, Troy, Saratoga and Boston.

The amateur mechanics were also at work on experimental machines in the following years. But I have not been able to find as much evidence of their activities there as I have in England. They were in many ways a peculiarly English phenomenon.

Pierre Lallement, who worked for Michaux in Paris, was the best-known unsuccessful American pioneer. His ideas, brought over from France and patented in New England in 1866, lay dormant for a year or two, and were at first thought to be an eccentric whim. But they must have had some impact on other inventors. As the news and details of the French craze filtered through into American newspapers and magazines, coach-makers and wheelwrights began to experiment and turn out their own velocipedes, and by early 1868 the velocipede industry was firmly established on the East Coast.

Makers mushroomed. In New York, Pickering & Davis, the Hanlon Brothers, the Wood Brothers, Mercer & Monod and Calvin Whitty were among the first; in Boston there were William P. Sargent and Company and the Kimball Brothers. For every manufacturer who made a name for himself there were dozens of other little inventors and improvers, each claiming to have discovered a valuable new principle. There was little doubt in the air that the French velocipede could be improved upon. 'A number of professional inventors are now laboring to bring it to American completeness,' says *Harper's Weekly*,[5] while the *Scientific American* boasts that 'like every other machine which we have copied from other peoples, this has been materially improved by American mechanics'.[6]

Basic design was inspired by Michaux, but the Americans added plenty of their own ideas. Pickering's velocipede had a brake over the back wheel which could be applied by pushing down hard on the saddle; Hanlon's was a racy upright machine with wheels of almost equal size, while MacDonald's Adjustable Bicycle adopted an altogether new steering system.

One sharp New York pioneer and maker, Calvin Whitty, realizing the enormous commercial potential of the velocipede, and seeing business booming, did a little research into the patent archives, found Lallement's designs and promptly bought the patent from him for $2,000. Licking his lips, he sent out infringement of patent notices to all the manufacturers in America, forcing them either to engage in expensive lawsuits or to purchase manufacturing rights from him. For a number of years, until the death of the mania, he prospered by collecting a royalty of $10 on every machine sold in the United States. He was at one stage even unsuccessfully sued by another maker, Stephen W. Smith, who in his turn claimed that all his other rivals, including Lallement and Whitty, had in fact stolen the design of the two-wheeled velocipede from him.

Just as in England and France, the first professional velocipede manufacturers were usually craftsmen willing to innovate for profit. To support their enterprises they needed the skills of other craftsmen. It was not a cheap or easy business:

> A manufacturer requires draughtsmen to prepare models for the foundry, blacksmiths to do the forging, wheelwrights for the wheels, machinists to turn and fit the work, foundrymen to cast

the pedals and braces, boltmakers to make the nuts and bolts, saddlers to prepare the seats, and painters and varnishers to finish the machine for the wareroom. The wear and tear in the ordinary use of the velocipede is so great as to require the very best of materials in its construction.[7]

The velocipede was a runaway success in America. 'The art of walking is obsolete,' says the *Scientific American*. 'It is true that a few still cling to that mode of locomotion, are still admired as fossil specimens of an extinct race of pedestrians, but for the majority of civilized humanity, walking is on its last legs.'[8]

Riding-schools were quickly opened to teach eager pupils the art of velocipeding, and the shortage of machines provided a fine opportunity for the owners of the schools to hire out machines by the hour, and bring in enormous profits. Gymnasiums became velocinasiums, and small books of riding instructions were put out to help the learners. Goddard gives the following instructions:

In learning, be careful to keep the shoulders straight and the head back. An erect position upon the bicycle is as necessary for grace and ease as upon the horse. Avoid looking at the wheels; accustom yourself to look ahead ...

Take things as easy as possible. The greatest difficulty with beginners is to restrain the unnecessary expenditure of muscular power. They ordinarily perform ten times the amount of labour requisite.

If you finish your first trial covered with dust and perspiration,

'It is very amusing to watch the eager pupils going through their novitiate. The beginners mount, struggle, perspire, and tumble in all directions and shapes, and blunders, awkward movements, collisions and shipwrecks follow each other in constant succession.' A scene in a riding-school in New York City.

64 King of the Road

with a bumped head, jammed feet, tired arms, sore muscles, let your faith remain triumphant and your determination and expectation to master the vehicle increased ...[9]

In Boston there were soon twenty schools and rinks; the two best and largest in the country were in Harvard Square, Cambridge. One writer claims that there were 10,000 pupils and 'graduates' in New York alone. The schools were open at almost all hours of the day and night, but there were still disappointed applicants queuing up. Velocipedes appeared in Detroit, Chicago, St Louis, San Francisco and New Orleans and in Texas. They seemed to have become an integral and unquestioned part of everyday life:

In New York, no matter where you go, a velocipede is sure to whizz past you. The school boy rides up 5th Avenue in the morning with his books strapped before him. In Broadway, where stages, wagons, carts, trucks and carriages clog the streets from morning till night, the iron steed may be seen gracefully cutting its

... Frederick Hanlon, the distinguished acrobat, seems to have transferred all his gymnastic and flying trapeze skill to the veloce, and has therefore justly earned the name of Champion Velocipedist of the world. He seemed to manage his steed with the utmost ease,' said the Velocipedist *in February 1869.*

'The Velocipede Mania', a satirical American interpretation of the death of the horse.

way among the larger vehicles.[10]

The advantages of the velocipede were obvious enough:

It takes men from the bar-rooms out into the pure air, into God's light and sunshine, and braces their lungs with the very breath of Heaven. It stimulates them to save what they would otherwise spend foolishly ... It is an inducement to young men who work in close apartments to spend more time in the open air, and furnishes them a means of healthful, invigorating and pleasant exercise.[11]

The velocipede's sudden popularity was encouraged by the showmanship of the makers and by its entertainment value. Just as in Paris, it was seen on the stage and became a character in plays. At Crosby's Opera house in Chicago the audience was treated to a spectacle between the music-hall acts: 'The velocipede has been introduced, mounted by a young and fascinating lady, and her sylph-like evolutions have created such a sensation that there are always crowded audiences, instead of rows of empty seats and boxes.'[12]

At the opening of their new school at 65 10th Street, in New York, the famous acrobats, entertainers and velocipede manufacturers, the Hanlon Brothers, gave an exhibition of their skills, complete with a brass band: 'Frederick Hanlon, a high-priest worthy of offering incense on the altars dedicated to the cause of velocipeding, appeared equipped in raiment suited to the occasion, and mounted on his favourite thoroughbred, of pure American origin.'[13]

In Prospect Park, Brooklyn, a series of bicycle races was held as part of a grand velocipede tournament, while at the Apollo Hall, on the corner of 28th Street and Broadway, 'one of the most brilliant exhibitions of skill in velocipedestrianism that has ever taken place in the city' was staged:

> Dodsworth's band was present, and the evolutions of the skilful riders were rendered more pleasing by the splendid music, The tournament opened by the entrance upon the floor of twenty-five of the most expert riders in the country, whose advent called forth immense applause, renewed as the graceful evolution of the performers excited and delighted the admiring assembly.[14]

'Many people have expressed doubts as to the real utility of the velocipede,' says Goddard. 'We believe in the utility, convenience and economy of the innovation, as well as in its capacity for affording amusement and developing strength and skill; and we believe as now improved, it is destined to mark an era in the history of vehicles.'

The bicycle certainly looked as though it had come to stay, and would progress and improve and be increasingly used. In May 1869 *Harper's Weekly* published a cartoon showing the whole of a city on wheels; old and young, ladies and gents, bakers and soldiers. The stables are empty, boarded up and to let, while the horses are being sold off at the horsemeat market next door.

This kind of light-heartedness was balanced by the more serious proposition of Mr Charles Dana, a journalist on the *New York Sun*, who suggested the building of an elevated railway from one end of Manhattan to the other, to enable a good velocipede-rider to get from Harlem to the Battery in about half an hour. *The Scientific American* took the whole velocipede question just as seriously. 'The question is getting to be an interesting one,' it says, 'as to how extensively the social system is to be revolutionized.'[15]

But something went wrong. The driving force behind velocipedomania in America was fashion and the desire of the makers for quick profits, rather than a patient interest in working out the solutions to a difficult mechanical problem. The initial impetus soon faded. The manufacturers got bored with making the same style of velocipede; they did not apparently believe in its future strongly enough to extend and develop new models. 'Though the American carriage-makers all dropped the veloce in a hurry, with a feeling of contempt for their own folly in having interrupted their proper business in behalf of such a deceptive toy,' says Karl Kron in *Ten Thousand Miles on a Bicycle*, 'the less excitable Englishmen kept pegging away at it, both on the road and in the machine shop, until the modern bicycle was evolved.'

In spite of the intensity of the craze, and the serious and optimistic forecasts that were made for the velocipede, by the end of 1871 velocipedomania in America was dead and forgotten. The fashion passed without a sport beginning. Makers could not sell any more machines, and businesses went broke. Such a dramatic fall from fashion did not inspire the manufacturers' confidence in the viability of the bicycle.

In England

> Amongst machines of recent introduction, none promises to secure so much health, strength, and amusement, to the youth of this country as the modern velocipede. It is already being patronized by all ranks; it is not too expensive for the purse of the peasant, nor too insignificant for the attention of the prince.
>
> Velocipede exercise is especially beneficial to those whose occupations and circumstances compel them to spend the greater portion of their time indoors. If clerks and shopkeepers were to take a six-mile run on a velocipede daily, they would derive an immense benefit thereby. Also ladies, who have not sufficient exercise, would, with a few months' regular and moderate running, become strong and robust.

'The "New World" Pleasure Velocipede': an American invention which turned the velocipede into a roundabout. 'The pleasure of the exercise is enhanced by association ... in looking at the picture one is seized with desire to mount and enjoy the exhilarating sport ... Probably no more durable, useful and attractive application of the principle of the velocipede than this has been brought out.'

> If the velocipede continues to gain popularity, as it has lately done, in England, both this and succeeding generations will, on the score of health, reap a most decided benefit; our countrymen and countrywomen will become possessed of clearer heads and more vigorous frames, doctors' bills and doctors' pills will become things of the past ...[16]

In England, velocipedomania was not so contagious as it was in Paris and New York, perhaps because the English mechanics had been working on their own velocipedes with considerable energy for some time, and were less likely than the Americans to snap up someone else's novel idea. Also they were scattered all over the country and not concentrated in London.

Interest in the new two-wheeled velocipede was slow, as news of the crazy excitement in Paris and New York filtered slowly through into English newspapers and magazines. It did not seem to offer immediate advantages over all the other kinds of velocipedes already suggested, and the English were quite accustomed to reading about short-lived crazes in Paris.

But Paris was not ignored. The first picture and report of a Michaux

68 King of the Road

velocipede appeared in the *English Mechanic* on June 28th, 1867. 'I have lately seen one in Paris that I think may give a notion to your readers who take an interest in the matter,' writes the anonymous correspondent. A few were brought into England, and in Liverpool the firm of Samuel & Peace was importing Pickering's American velocipede early in 1868; there was even a Liverpool Velocipede Club in existence as early as March of that year.

Rowley Turner was the Paris agent for the Coventry Sewing Machine Company, which had been founded in Coventry in 1861 as the European Sewing Machine Company by his uncle, Josiah Turner, James Starley and an American named Salisbury. Coventry, traditionally a silk-weaving town, was then suffering a disastrous economic slump and offered bright prospects and cheap labour for a small manufacturing industry. Starley, who before going to Coventry had been an engineer and designer with a London sewing-machine company, Newton, Wilson and Company, was persuaded to join the new firm as works manager.

The reason they chose Coventry was not philanthropy, as James Starley's biographer makes quite clear:

> Starley made known the improvements he had made and was still able to make in the sewing machine, and Salisbury was cute enough to understand their value. There is no doubt that Salisbury, who was an American, used his efforts to make capital out of Starley's ingenuity, and he being acquainted with a Coventry man, to whom he expressed himself pretty plainly, and who intimated that cheap labour could be obtained in the city, an introduction was arranged with Mr John Newark, a well-known gunsmith in Coventry.[17]

The European Sewing Machine Company did not prosper at first, and 'several influential local gentlemen', frightened at the prospect of there being no profitable industries in their city in which they could invest their money, determined to line their own pockets by underwriting the company, which changed its name to the Coventry Sewing Machine Company in 1863.

As a student in Paris in 1866, Rowley Turner had learned to ride a velocipede, and at the time of the 1867 International Exhibition he had seen the success of the Michaux machines. He was soon one of the mad young experts of the velocipede fever, and fever quickly turned to

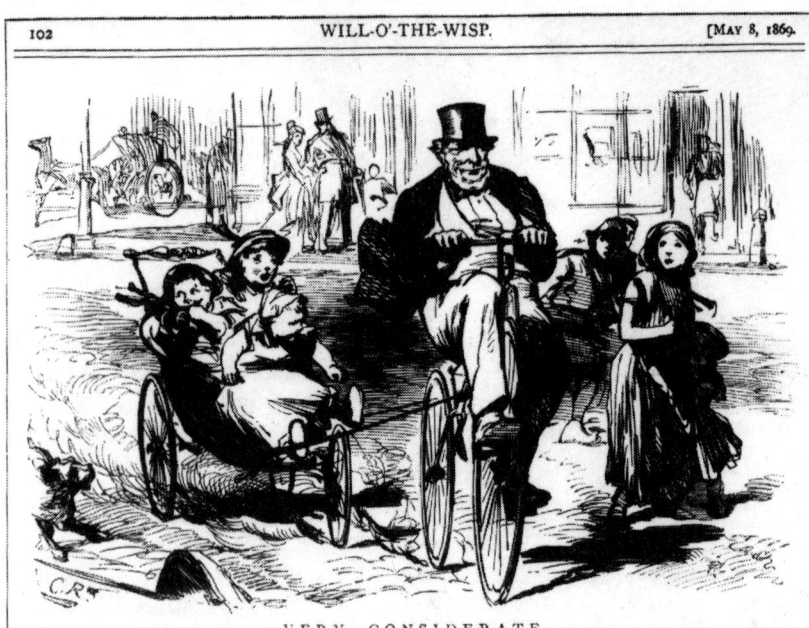

Will-o'-the-Wisp, a satirical magazine similar to *Punch,* made no secret of its opinion of 'those ridiculous velocipedes'.

A velocipede made in England in 1869 by K. W. Hedges. The brake is applied by twisting the handlebars, thus tightening the cord and pressing the lever on to the back wheel.

business. 'In 1868,' he says in a letter which he wrote in 1891 to the paper *Wheeling*, 'I put capital into the velocipede, and with the late M. L. Pascaud, the proprietor of a gymnasium in the rue Vaugirard, and a M. Cuissard, established a firm in my name. We built a large riding-school, stores and workshops in the rue Bonaparte.'[18]

Business was brisk. The company was not able to keep pace with the orders that poured in from all over the world. They decided to contract out some of the work. Late in 1868 Rowley Turner took a velocipede from Paris to London, astonishing Londoners by riding it over London Bridge and down Cheapside on the way to Euston Station, where he caught a train for Coventry, and at the other end of the line once more surprising the people who saw him riding to the works of the Coventry Sewing Machine Company at Cheylesmore. Turner seems to have taken the initiative in the affair, but perhaps he also received some encouragement from James Starley, for Starley had already dabbled in velocipedes, and was fascinated by almost any new mechanical contrivance.

The curiosity of Josiah Turner and James Starley was quickly channelled into a business venture. Rowley Turner convinced them of the great demand for velocipedes in France, and a meeting of shareholders was called to persuade them of the wrongness of their initially hostile reaction to the idea of making what most of them considered to be just the latest piece of Parisian frippery.

70 King of the Road

I Tolled You So!
Jocose Velocipedestrian – 'What's to pay, guv'nor?'
Matter-of-fact pikeman – 'Carn't yer read – Anything having two wheels, drawn by a horse or an ass – 3d! Take it through, and down with the thruppence!'

The enterprise changed its name to the Coventry Machinists' Company and set about making the first batch of 400 velocipedes for Turner to sell in France, encouraged by the possibility that they might also sell in England. Turner travelled around England ordering other components, lanterns, bells, oilcans, spanners and saddles from other makers.

James Starley was the mechanical genius behind his company. He never claimed that he had played any part in the actual design or invention of the original two-wheeled velocipede, but he was quick to understand its potential and was fascinated by it. The company started manufacturing velocipedes towards the end of 1868 and went into full production in February 1869, after receiving the sanction of the shareholders.

The response was immediate. Large orders came in from France and England. Starley began to put all his energies into improving the velocipede; each batch that left the factory in Coventry was a slight improvement on the last. James Starley, probably the most energetic and inventive genius in the history of bicycle technology, had found his vocation, and the industry that was to make Coventry the world's most important bicycle manufacturing city was founded.

London lagged behind Coventry and Liverpool in its enthusiasm for the new velocipede. But not for very long. In January 1869 the energetic Rowley Turner appears again, this time down in London demonstrating a French velocipede at a gymnasium owned by Charles Spencer, a partner in the firm of Snoxell & Spencer, manufacturers of gymnastic apparatus, probably trying to persuade Spencer to buy, or act as an agent for, some of the velocipedes he had ordered in Coventry.

John Mayall, later a keen bicyclist and racer, wrote a colourful account of the occasion, which was published in 1875 in a short-lived magazine called *Ixion – A Journal of Velocipeding.* Turner, 'a slender young man', brought in a foreign-looking packing case and superintended its opening:

> Mr Turner took off his coat, grasped the handles of the machine, and with a short run, to my intense surprise, vaulted on to it, and putting his feet on the treadles, made a circuit of the room. We were some half-dozen spectators, and I shall never forget our astonishment at the sight of Mr Turner whirling himself round the room, sitting on a pair of wheels in a line, that ought, as we innocently supposed, to fall down immediately he jumped off the ground. Judge then of our greater surprise, when instead of stopping by tilting over sideways on to one foot, he slowly halted

'It is confidently predicted in fashionable circles that Rotten Row will be completely given up to velocipedes, and that horses will be nowhere.' Cartoon from *Fun*, 1869.

and turning the front wheel diagonally, remained quite still, balancing on the wheels. I turned to Mr Spencer and exclaimed – 'By Jove, Charley, there's a balance!'

But when Mr Turner started off again, whirled around the room and halted again as before, we spectators all burst out in admiration; and when he coolly vaulted off by throwing one leg backwards, we clustered round him expressing our great astonishment and delight. He gave us a rapid explanation of the process of keeping the machine from falling whilst in motion by the management of the guiding handles; but we were too much absorbed by wonder to fairly seize and comprehend his explanation ...[19]

Mayall and Spencer soon learned to ride the velocipede. 'We were so charmed by the new machine that we devoted the evening to it,' says Mayall, 'and before I left the gymnasium, I succeeded in getting round the room with it by myself ... '

Back early the next day, they perfected their technique, and the following week-end they went to Regent's Park, where they had an altercation with a park-keeper, and then rode to Spencer's house in the Holloway Road. Mayall soon found that riding in the streets was a very different matter from riding on the smooth boards of the gym: 'The change of sensation when I first fairly tried to ride on the roadway almost bewildered me; there was a strange feeling of vibration ...' People in the streets were of course astonished by this man on a bicycle, but Mayall was afraid that the shouts he heard were more of derision and ridicule than of delight or encouragement.

Only a few days after his first encounter with the new velocipede, John Mayall set out by himself to try to ride the fifty-three miles to Brighton. Not surprisingly, he could only get as far as Redhill, a distance of about twenty-five miles, and after giving the station-master a demonstration of riding on the platform of the station, he collapsed on a bench and later took a train back to London.

But he was determined to arrive in Brighton. 'Extraordinary velocipede feat!' headlined *The Times* on February 20th:

On Wednesday, Mr John Mayall, son of the well-known photographer, accomplished the journey from London to Brighton on one of the new two-wheeled velocipedes. He was accompanied by two friends, Mr Spencer and Mr Turner, also on velocipedes. They had a preliminary run round Trafalgar Square, and then started off at the rate of 8 miles an hour on roads which proved to be generally good, but against a very strong wind all the way. They kept pretty well together as far as Crawley [30 miles], after which Mr Mayall took a decided lead, and arrived in Brighton

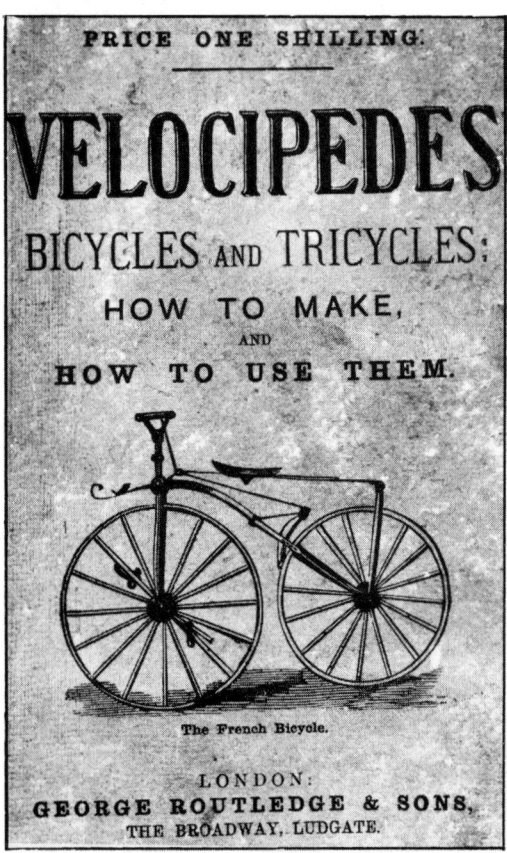

The cover of one of the many little books about velocipedes published in 1869; the title shows that it was still thought to be possible for a skilful mechanic to make his own bicycle.

The first advertisement for a bicycle appeared in the *English Mechanic* on February 19th, 1869, and probably advertised machines made either in Coventry by the Coventry Machinists' Company or imported from France.

in time and in good condition for dinner, and the second part of Kuhe's concert at the Grand Hall.

The ride helped to show that the velocipede was a serious and practical road vehicle, and not just a plaything or a piece of gymnastic apparatus, although *The Times* forgot to mention that Spencer and Turner finished the trip riding in a coach!

Spencer lost no time at all in capitalizing on the publicity. He was evidently full of enthusiasm and ambition, and on February 19th Messrs Snoxell and Spencer are advertising themselves in the *English Mechanic* as 'Velocipede Manufacturers' and offering velocipedes for sale for the high price of £10. They could not have established their own works in this short space of time, and it is obvious that the machines sold by them were in fact those made in Coventry by the Coventry Machinists' Company.

Mayall, Spencer and Turner were not lone pioneers; they were not even the first riders in England. As we have seen, Pickering's American velocipede had already been imported into England by the Liverpool firm of Samuel & Peace right at the beginning of 1868, and a club, the Liverpool Velocipede Club, almost certainly the first active club in England, was already in existence as early as March of that year. Its members were probably stimulated by the discussion about the formation of velocipede clubs which had been going on in the pages of the *English Mechanic*.

In May 1868 the first bicycle-race in England was held at Hendon, and the prize of a silver cup won by Arthur Markham. And nearly a year later, in March 1869, two members of the Liverpool club easily outdid Mayall in his London-to-Brighton run by riding from Liverpool to London in three days, the longest bicycle tour made until that time, though longer trips had been made on four-wheeled velocipedes. *The Times* also reported this exploit:

> Their bicycles caused no little astonishment on the way, and the remarks passed by the natives were almost amusing. At some of the villages, the boys clustered round the machines, and where they could, caught hold of them and ran behind until they were tired out. Many enquiries were made as to the name of 'them queer horses', some calling them 'whirligigs', 'menageries' and 'valaparaisos'. Between Wolverhampton and Birmingham, attempts were made to upset the riders by throwing stones.[20]

According to one account, James Starley himself was a pioneer rider. Later in 1869 he and William Hillman, an employee, rode from London to Coventry in one day, 'probably the first time it had ever been accomplished within the time on any machine of mechanical locomotion. The journey however severely punished the riders, and compelled them to be idle for a day or two.'[21]

Charles Spencer went on to become an ardent bicycle pioneer and journalist, and President of the Middlesex Bicycle Club. His gymnasium became the first school for teaching bicycling, and in June 1873 he was one of a party of four bicyclists, members of the Middlesex Bicycle Club, who rode for the first time from London to John-o'-Groats, a marathon for those days of about 800 miles, in a fortnight. In 1870 he published a book called *The Bicycle: Its Use and Action*, which is mainly a guide for beginners:

> The fittest use of the Bicycle is not to treat it as a toy, but to use it as a vehicle, as an ordinary means of transit from one place to another ... Thus, starting through the crowded streets at evening, as is my wont, and working at moderate speeds through the omnibuses, cabs, drays etc. till gradually the road gets clearer, extra speed may be put on ...
>
> This has been my practice for months on returning from business in the City to my residence at Harrow-on-the-Hill, and I can assure my readers that the 'Hill' occupies a very conspicuous part in the affair, particularly in wet or foggy weather, when it is a very different thing indeed to travel along dark, sloppy and hilly

THE NEW
TWO-WHEEL VELOCIPEDE.

MESSRS. SNOXELL and SPENCER, VELOCIPEDE and GYMNASTIC Apparatus Manufacturers, having introduced the best PARIS Model of the NEW TWO-WHEEL VELOCIPEDE, and having made several important improvements thereon, are now prepared to execute orders to any extent.

The VELOCIPEDES now offered are made of the best materials throughout; they are well tested, and admit of the greatest speed, with the least exertion, that have yet been offered to the public. Purchasers can have instruction, by proficient performers, in their large Practice Room, and on that Velocipede most suitable to the purchaser. Gentlemen are invited to inspect them in use at Messrs. S. and S.'s Factory and Practice Room, 35, Old-street, St. Luke's.

PRICE LIST.

		£	s.	d.
No. 1, Front or Guide Wheel 32 inches high	. . .	10	0	0
No. 2 ,, ,, ,, 36 ,, ,,	. . .	11	0	0
No. 3 ,, ,, ,, 40 ,, ,,	. . .	12	0	0
No. 4 ,, ,, ,, 48 ,, ,,	. . .	14	0	0

THE TRADE SUPPLIED.

ADDRESS:

MESSRS. SNOXELL & SPENCER,
VELOCIPEDE AND GYMNASTIC APPARATUS MANUFACTURERS,
35, OLD STREET, ST. LUKE'S, E.C.
(Three minutes' walk from Aldersgate Station, Metropolitan Railway.)

roads, to gliding swiftly round the brilliantly lighted and smooth arena of the Agricultural Hall.[22]

The outbreak of the Franco-Prussian War gave a huge boost to the English trade; all of the Coventry Machinists' Company's velocipedes were directed at the English market, and other manufacturers began to see the possibilities of the trade which had been pioneered in Coventry. Rowley Turner's Paris business must have been destroyed in the general upheaval at the beginning of the War, and as Paris was being encircled by Prussian troops Turner himself apparently escaped from the danger on one of his firm's own velocipedes.

So, after its slow start, velocipedomania did finally hit England. Its repercussions were immediate. 'A New Terror in the Streets,' shrieked *The Times* on March 24th, 1869:

> We are already beginning to taste the first fruits of the velocipedomania. A summons, applied for by the inspector of nuisances, was issued at Clerkenwell Police Court on Monday against 'a comic singer' for driving a velocipede along the foot pavement at the rate of 10-12 miles an hour. Whether the comic singer was unskilful in the management of the machine, or whether it became uncontrollable, will not be known until the case comes on for hearing; but we learn that he knocked down three persons, ran over the foot of another, attempted to escape and was with difficulty captured by the police. If this is the kind of thing we are to expect from velocipedes, a pleasant prospect is opened for pedestrians ...

The Sphinx, a Manchester paper, was even more hysterical:

> The velocipedomania has broken out here with alarming violence. A mad dog can be avoided, because he runs straight, but a madman on a velocipede runs anything but straight, and when he meanders along the footpath at a rate of 10 miles an hour, he becomes a dangerous nuisance. If babies want to be wheeled along the footpath, they must go in perambulators, and not on velocipedes.[23]

The oppressive hand of respectability and law and order, which was to prove the main enemy of the sometimes irresponsible bicycle-riders in the pioneering days, was already at work. But the pastime and the sport were too popular to be put down. Bicycle clubs were formed, races were held, exhibitions of indoor riding were organized and profitable riding-schools were opened, in London, Liverpool, Manchester and Birmingham. Just as in Paris, but with less festivity and excitement, the novelty of the velocipede caught people's attention and held it.

The velocipede was ridden by all kinds of people, from the son of Queen Victoria to such working men as could afford to buy one; it became for a short time the focus of attention in cartoons and music-hall acts. Plays, songs, poems appeared and it encouraged *risqué* sexual repartee. Overnight it became fashionable, though that is not the same thing as saying that it became respectable. Upper-class society was quite capable of being interested in it without approving of it, but most of the early riders seem to have been middle-class, engineers, mechanics, tradesmen, shopkeepers.

The Coventry Machinists' Company went on manufacturing. Other small companies sprang into existence. By the end of 1869 there were at least ten velocipede-makers in London, another ten in Wolverhampton and a couple of dozen more spread out over the rest of England. For a short while in 1868-9 blacksmiths, coach-builders and wheelwrights turned out component parts which could be bought by the smaller manufacturers or by the many people who were still making their own machines. It was easy to buy a set of plans which explained exactly how to 'do it yourself'. But the professionals soon took over. Gradually the heavy boneshaker became lighter and stronger, and slowly the price dropped. By the end of 1869 a second-hand velocipede

The velocipede quickly penetrated into the popular culture of the time, and songs about bicycles were written throughout the rest of the nineteenth century.

Although the boneshaker was ridden in England mainly by people at the other end of the social scale, the upper classes also showed some interest in it. This picture shows Prince Leopold, the youngest son of Queen Victoria, at Balmoral in 1870.

could be bought for about £3.

In the autumn of 1869 the International Velocipede and Loco-Machine Conference was held at the Crystal Palace, Sydenham. There were lectures, demonstrations, races and an exhibition, and a great deal of information was exchanged between manufacturers. One amateur velocipede-maker from Coventry complained about the high price of renting space at the Exhibition, suggesting, quite rightly, that it excluded people such as himself who could not afford it. And it does seem that, for the first time, it was the trade rather than the individual inventor which was considered to be more important.

There was by no means unanimous agreement about the best and most efficient style of velocipede, and although the races helped to prove conclusively that the two-wheeler was the fastest and most versatile, and that was the type everybody talked about, there were still plenty of three- and four-wheelers. Several of the machines shown were serious attempts to improve the standard French style. One was driven by cranks to the back wheel, and another, which won a prize, was the 'Phantom', designed by Messrs Reynolds & Mays, and put into production by the 'Phantom' Veloce and Carriage Wheel Company in London.

The worst aspect of the two-wheeled velocipede was that the front wheel would habitually clean itself continually against a rider's calves when he turned corners, making it absolutely necessary for him to wear high leather boots to avoid tearing his trousers and legs. The 'Phantom'

THE BICYCLE,
OR
The Wheel and The Way.

"SHE WAS A 'PHANTOM' OF DELIGHT
WHEN FIRST SHE BURST UPON MY SIGHT."

THE "PHANTOM" VELOCE AND CARRIAGE WHEEL COMPANY, Limited,
10, King Street, Tower Hill, London, E.C.
1870.

The 'Phantom' bicycle was an attempt to overcome the difficulties of steering and pedalling the front wheel of the velocipede at the same time.

overcame this problem; the whole framework pivoted in the middle, leaving saddle and pedals more or less in line with each other. It also had the first metal-spoked suspension wheels used on an English bicycle, and solid rubber tyres. But these advantages were offset by its erratic steering, and it was not very successful.

Invention did not stand still. The trade expanded and interest in bicycling grew and grew. People did longer and longer journeys. As bicycles got lighter and faster and their riders more skilful, the most immediately obvious way of gaining more speed was to make the driving-wheel bigger, thereby covering more ground with each pedal stroke.

Catalogues, books and newspapers followed the bicycle on to the market. They give basic information about the history of the velocipede and describe how it is made and how to ride it. One is called *The Modern Velocipede, Its History and Construction*, and another, which is partly a do-it-yourself manual, is *Velocipedes, Bicycles and Tricycles, How To Make and How to Use Them*. They communicate enthusiasm and optimism; they are carried along on the wave of inventive energy characteristic of the period, and mostly foresee a great future for the bicycle.

The seriousness of the bicycle could easily be seen reflected in the bulging bank accounts of the overworked manufacturers. It was no longer a toy, and velocipedomania no longer a trivial affair but an important social movement. 'The progress of the Bicycle seems steady and sure,' says J. F. Bottomley-Firth in *The Velocipede: Its Past, Present and Future:* 'it is of course quite clear that if they come into very extensive use, the conditions of life must undergo a change ... The winch-axle bicycle is undeniably the great locomotive invention of the age.' 'Perhaps,' comments another writer, 'the Velocipede movement may ultimately lead to the production of that reliable means of daily migration which is all that is required to induce, on the part of some of those who are in the city pent, a selection of residences a little way out of the smoke.'

But there are still a few critics around. 'The Bicycle tested ... and condemned' is the title of one long attack in the *English Mechanic*:
> ... the exertion required on the bicycle is, to my mind, of too concentrated a nature, and tends to pull one to pieces, rather than to afford a healthful exercise ... Bicycle riding, if gone in for to any great extent, results in depression, in exhaustion and in wear and tear ... Unless anyone is possessed of legs of iron and thighs of brass, I would strongly recommend him to look before he leaps into the saddle of a bicycle.[24]

Why did the bicycle make such an extraordinary headway during 1868 and 1869? How can we explain its sudden flowering?

Undoubtedly, novelty was its biggest initial selling-point. But it was not a totally new idea, only a novel solution to an old problem. Right from the earliest Michaux machines, it is quite clear that bicycles were being produced because the idea that they could be very useful was already quite common. People were interested in getting around more easily and cheaply and were less and less prepared to accept restrictions on their mobility.

The writer of a serious and perceptive little book produced primarily as an advertisement by the 'Phantom' Veloce and Carriage Wheel Company in 1870 asks himself the same question. It is 'a prominent feature of the present day that new ideas are taken up with astonishing rapidity', he says:
> The tendency of the times is to rush after novelties with an enthusiasm and eagerness utterly incomprehensible to steady-going old stagers ... Perhaps no better illustration of this characteristic can be found than is afforded by the remarkable spontaneity with which all classes of the population have been

seized with the bicycle mania, as it has been rather rashly designated by the professedly more sober-minded among the community. In much less than a couple of years the country has become totally overrun by this new saddle horse ...

Why is this, he wonders, when bicyclists have been legally repressed and ridiculed, when they have been 'chaffed, cajoled and bullied, when everything has been said and done by the churlish among mankind everywhere, envious at the coming in of a pleasure they are too stupid or too awkward to take part in, to dampen and, if possible, destroy this new delight to others'?

His answer is accurate and illuminating:

The reason is not far to find to those who will look in the right place for it: there is that in the bicycle which ministers to a want in every man's nature — every young man's, at least. The desire to 'get on' is concurrent with and united to an ambition to see, to visit, and to enjoy the most of the world around us, and the bicycle assists its owner in accomplishing the objects involved in such an ambition, by enabling him to travel over more ground with far less fatigue and a great deal more pleasure than if he depends upon his feet alone ...

Thoughts like these are voiced time and again over the next fifty years, as more and more people learn about the benefits of the bicycle and take advantage of them.

As the bicycle evolved, the front wheel grew larger to gain greater speed, while the back wheel grew smaller to save weight. This wooden-wheeled boneshaker was probably made in about 1870, and is a transitional machine.

CHAPTER 4
THE CULT OF THE ORDINARY

Although it was not yet realized, the revolution in transport had begun. The first high 'penny-farthing' bicycles were already on the roads, darting and swerving like swallows heralding the summer of the buses and cars and motorcycles which were soon to transform country life. But how fast and dangerous they looked! Pedestrians backed almost into the hedges when they met one of them, for was there not almost every week in the Sunday newspapers the story of someone being knocked down and killed by a bicycle, and letters from readers saying cyclists ought not to be allowed to use the roads, which, as everybody knew, were provided for people to walk on or drive on behind horses. 'Bicyclists ought to have roads to themselves, like railway trains' was the general opinion.

Yet it was thrilling to see a man hurtling through space on one high wheel, with another tiny wheel wobbling helplessly behind. You wondered how they managed to keep their balance. No wonder they wore an anxious air. 'Bicyclist's face', the expression was called, and the newspapers foretold a hunchbacked and torture-faced future generation as a result of the pastime.

Cycling was looked upon as a passing craze and the cyclists in their tight knickerbocker suits and pillbox caps with the badge of their club in front were regarded as figures of fun. None of those in the hamlet who rushed out to their gates to see one pass, half hoping for and half fearing a spill, would have believed, if they had been told, that in a few years there would be at least one bicycle in every one of their houses, that the men would ride to work on them and the younger women, when their housework was done, would lightly mount 'the old bike', and pedal away to the market town to see the shops.[1]

When the Ordinary or 'high' bicycle was the only kind of bicycle in existence, it was simply known as 'the bicycle'. Only when the various 'safeties' started to come on to the market, experimental and

W. H. J. Grout, bicycle-manufacturer of Stoke Newington, London, a bicycle pioneer, photographed with a Grout Tension bicycle of the early eighteen-seventies.

strange-looking machines, did the Ordinary bicycle get its name, and only much later, when 'safeties' were accepted by everyone as completely normal, was it unkindly referred to as the 'penny-farthing'. But it was, in reality, very far from ordinary. In fact, it is one of the most extraordinary machines ever made.

People are often puzzled by it. They want to know how and why it happened, and ask how it was possible to climb up on to it; wasn't it dangerous, didn't it capsize? It is easy to understand their bewilderment. The Ordinary hasn't been properly explained in the past. It has been laughed at more than it should have been, and its real mechanical and social importance hidden behind a facade of patronizing sentimentality.

It developed logically and for very good reasons. There was no adequate chain technology in the early eighteen-seventies, and although there were a number of rear-driven machines being experimented with, none of them seemed to offer such a promising future as the velocipede driven by the front wheel. The best way to get more speed out of this bicycle was quite simply to make the front wheel, the driving-wheel, bigger. For every turn of the pedals, the wheel thus covered more ground. The wheel grew in fact as high as the length of a tall man's legs would allow, and the biggest wheel which could be ridden worked out at about sixty inches high.

Yet even after these reasons have been given, and the elegance and simplicity of its particular resolution of difficult ergonomic problems explained, there remains a lingering doubt about its plausibility. It is not hard to understand why people thought the early riders were a bit soft in the head. Perhaps the fact that it has this strong air of implausibility helps to explain why it had such a hold over the men who pioneered it and understood its usefulness, and why they found it so attractive in spite of quite fierce opposition, and were so reluctant to give it up when other designs proved to be both faster and safer.

For the Ordinary did become almost a cult. A small group of enthusiasts propagated it and improved it. They rode it compulsively. They organized their own clubs, each with its own badge, they wore special uniforms, had a special language and special habits, and they organized races.

The early Ordinary-riders had a strong sense of their own identity and importance. They were adventurers and explorers, opening up a completely unknown territory of experience with tremendous energy and persistence. Most of them came from cities and towns, and city people had not been in the habit of moving outside their own districts very much. Before the bicycle, it had been expensive and time-consuming for them to get away. Few of them could afford to own a horse; England was still a stationary society.

But the bicycle changed this. On Saturdays and Sundays cyclists met together and set off on empty roads for the countryside, returning in the evenings full of the pleasures of their new experiences. Sometimes they went away from home for a week or so at a time, and rode the old stage-coach routes between the major cities, journeys which had hardly been made since the coaches died with the coming of the railways:

> ... on these early runs they were really exploring, they were adventuring into what was to them the absolutely unknown. Every bend in the road was full of pleasant speculation as to what was round the corner; the uncertainty as to the state of the roads and the certainty of some of the riders having headers made each run an adventure.[2]

Touring over hitherto undreamed-of distances, they were proud of their mastery of a difficult machine and of their independence, which set them apart from the sedate and conventional people who preferred to travel by train. It was a young man's sport and a young man's adventure. Perhaps it is this pioneering spirit which gives the riders in the old photographs their look of confidence and pride, the sense of

taking part actively in a new and dynamic way of life.

Just how much of an adventure it was can be imagined from the fact that there were no easily available road maps in the eighteen-seventies. Bicyclists had to make their own, discover which roads were good and which were bad, and pass on this often hard-earned information to others. Early bicycle books give a lot of space to describing the state of the roads: 'Andover to Amesbury is a difficult road,' we read, 'there are two high hills to cross; the road is rough in many places, a lot of walking is necessary in either direction.' And again: 'Wells to Glastonbury is a fair road in dry weather, but being oolite, it is dangerously greasy and rutty when wet.' Even the distances between places were not well established; there were not many signposts, and when he asked a country labourer the distance to the next town, the bicyclist was more likely to learn how long it took to walk than how many miles it was.

The state of the roads was a continual preoccupation for bicyclists until the turn of the century. They were neglected because it was too expensive for local authorities to look after them, and the laws that put pressure on them to do so were often impossible to enforce:

The surface was sometimes macadam, nearly always so in larger towns, whilst in the southern counties, it was either sandy gravel or chalk. In summer every road became very dusty if a wind blew, and if the dry weather was at all prolonged the sand roads became terribly loose and cut up ... In wet weather, the macadam, and to a lesser degree, the chalk, became very slippery and accounted for many croppers, whilst the sand would be lifted

'... The loneliness of those roads. It is past all belief to those who never cycled over them and only know the whirl of traffic that congests the highways today. Perfect quiet reigned out in the country, miles would be covered without meeting a vehicle, and those that were met were mostly farmers' waggons slowly drawn by heavy horses.' Two West London club members on the road in the early eighteen-eighties.

Fitted with Lever Tension Wheels, India Rubber Tyres, Improved Rudder, Registered Cliptail Sliding Spring, &c.

With his 'Ariel', James Starley introduced the first English Ordinary bicycle, and a novel system for tensioning a metal-spoked wheel. Its brake was on the back wheel.

up by the splash of the water into pedal and other bearings; any chain-driven machine suffered intensely, the block chains simply sucking in the grit until they became so gorged with it they were literally incapable of bending and were little short of bars of solid metal.[3]

With such roads, it was not surprising that a great deal of the energy of bicycle-manufacturers was later directed towards softening their impact and the terrible vibrations that they caused. Sprung frames, front forks and saddles, and eventually the pneumatic tyre were all introduced to make cycling faster and more comfortable.

But in the days of the Ordinary, riders tended to favour the roads that the knew were rideable, flat and well-surfaced, such as the London-to-Portsmouth road, which was the busiest cycling road anywhere in the country. Two of the villages on the road, Ripley and Cobham, soon became the Meccas of London cyclists, with a long and colourful tradition behind them.

One old cyclist recollected that it was the habit to dump broken stones across the roads and leave them to be worn in by the passing traffic; this was manageable perhaps for carts and wagons, but disastrous for bicyclists. The time usually chosen for this dumping was the early summer so that the tourist traffic would do its fair share of the rolling: 'The loose stones often caused riders to fall. They were the chief source of our numerous croppers, for our saddles were placed as close as possible to the upright forks with the idea of getting as much weight and force on the pedals as possible, and as little on the tiny and light back wheel.'[4]

In such a position, of course, riders were extremely unstable on a bad road, and the 'cropper' or 'header', a heavy fall forward over the handlebars, could be a very nasty experience, and sometimes caused quite serious injuries to noses, skulls and wrists. Newspapers of the time contain an alarming number of reports of fatal bicycle accidents and, although most good riders learned to fall properly, there was always the strong possibility of a 'cropper' happening. Most riders seem to have taken them more or less as a matter of course.

If the rough roads made bicycling dangerous and often caused damage to both riders and machines, and were a constant source of grumbles, there was always the consolation of the countryside. England in the eighteen-seventies was still a rural paradise which, except in the industrial Midlands and North, had hardly changed since the Middle Ages.

There was soon very little of this unspoiled England which had not been explored. Rides were made right up into the far north of Scotland and down to the southern tip of Ireland, and bicyclists were almost the only strangers who were seen in these distant parts. They were like messengers from the outside world. 'The loneliness of those roads,' reminisced G. H. Smith, 'is past all belief to those who never cycled over them and only know the whirl of traffic that congests the highways today. Perfect quiet reigned out in the country, miles would be covered without meeting a vehicle, and those that *were* met were mostly farmers' wagons slowly drawn by heavy horses.'[5]

In America the emptiness and vastness was even more impressive, and bicycling took root at first in New England, where the towns were a rideable distance apart and the roads at least existed. There, a lull in bicycling enthusiasm followed the sudden fall from favour of the velocipede, and the Ordinary, exported at first from England, did not come into use at all until about the end of 1877, and was not manufactured in the United States until 1878, when the Pope Manufacturing Company started in business in Hartford, Connecticut. The first club there was the Boston Bicycle Club, founded the same year, and the second was in San Francisco, then still a small town not much increased in size since the Gold Rush days. 'Bicycling here being only in its embryonic stages, so to speak,' writes one East Coast rider, 'it

is in a rather chaotic and uncertain condition as yet.'

The lack of roads in the San Francisco Bay area made bicycling difficult, but the pioneers persisted. In 1880, when bicycling in England had already become a popular sport with thousands of followers, some members of the San Francisco Bicycle Club made the long trip round the south end of the San Francisco Bay. 'This was only possible in the spring or autumn,' writes one of them to an English magazine, 'when the condition of the roads allowed it. The rainy winter months convert the earth roads into bottomless quagmires, and the long rainless summer months reduce them to a condition of dust that precludes riding. We can always find 10 or 20 miles of good riding, however, in the vicinity of Oakland, and we are thankful for small favours.'

The Ordinary-riders in England found themselves in a predicament. They simply wanted to ride their bicycles wherever they fancied and most of them were quite well-behaved people. But the general public reacted with horror and they met with hostility from many different quarters. The speed and style of the new vehicle was thought to be flashy and irresponsible in town and an intrusion into the placidness of the countryside. Some people just thought it was a joke.

Little boys tried to knock bicyclists down in the streets. People in charge of horses complained that bicycles surprised and frightened them, as they did not make any noise as they approached. Religious people complained because they saw bicycles on the roads on Sundays, and one vicar even went so far as to make it publicly known that he would not welcome anyone who came on a bicycle into *his* church. Bicyclists repudiated accusations of irreligion:

> This exercise is often of great benefit to both body and mind, and I am satisfied that very often more good to the soul is derived from communion with nature in summer, than by sitting in a stifling atmosphere in church, probably longing for the end of the service. The amount of cant and hypocrisy on this subject is very edifying! The richer classes especially think nothing of equally breaking the Sabbath by driving to church in their carriages.[6]

A group of American bicycle pioneers on the road outside Readville, Massachusetts, taking part in the first two-day cycling tour in America; September 11th, 1879. The first five figures are: Charles Pratt, a writer and organizer of the League of American Wheelmen in 1880; Col. Albert Pope, the head of the Pope Manufacturing Company; L. H. Johnson, one of the first Amateur Champions; Josiah Dean, a racing man and co-editor of *Bicycling World*; Geoffrey Fairfield, the President of the Weed Sewing Machine Company of Hartford, Connecticut, who manufactured bicycles for the Pope Manufacturing Company. Right at the end of the line is Frank Weston, the publisher and editor of America's first bicycling paper *The American Bicycling Journal*.

84 King of the Road

Many of the people shown in the illustration on page 83 took part in the second two-day tour which was held a month later. They posed for this picture in Wellesley, Massachusetts.

The cover of *Bicycle Riding: Its Theory and Practice,* published in 1878.

The cover of Charles Spencer's *The Modern Bicycle,* published in 1876.

Above all, some policemen and magistrates earned themselves bad reputations for their hostile attitudes. By-laws varied from place to place and were often loosely defined; for some time the legal status of the bicycle itself was in question. Was it a carriage or a cart? What sort of rights did it have on public roads? Should a rider pay tolls on the turnpikes or not?

The law began to put pressure on riders. They were not to ride on the footpath. They had to ring a bell continuously as they rode to warn other users of their approach. They had to carry a light after dark, and they could be prosecuted for 'furious riding', which applied mainly to organized racing, but was always hard to define since what was a quiet spin in the country to a fit athlete might easily appear to be 'furious riding' to an unsympathetic magistrate. Riders were fined for often trivial reasons, although most of them accepted a fine for footpath riding as an occupational hazard.

But there were some policemen, it seemed, who thought they had an automatic right to stop a bicyclist in their village just for being there. It began to look as if the peacable bicyclist was the object of organized repression. 'No class or association of whatever description appear to have been subject to such unjust treatment, without giving the slightest provocation, as bicyclists have frequently met with,' complained *The Bicyclist* for October 1876. 'It is clearly proved that frequent attacks upon bicyclists have not been mere showers of empty chaff, but have taken the form of dastardly attempts to peril both the life and limbs of the rider.'

The Bicyclist went on to give details of 'an act so fiendish and murderous that nothing short of a long term of imprisonment would seem to justly punish the offender'.

On 26th August, a number of bicyclists were making their way along the high road at Hendon, when they overtook the St Alban's

[sic] coach. On top of the vehicle was Henry Cracknell, guard to the coach, who had provided himself with an iron ball connected with a long rope. As the bicyclists overtook the coach this person launched the missile in question against the machine of Mr Gee, the Hon. Sec. of the Trafalgar Bicycle Club, and he was the next moment lashed over the shoulders by the driver of the coach ... Mr Mitchell, who followed him, was caught by the rope, and his bicycle overturned and he himself thrown to the ground with great violence. He was then dragged some distance until the rope broke. His clothes were torn, his leg bruised and his bicycle damaged.

The prosecution of Cracknell and Parsons, the driver, was a test case. The court-room at the Edgware Petty Sessions was crowded with bicyclists and coaching people, 'all of whom listened to the proceedings with great interest, and frequently gave vent to their feelings by stamping, hissing and cheering'. Mr Gee admitted that he had sworn at the coach-driver who would not allow him to pass; the coach-driver claimed that he had had a lot of trouble in the past with bicyclists frightening his horses, and therefore felt justified in 'taking preventive measures'. But the magistrate did not consider this was a good enough reason for assaulting strangers, and they were found guilty. Cracknell was fined £5 and Parsons £2. 'We think to charge £5 for the chance of killing a man is holding human life too cheap,' commented the *Bicycle Journal* drily.

But the conviction was a moral victory:

The bicycle atrocity is avenged, and riders may now go their way, feeling assured that they have an equal right with all others on the Queen's Highway ... But we urge upon bicyclists the palpable prudence, nay, the absolute necessity, of so riding along the public thoroughfares as to avoid, as much as possible, giving offence, causing horses to shy, or getting in the way of traffic. There are some bicycle riders who ought to bear the blame of most of the charges made against the bicycling community.[7]

For some time, public feeling was so strongly against the bicycle and the people who rode it that it seemed possible that legislation might be introduced to stamp it out altogether. Bicyclists had to fight for their survival.

The turning-point was reached in 1878, when the bicycle was properly defined legally and defended in a humorous and friendly leading article in *The Times*.

The bicycle has come to the front and is fighting for existence ... It has now surmounted the difficulties of construction, and adapting itself to human capabilities. It augments at least threefold the locomotive power of an ordinary man. A bicyclist can perform a journey of a hundred miles in one day with less fatigue than he could walk thirty ... Bicyclists are become a power.

The legislature would be very unfaithful to the courageous principles which have hitherto guided it in the treatment of discoveries and improvements, if it showed any prejudice in this matter. That would be a great injustice to the men, most of them still young, who have won for themselves a great convenience, and no less pleasure, at no cost whatever. Society used to be divided into the equestrian and the pedestrian orders. These people have found a third rank. Their success proves what men can do. They have attained the speed of a horse, leaving the flight of an eagle open to nobler, or wilder, aspirations.[8]

As more and more people owned bicycles, opposition became more and more difficult to sustain. In the countryside, innkeepers and blacksmiths became more friendly when they realized that riders brought them business and were after all quite nice people. *Bicycling News* remarked on September 1st, 1876 that:

Bicycling is steadily outgrowing prejudice and bicyclists are becoming of such importance as travellers that even the rural

86 King of the Road

The start of a bicycle race from Bath to London in 1874.

CITY BICYCLE SCHOOL.

The proprietors have great pleasure in announcing that they have opened premises in the

HEART OF THE CITY,

as a Bicycle School, **larger** and **more commodious** than **any other in existence.**

In making this announcement they do so with the conviction that they are meeting

A GREAT PUBLIC WANT

during the rise and development of the

ART OF BICYCLE RIDING,

and appeal to all Bicyclists, and intending Bicyclists, for their

SUPPORT AND ENCOURAGEMENT.

This school is open to enable intending riders to learn privately, at a

MODERATE CHARGE,

and to extend to riders the opportunity of perfecting themselves and

LEARNING ACCOMPLISHMENTS

under the tuition of a professional rider of great experience.

Terms—1s. 6d. single lesson ; or efficient riding guaranteed for 10s.

Practice, on Spider Machines, 1s. first hour, 6d. second hour, &c.

Address:—**CHEQUER YARD,**
(Exactly opposite Aldgate Metropolitan Station.)
Manager—Professor T. QUINTON,
Champion Ornamental Rider.

Advertisement – 1878.

Briton distinguishes in the lately ridiculed rider of wheels, one of a class who will benefit the towns and villages throughout the land.

When bicyclists shall have imparted to others the knowledge which they themselves possess, that a bicycle, costing less than a horse in the first place, and maintained at an outlay exceeded by that ordinarily paid for shoeing a horse, will carry a man further in a day than he can ride a horse and do it with less fatigue to himself, they will be looked upon as men whose comfort is worth studying. They have given roadside houses new leases of life, and transformed dull, unvisited villages into places whose inhabitants have only to look out of doors at almost any time of day to see people from beyond the confine of their own parishes.

When velocipedes have become more numerous than horses upon our great roads, we may hope to see the British Government wake up to the importance of the bicycle as an instrument by means of which men may rapidly, easily and safely move from place to place.

In the face of such hostility, it made all the more sense to join a club. A club gave protection and companionship and would help a member who got into trouble with the law. From the foundation of the Pickwick Bicycle Club in Hackney, London, in 1870, for many years the oldest surviving club, the growth of the movement was spectacular.

In 1874 there were 7 clubs in London and 22 in the rest of the country. By 1876 they had increased to 11 in London and 46 elsewhere, and by the end of 1877 this number had once more doubled. *The Bicycle Annual* for 1878 lists 64 London clubs and 125 in the provinces, and the *Cyclist and Wheel World Annual* for 1882, 184 in Greater London and nearly 350 in the provinces. The average size of the clubs in 1882 was about 30 to 40 members, but some of the biggest could boast more than 100 members. And then of course, there were thousands of riders who did not join a club.

As well as forming local clubs, which organized week-end trips and race meetings, and sometimes hired out machines to poorer members, it soon became obvious that an umbrella organization was absolutely essential to safeguard the interests of bicyclists in general, and after a good deal of squabbling the Bicycle Union, the predecessor of the Cyclists' Touring Club and many other national organizations, was formed in 1878. The growth of the Bicycle Touring Club, which changed its name to the Cyclists' Touring Club (C.T.C.) in 1883, was phenomenal. One year after its foundation it had 836 members, by 1880 3,356, and by 1886 it could boast 22,316 members, a number that was not exceeded until the great bicycle boom of the mid-'nineties.

A well-designed club uniform made sense because it was comfortable to wear; tight knickerbockers, high boots and a jacket without any flaps or frills. It was dark so that the dirt of the road and oil from the wheels would not show up. It was also good public relations. This more or less standard uniform, first worn by the Pickwick Bicycle Club members and later recommended by the C.T.C., was varied by the addition of individual club hats and badges. It gave the club members a sense of belonging and helped to identify them when they were out on the road:

> Bicycle riders can obtain more pleasure, and enlist more recruits by riding together in a compact and neatly dressed body than by each man wearing what pleases him and going where he likes. To see a dozen or score of men astride their silent horses, uniformly dressed, each rider in his place, and all regulating their speed by the captain as they glide smoothly and swiftly along a country lane is a sight fascinating to a stranger and gratifying to a brother cyclist.[9]

The clubs also had a bugler. He was supposed to sound a few notes to call the riders together. But bugles could sometimes do more harm than good to the name of bicycling. A group of excited, fast-riding, bugle-blowing city people riding new-fangled and ridiculous-looking machines did not go down too well in sleepy country villages on Sunday afternoons. *Bicycling News* thought the problem serious enough to devote an editorial to it, in its usual laconic style:

A benefit race organized for the victims of flooding in the Midi, held in the Tuileries Gardens in Paris in 1875. These races appear to have been more acrobatic than athletic.

PARIS. — COURSES DE VÉLOCIPÈDES, ORGANISÉES AU BÉNÉFICE DES INONDÉS DU MIDI, DANS LE JARDIN DES TUILERIES.

It cannot be necessary for each of three men riding in company to blow unharmonious blasts upon questionable instruments whenever he can manufacture, by diligent searching, an opportunity. There is a reprehensible practice gaining ground among some bicyclists which cannot be too strongly condemned. They do not hesitate to make their horrible noises immediately in front of strange horses, to the annoyance and also the danger of riders and drivers.[10]

The relationships between bicyclists and horses were full of complicated delicacy: 'Horses, it must be admitted, do not like bicycles,' said *The Times* leader.

There is no end to a horse's dislikes. A horse will be frightened to death by numerous objects and occurrences that, so far from creating the slightest alarm in other creatures, will escape their notice altogether. A horse will be very much frightened at a bit of paper, at a wheelbarrow by the roadside, at a hat or a jacket, a stick, a wisp of hay, a few weeds, a bit of dirt, a bush, a gap, a donkey or a cow ...

Some horses were quite agreeable, others were touchy. How to deal with the touchy ones was a problem, and the rules of the Cambridge University Bicycle Club, formulated in 1876, proposed one possible solution: 'If a horse, on meeting a bicycle, shows signs of restiveness, it is not always wise to dismount at once. To dismount *suddenly* is more likely to frighten a horse than to continue riding slowly by, *talking to the horse as you do so*.'

With dogs, who hated bicycles then as they still do today, no such sensitivity was called for. They either attacked you or they did not:

Was the dog hurt? was a question we read the other day in the *Hertford Mercury* as being asked during the hearing of a case in which a fishmonger had been summoned for permitting a dangerous dog to be at large, and which pretty little pet had, in attempting to bite an unoffending bicyclist, brought rider and machine on top of its canine person. Was the dog hurt? tenderly inquired the chairman of the bench of magistrates ...

Was the rider hurt? Was his machine damaged? Are bakers to be allowed to drive down bicyclists, and fishmongers' savage dogs to bring them down to earth with impunity? are the questions riders must ask themselves.[11]

Bicyclists themselves of course were far from blameless. Some of them persistently flouted the law by riding on the footpath whenever the road was a bit too rough for their liking, and raced down hills as fast as they could on every occasion. Among the clubs, there was a kind of snobbishness which some unattached riders found rather offensive. 'The clannishness of the bicycle riders is carried to the point of intolerance,' said the *Daily News* on August 23rd, 1876. 'A forlorn and solitary bicyclist, wearing no uniform or other token of club membership is contemptuously nicknamed "an outcast", and hardly recognized as having a clear right to a share in the Queen's Highway.'

The passion for order and military precision seems to have been overdone by some clubs: 'The uniforms adopted by some savoured more of the costumes worn by a German band, than by respectable Englishmen bent on enjoying themselves,' said a critic later. Mostly the uniform was intended to give an impression of respectability that could easily be shelved once the riders were out on the open road.

The bicycling clubs were vital to the existence of the pastime. Bicycling was essentially a communal activity; it was nice to ride with other people. Indeed, only a brave man would undertake a long trip by himself. The Saturday and Sunday club runs were the beginning of the modern 'week-end', when city people looked out towards the countryside and its pleasures as a way of recovering some of the health and strength they felt they had lost in the city. They were a way of refuelling

A faded photograph, but a fascinating period piece. Very few clubs would have had as many members as this in the mid-'eighties, and this is in fact a 'meet' of several clubs, lined up one behind the other. Probably taken in Colchester about 1886.

William Keen, bicycle-manufacturer, had his factory at the Angel Inn, Thames Ditton, on the Portsmouth Road. This group of bicyclists and tricyclists was photographed there about 1885. The man standing to the right of the tricycle may be Keen himself.

for the strains of the week ahead.

The clubs were such vital institutions in the eighteen-seventies and 'eighties that many people took up bicycling and tricycling so that they could take part in the social life that the clubs offered. It was a way of joining a magic circle of new activities, of making new friends, of adopting a new style of life. Club life was not just riding and racing, it was also talking, arguing, reminiscing, eating, drinking, writing articles for magazines, organizing dances, putting on plays and musical evenings. On winter evenings the club room, which was often in a pub, was a place where members could meet their friends. *Bicycling News* argued that not only was club life 'absolutely essential to cycling', but that 'its popularity today may be to a very great extent ascribed to club life'.

Most of the people who took up bicycling in the early days were more or less middle-class people, tradesmen, shopkeepers, manufacturers, clerks, the occasional Civil Servant, doctor or teacher. There were a number of distinctly upper-class clubs, but in general the upper classes thought it vulgar to be seen in public on bicycles, which were not only unconventional but not quite respectable. The upper classes had their own sports, cricket, tennis, riding, boating and polo. Poor workers could not at first afford the luxury of a bicycle costing £12 or £15, but as second-hand machines came on to the market for a few pounds many could, and a lot of the clubs had a strong working-class element, particularly in the north of England and the London suburbs.

The price of a bicycle varied considerably according to the quality and the finish. A 'Gentleman's' bicycle made by the Coventry Machinists' Company cost £16 in 1878, and there were ultra-light racing machines weighing hardly more than twenty pounds which could cost as much as £20-£25. But by 1884 'The Working Man's Friend', made by J. Devey and Company of Wolverhampton, could be had for as little as £4 10s. Obviously, with such a price range, few people could easily claim that it was impossible for them to afford a bicycle.

Bicycling was, in general, a leveller of classes. The new city suburbs were the heartland of the bicycle, where the old rigid class distinctions were being redefined in terms of money and social status. It was the new urban proletarian and white-collar worker above all who felt himself to be in need of the intense exercise and pleasure which the bicycle could give, and he was the kind of man who seized the new opportunity with relish. *Wheel World* had this to say in 1880:

> Thousands of cyclists are to be found flitting round the country on their glittering wheels; their open and trammelless existence begets a freedom of manner peculiarly characteristic.
>
> The man who is cooped up all the year round in the Metropolis, with nothing more cheering than a perspective of chimney-pots to gaze upon, will find his health improved, his mind expanded, and that modicum of artistic appreciation of Nature's beauties which he possesses vastly enlarged and enlightened by an occasional run into the country, away from the busy hum of men. Thus it is to the dwellers in the cities as much or more than to those resident in the country that cycling offers such numerous charms. Since the first use of the hobby-horse to the present time, the pleasures of independent locomotion have been acknowledged. Fettered by neither time nor tide, the cyclist wanders at his own sweet will. The slight dash of Bohemianism serves only to enhance the enjoyment of the journey.[12]

The bicycle was also very practical, for it shortened the time it took to get to work every day. 'To working men it is an incalculable boon,' comments *Bicycling News*, 'for it enables them to live further away from their work, and to substitute for themselves and their families a cheap and healthy home at a moderate distance from their town for the expensive insalubrity of the urban rookery. The social importance of this benefit can hardly be overestimated.'[13]

Ever since the first machines of the amateur mechanics, the essential

---

The photographer photographed; a picture taken by the Thames about 1885.

'When he deliberately starts out for a ride of pleasure or exercise, and especially on a Sunday, the wheelman should attire himself properly, and as neatly as possible. Dress, as it is neat or shabby, tells amazingly either for or against bicycling. Moreover, the better a man is dressed, the more he will respect himself ... ' (*Wheel World,* September, 1882.) In this picture of a London club taken in the Upper Richmond Road, Putney, about 1885, the tricycle is already a serious rival to the Ordinary bicycle.

The Cult of the Ordinary 93

Mastering the Ordinary was no easy task. Mounting was the hardest part. Left foot on the step, backbone up between the legs, scoot forward with the right leg, straighten up the left when you've got up enough momentum, slip forward on to the saddle, and only then start pedalling. A picture taken about 1885.

94 King of the Road

'Racing on Ordinaries', a drawing by George Moore, the best of the cycling artists of the eighteen-eighties and 'nineties.

problem in bicycle design had always been the same, to find an efficient mechanical system to harness the energy of the human body, with as little wastage as possible. Weight and friction were the two main sources of waste of energy. By 1870 the two-wheeled bicycle had been accepted almost universally as the most efficient system available at that time, and bicycle-makers directed their inventive skills to improving and refining it.

James Starley, William Hillman, Dan Rudge, W. H. J. Grout, Thomas Marriott, Fred Cooper and other pioneer manufacturers were all riders. They were not producing bicycles for distant and anonymous consumers but for people like themselves. They understood the problems of mounting, steering and pedalling freely and easily, and applied what they learned from their own experience to the machines they manufactured. Weight could be saved in the wheels and the 'backbone'; friction cut down by using roller or ball-bearings in the hubs; a much better steering head could be made and a more efficient brake, and rubber had to be used on the tyres.

Making a light wheel was a severe test of mechanical ingenuity; the wooden-spoked and metal-rimmed boneshaker wheel had been painfully inadequate to take the jarring and jolting of bad roads. Messrs Reynolds & Mays had used metal spokes in their 'Phantom'. These were in pairs, attached at the hub and at the rim through an 'eye'. They were tightened by moving the flanges of the hub farther apart. The

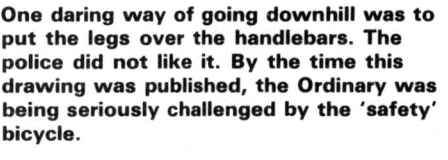

One daring way of going downhill was to put the legs over the handlebars. The police did not like it. By the time this drawing was published, the Ordinary was being seriously challenged by the 'safety' bicycle.

wheel was not especially successful.

Other experiments with suspended, as opposed to compressed, wheels had been made in France. In 1870 James Starley and William Hillman patented the 'Ariel' bicycle, which included all the latest ideas in bicycle design, and was sold first by Starley & Smith in Coventry and later made under licence by Haynes & Jefferis, the company to whom Starley, now independent of the Coventry Machinists' Company, sold many of his ideas. The wheels of the 'Ariel' were called 'Lever Tension' wheels, and the spokes were radial and held in tension by a pair of levers attached to the hubs and rims. The levers took some of the strain off the spokes since they could transmit much of the pressure applied to the pedals directly to the rim. Smith and Starley, sure of the rightness of their idea, offered to fit these wheels, with rubber tyres, to the hundreds of wooden-wheeled boneshakers that had been discarded by their owners. 'The principle of Lever tension and mode of suspension adopted,' they claim in the 'Ariel' catalogue, 'is *the only correct plan* for wheels which are propelled by leverage upon the axle ...'

In 1871 W. H. J. Grout introduced his version of the 'Tension' wheel. The spokes were radial and each was individually adjustable by a nipple at the rim. Other makers also advocated this method. Starley claimed that it wasted power, and an argument developed that was known as the Battle of the Wheel. But Starley himself had the final say: in 1876, he produced the 'Tangent' system, in which the wheel was held completely rigid by the spokes being tensioned in four different directions. Starley's 'Tangent' system is still universally used, and is still the strongest way of building a bicycle wheel.

The 'Ariel' set new standards in bicycle-manufacture. It was the first all-metal English bicycle to be mass-produced and weighed about fifty pounds. At £8 it was expensive, but not exorbitant. It was the first English Ordinary bicycle, and introduced for the first time in a systematic way the idea of the size of the front wheel being variable to suit the length of the rider's leg. 'Respecting the special and comparative merits of the "Ariel" and its capabilities,' declare the manufacturers, 'we might dilate at considerable length, but will simply declare it to be at once *the lightest, strongest, safest, swiftest, easiest, cheapest, best finished and most elegant of modern Velocipedes.*'

Starley is certainly not anxious to conceal his leading role in the field, although he never suggested that he had 'invented' the bicycle:

> Bicycling has fairly taken rank as one of the healthiest and most enjoyable out-door sports of the English gentleman. We have bestowed great care and attention in order that the amusement might become entitled to such distinction, and henceforth our chief efforts shall be given to maintaining and increasing its popularity, by the production and supply at the most moderate rates, of what we beg respectfully, yet confidently, to submit as THE PERFECTION OF PEDO-MOTIVE MECHANISM.[14]

The bicycles made by Thomas Sparrow, a smart London maker who soon had a showroom in Piccadilly, were tested and proved in June 1873. As we have seen, Charles Spencer, and Messrs Hunt, Leaver and Wood, members of the Middlesex Bicycle Club, set out to ride from London to John-o'-Groats, the most northerly point of the British Isles, about 800 miles away, the longest distance ever attempted. This was to form 'some idea of the distance which could be tracked on a Bicycle without preliminary training, and on the ordinary turnpike roads'.

They did it in fourteen days almost without incident, except that five miles from Newark they met

> an intoxicated yokel driving a half-broken horse, and one of our party, who was behind, kindly vaulted off his bicycle to allow more room to pass; in return for which civility, the bumpkin got down from his trap, and quite unexpectedly and unprovokedly knocked the bicyclist down, giving his opinion 'that such damned things ought not to be allowed'.[15]

The ride received a good deal of publicity in the newspapers. 'A more

"THE DELIGHTFUL FREEDOM AND COMFORT OF THE BALANCE."

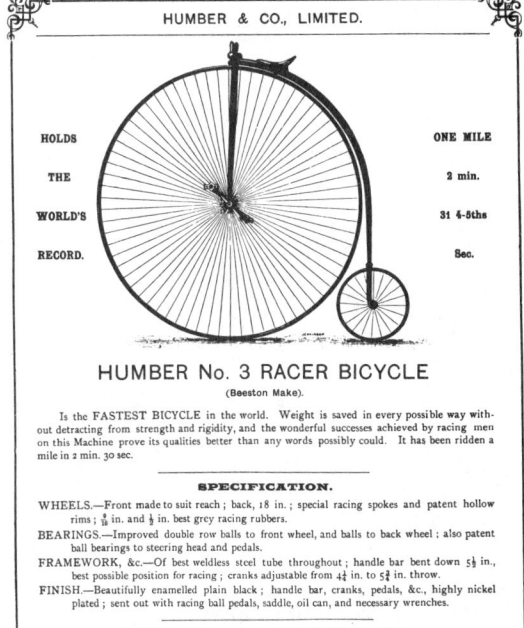

extraordinary journey had seldom been recorded,' said the *Daily Telegraph*.

A distance of 800 miles has been covered, at a rate of 60 miles a day. To say that the work would tire a horse is a feeble description of it. The strongest horse would *break down* under such a journey. Bicycle riding at the rate of 60 miles a day must have a fascination of its own ... You are a self-contained man, with all your resources under your own control.

Bicycle racing was the high point of the cult of the Ordinary. It stimulated design, improved construction, tested reliability. It obsessed some racers, drew huge crowds, established new popular idols and was the arena for many extraordinary athletic feats.

Bicycle racers proved they were stronger than horses by beating them over measured distances. Mostly they raced against each other and against the clock. Track and road races were organized by clubs and athletic societies, and the crack riders competed against each other for national titles over all distances and times from one mile to twenty-four hours, and place-to-place records were set up and constantly attacked over the rough and unpredictable main roads.

The journals of course were full of superlatives when records were broken, manufacturers full of pride. At Lillie Bridge Track on October 19th, 1874 David Stanton beat John Keen over 106 miles with a time of 7 hours 58 minutes $54\frac{1}{2}$ seconds, 'the most extraordinary performance on record of any man, animal or machine'. In the same year 5,000 people watched a fifty-mile race between the same two riders in Wolverhampton.

In February 1876, the *Bicyclist* claimed, there were between 15,000 and 16,000 people at the Wolverhampton track to watch the one-mile championship race between Keen, Cooper and Moore, 'one of the largest gatherings ever known in this district to witness an athletic performance of any description'.

On September 12th, 1878 F. Smythe, 'despite rain, wind, and heavy roads, covered no less than 218 miles in less than 24 hours'. And on August 2nd, 1882 H. L. Cortis, the idol of the English bicycle-riders,

The dangers of cycling in 1882; an advertisement for Bown's tyre-sticking gum. A testimonial reads – 'Without doubt possesses powers of tenacity unequalled in our experience, and we unhesitatingly pronounce it the very best process of the kind before the public. No pressure that we can bring to bear has in any way succeeded in parting the india rubber from the metal.'

Humber advertisement; about 1883.

became the first man to cover more than twenty miles in an hour on a bicycle.

As the bicycling public responded with such enthusiasm, and the attractions and usefulness of the bicycle were demonstrated more and more convincingly, the industry flourished. Coventry became the undisputed headquarters of ideas and expertise, and the Coventry Machinists' Company and the now independent James Starley the acknowledged kings of the trade. Many of the manufacturers who were later to be well known started their careers working close to Starley, and the Coventry firms had a way of serving as schools for the apprentices of the expanding industry.

New firms were started in London, Birmingham, Sheffield, Nottingham, Glasgow and Wolverhampton, the home of the cheap bicycle. Other light-engineering firms saw the opportunity and turned over part of their production to bicycles. 'In the Midlands, the obscure shops wherein a few boneshakers were formerly thrown together have given place to great factories, from which hundreds of accurately fitted bicycles are issued every week.'[16]

In 1874 there were about twenty firms making bicycles in England, but there was still no firm basis for confidence in the future of the industry. 'The circumstances of that time were very peculiar. No one had what we may call a legitimate confidence in the future success of the bicycle. It was thought to be only a passing whim, and even Starley himself did not believe that its foundation would be made sufficiently solid to enable a firm to exist permanently on its manufacture alone.'[17]

H. H. Griffin's *Bicycles of the Year 1878* lists sixty-eight makers, and says that there are over 100 in existence, and describes the Coventry Machinists' Company as 'the largest makers in the world, employing over 100 workmen at Coventry, and with unrivalled showrooms in London'.

The bicycle began to play an important part in the economies of these cities. People did not just ride bicycles; they also began to earn their livings making them. When a new Highway Act was being discussed in Parliament in 1878, which threatened to make life extremely uncomfortable for bicyclists, to the point of making it impossible for them to ride in some areas, it was seen as a political issue of great importance. Riders and makers protested equally loudly.

A deputation went to Westminster to see the Home Secretary. The influential and highly respectable members of the deputation were Mr Cobb of Trinity College, Cambridge, President of the University Bicycle Club, Mr Hutchings, the solicitor to the newly formed Bicycle Touring Club, and Mr Salamon, the chairman of the Coventry Machinists' Company.

In 1873, they argued, the only important bicycle-manufacturer in England had been the Coventry Machinists' Company, making only five bicycles a week;

> ... now there are 14 makers in Coventry. The present weekly wages paid to makers of bicycles in Coventry ranges between £1,500-2,000. The amount of capital invested in plant and machinery may be estimated at about £1 million and the value of bicycles throughout the country at between £60-80,000. In London there are upwards of 10,000 bicycles, and in the whole country about 50,000.[18]

The senior Member of Parliament for Coventry also had something to say in Westminster about the effect of the bicycle trade on the economy of his city.

When a grand 'meet' of bicyclists, a kind of communal celebration of the sport, and a display of riding skill and club solidarity, was held at Hampton Court in August 1876, riders came from all over London. Such an event could not but impress onlookers and help to dispel their unfriendly prejudices:

> When a meet of bicycle riders is found capable of mustering

750 machines all told, representing probably a money value of no less than £15,000, it is no longer possible to shut one's eyes to the fact that bicycling has become a great national pastime. By degrees, the spectacle of a bicycle has become so familiar that people, as a rule, take no more heed of it than of a man driving or on horseback. Indeed, there is now hardly a road out of town where many a score may not be counted in a day passing and repassing.[19]

Soon the bicycle had become a household object, although the club members and racers saw themselves apart from the common run of riders. Public hostility was largely overcome, and thousands of men discovered a new kind of pleasure, healthy exercise and a new mobility.

The technical improvements that were made in the evolution of the Ordinary bicycle had an importance outside the cycling world. Ball-bearings were used extensively in it for the first time; hollow drawn tubing for forks and backbones was perfected, and an enormously strong tangent-spoked wheel was designed. Hollow rims were introduced and the rubber used for tyres was enormously improved.

In its perfected form, reached in about 1880, the Ordinary bicycle was the most efficient machine ever devised for the harnessing of human muscle-power. It was one of the high points of communications technology in the nineteenth century. Never before had so many people been able to travel so quickly and so easily from place to place under their own steam. The record-breakers who were lowering their times over measured distances each year could quite accurately describe themselves as the 'fastest people in the world'.

In the late eighteen-seventies a roadster usually weighed about thirty to forty pounds, but racing machines were soon made as light as thirty pounds. The Ordinary was beautifully simple and efficient; one of its main attractions was that there was so little that could go wrong, and that every rider could be his own mechanic. Only serious injuries like buckled wheels and fractured backbones had to be repaired professionally.

The position of the rider was ideal for using the power of his legs to maximum effect. While he pulled against the handlebars, his upright position gave him good leverage on the pedals, and the circular motion of his legs was comfortable and natural, like two pendulums swinging, a crucial factor in bicycle ergonomics. His energy was transmitted direct to the road with hardly any loss of power; the trouble with any system of gearing up or levers was that there was a huge loss of power through friction.

But the extinction of the Ordinary was implicit in its design. It had two insuperable disadvantages, which combined to kill it. First, it was difficult to get on and off and was therefore dangerous, particularly for town riding, on top of which it was dangerous even when the rider was successfully in the saddle. Second, it would not go fast enough as the driving-wheel turned only once for each turn of the pedals. A champion on a sixty-inch wheel might do almost twenty miles an hour with great effort, but a little guy on a fifty-inch wheel had to pedal very fast to keep up with himself going downhill. Attempts were made to gear up the front wheel as early as 1870, but they did not seem to catch on.

While the members of the cult of the Ordinary defended their favourite machine against all others, even from the early eighteen-seventies other designs began to appear on the market. Tricycles were safer for older people and thought respectable for women, and experimental 'safety' bicycles were made as early as 1870, and began to appear in increasing numbers in the late eighteen-seventies. The Ordinary-riders thought them sissy at first. 'Tricycles and safeties,' they said, 'are for old men, ladies and cripples.' But as their own experience and races proved that tricycles were a lot of fun and that 'safeties' promised to be even faster than Ordinaries, they were forced to change their minds.

The arrival of the safety bicycle meant the end of an era, the arrival at middle age of a whole generation of bicycle riders.

The Cult of the Ordinary 99

About 1882 Mr Pearce, of Hammersmith, London, designed, patented and built this huge two-up monocycle, which was never a success.

ENGLISH MECHANIC
AND MIRROR OF SCIENCE

Engineering, Building, Inventions, Electricity, Photography, Chemistry,

VOL. IX.—No. 229. FRIDAY, AUGUST 13, 1869. [PRICE TWOPENCE.

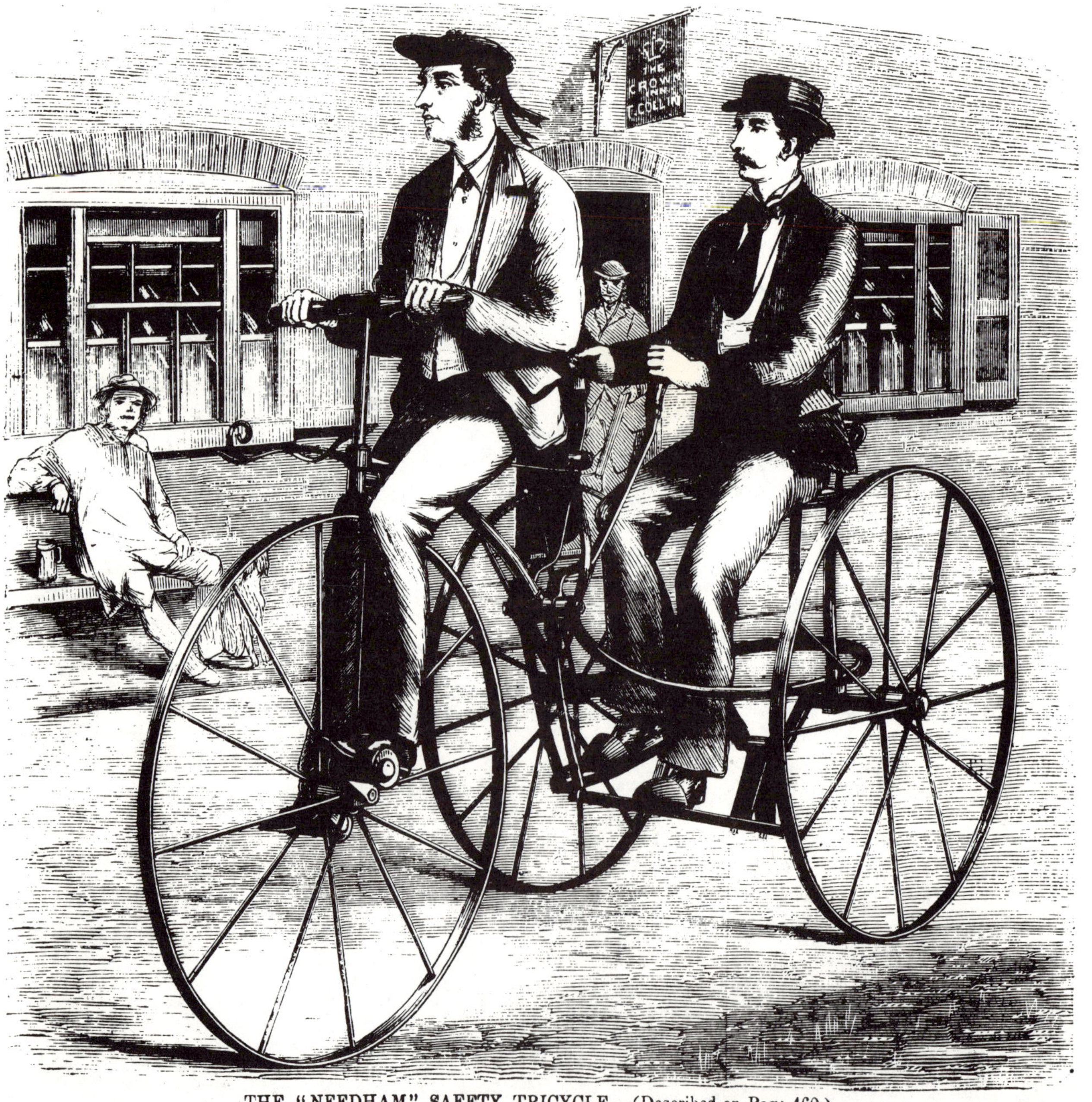

THE "NEEDHAM" SAFETY TRICYCLE.—(Described on Page 460.)

CHAPTER 5
TRICYCLING AND 'SOCIABLE' CYCLING

The tricycle is somewhat different from the bicycle. It appears to add dignity, or rather we should say, not to be so undignified, as a bicycle. Given a neat and appropriate costume there is nothing undignified in actually riding a bicycle; but riding in trousers and a tall hat; taking innumerable hops preparatory to mounting; getting oily fingers, dismounting for stones and then painfully shoving one's machine along over bad roads, all tend to lower one's dignity in the eyes of the public. Thus it is that the practical use of the bicycle is greatly handicapped, to say nothing of the state of perspiration into which the exercise of bicycling throws most men.

The tricycle, on the other hand, allows of being ridden in ordinary costume without the rider being very noticeable; it can be gracefully and easily mounted, and the fear of loose stones is not a painful and ever present feeling on the part of its owner. Altogether it is a machine better suited to staid middle age, or professional life, than the bicycle.[1]

To a man advancing towards middle life the possibility of an accident resulting in a broken limb is not to be risked. Such a man is presumably a husband, father, and head of a business establishment; by him a bicycle should be let alone, to him the tricycle recommends itself.[2]

As the early bicyclists, the members of the cult of the Ordinary, toured on the roads of England and raced on the tracks in the eighteen-seventies, they tended to forget that there were other kinds of man-powered machines, that their own bicycles had been made possible by a long history of experimenting and invention.

For eight years or so, between 1869 and 1877, almost all the energy of bicycle inventors and makers went into improving the exciting new bicycle, and other kinds of velocipedes were hardly used and almost forgotten. Riders were so full of the excitement and potential of their new machines that they had little time or reason to think about other possibilities. Since they had discovered a bicycle on which they could

The designer of this three-wheeled American velocipede, an early tricycle, attempted to overcome the rigidity and jarring of the three-wheeler by making the two rear wheels pivot at the point where they connected with the backbone.

Mr G. Scopes sent a photograph of this large boneshaker tricycle to the *English Mechanic,* and they published it on August 19th, 1869. 'It will not require much description,' he says, 'as I think it is clear enough for anyone to understand.' This machine survives in a private collection.

102 King of the Road

An old, retouched photograph of James Starley riding on one of his early Salvos in 1878.

A velocipede designed by W. Jackson, of Caroline Street, Pimlico, in 1870, looks surprisingly like later 'sociable' tricycles, and bridges the gap between the heavy old velocipedes and the light tricycles of the late eighteen-seventies.

travel 100 miles in a day, they had every reason to look back at the clumsy and old-fashioned three- and four-wheeled velocipedes with a smile. They were things of the past. The bicyclists were modern, they had progressed, they did not want to look backwards.

But the Ordinary bicycle showed a way forward without giving everybody an equal chance of following it. It was a marvellous machine for athletic and bohemian young men, but it discriminated terribly against older people, staider people, people afraid of falling, and most of all against women. And 'respectable' people, through nobody's fault except their own, held aloof because of the bad image of the bicycle.

The amateur mechanics, although they had all been men, and most of their velocipedes had demanded the kind of athletic effort that only a young man could make, had not ignored their fathers and mothers, wives and sisters completely. There were dozens of machines which could be driven by two or three people, where it did not matter if one person was less strong than the others.

There were, indeed, a great many riders who had always preferred the stability and safety of three or four wheels. Until the sudden popularity of the boneshaker, almost all velocipedes had been made in this way, and many mechanically minded people were puzzled at first by the claim that a two-wheeled machine could be driven forward without falling over. They did not believe it until they had seen it. The success of the two-wheeled bicycle did not come out of the blue, and although it made a strong initial impact, it did not win over all the advocates of three and four wheels overnight.

It was obviously a breakthrough, that was undeniable, but it did not immediately drive all other competitors into a limbo. During the early eighteen-seventies some of the old velocipede-makers were still mulling over their earlier ideas.

Three-wheeled 'tricycle' boneshakers appeared in France, the United States and England very soon after their two-wheeled relatives. They were a part of velocipedomania. The reason for making the tricycle was quite simple:

Sir — I believe it is generally admitted that the two-wheeled or American velocipede has many advantages over the others, both as regards simplicity and speed; but it has also its disadvantages, viz — starting it, which must be very difficult without help, and the attention required to prevent upsetting when in motion. I would,

The Singer tricycle, of 1879, was an Ordinary bicycle going backwards, fitted with two front wheels and a complicated but not inelegant lever-drive. It was a three-wheeled version of Lawson's 'safety' bicycle, which is illustrated on page 123.

therefore, suggest that instead of one wheel only behind the driving wheel, there should be two thus making it self-supporting ...[3]

One writer to the *English Mechanic* gives a graphic account of his own introduction to tricycling:

> I am a little fat chap, and being somewhat stricken with the velocipede mania, I was very desirious of obtaining one that should combine elegance with speed, and at the same time would not require too much exertion ...
>
> You must remember that a naturally stout man not only does not look well upon a bicycle, but is really out of place upon one, and for that reason I wanted to obtain a tricycle. I sent to our village blacksmith and gave to that worthy man my orders to make a 'little pony' after the sketches I gave him. The result is beyond expectation ... the cost has been near £6.[4]

Another writer complains in 1870 that although the bicycle leaves hardly anything to be desired 'there is a large class of people, both young and advanced in years, desirous to make use of this kind of locomotion, who cannot or will not adventure themselves on two wheels'. It may have been for such people that W. Jackson designed his large-wheeled velocipede in 1870, a machine which looked forward to the 'sociables' that would appear within ten years.

'Velox', in his *Velocipedes, Bicycles and Tricycles*, thinks that tricycles may become more popular than bicycles; 'they permit the body to remain in a sitting posture when going downhill and when the machine is at rest. An artist can sketch from the front seat. It can be taken to a shady nook while the luncheon or quiet pipe is enjoyed, and what is lost in speed is made up in comfort.'

But whereas men could ride the boneshaker tricycle, women, as usual, were still prevented from this by the design and had to ride a machine without a backbone, in other words one of the unfashionable old treadle-driven velocipedes. J. F. Bottomley-Firth sees some more advantages of the tricycle:

> To the artisan or trader, or even to the professional man, who leave suburban houses early in the morning, the tricycle will no doubt recommend itself. It enables them to carry considerably more luggage, and also if they think fit, they may on a wet day avail themselves of an umbrella ...
>
> To the commercial traveller or to the tourist, the tricycle will prove itself invaluable, as apart from the immense advantage of being able to carry their own luggage with them, they can stop when and where they please, without perilling their limbs by jumping off. The tourist may balance the steering handle and rest to enjoy a fine prospect, or he may eat his bread and drink his wine under the shade of the nearest tree ...[5]

'Velox' already had his finger on the tricycle's most fundamental limitation: 'The speed of tricycles will as a rule be less than that of the two-wheeled velocipedes. The expenditure of forces must always be greater where three wheels have to be forced along than where there are two only ...'

The tricycle, it was apparent, had a different character from the bicycle, and different capabilities, and could be sold to quite a different sort of customer. A maker who could come up with a really good tricycle would do very well for himself. One who did try, and has a good claim to being the first person to make a new move in tricycle production in the later 'seventies, was William Blood of Dublin, who patented a tricycle in November 1876 which was built by Carey Brothers of Dublin, and was moderately successful.

The early years of the tricycle trade, however, were dominated by the energy and ideas of James Starley of Coventry. If, in general, the history of the bicycle is not star-studded with the names of great individualists and geniuses, and is much more the history of the gradually changing and developing ideas of ordinary mechanics and engineers, Starley is certainly one man who does stand out as an astonishingly gifted inventor.

Starley was the first inventor to put a tricycle successfully into production, and did more than any other individual to advance and develop it subsequently. He understood, as the *Cyclist* put it on October 22nd, 1879, that 'by the adoption of the "Spider" wheels and other improved parts of the bicycle, together with a little careful consideration and application of mechanical principles, a machine could be constructed which would travel easily, comfortably and safely.'

Although at first Starley borrowed his ideas from bicycles — light, strong wheels and hollow tubing — later on the process would be reversed; ideas would flow back into bicycle design from the more complex mechanics of the tricycle.

In Coventry, the centre of the bicycle industry, Starley must have been aware of complaints about the exclusiveness of the bicycle as it grew more and more popular. People who could not ride started to get a little bit jealous. His biographer says:

> The principal result of this growing popularity was a widespread feeling among those who were physically unable to ride a bike that a machine was required which would allow them to enjoy the pleasures of the wheel steed. The charge made against cyclists was that its frequent practice engendered an unsociable feeling among the privileged few ...[6]

Starley first of all designed, in 1872, a women's 'Ariel', a peculiar machine, a kind of side-saddle Ordinary, with two cranked treadles both on the same side of the big front wheel, and an offset back wheel and backbone. The machine was an attempt to give a woman in long skirts the opportunity to ride on a big wheel.

It was hard to ride and was a failure, although great hopes were held out for it. But Starley made one failure the basis of another success by redesigning the 'Ariel'. He added another small wheel in front for stability, added a larger, redesigned crank mechanism and a completely new steering system, and called the machine the Coventry Lever Tricycle.

First sold under licence by Haynes & Jefferis in March 1877, it was an immediate success: 'As soon as the nature and capabilities of the new machine were understood, orders came in very rapidly; and the high praise which it met with was sufficient to prove that Starley had at last succeeded in inventing the very machine that was required by those who were waiting to enter the ranks of cyclists.'[7]

In May 1877 Starley added another large wheel, an extra double-throw crank, and thus turned the Lever Tricycle into the first 'sociable', a quadricycle which he rode with one of his sons in and around Coventry.

The difficulties of handling a machine with two large driving-wheels quickly became apparent, difficulties which were well known to coach- and cart-makers, and of course to the amateur mechanics. Because of the problem of steering round corners with both wheels fixed securely to the cranked axle (the inside wheel will always rotate more slowly than the outer), Starley arranged the big quadricycle so that the driving axle was split in the middle; the left-hand rider drove the left wheel, and the right-hand rider the right. The result was predictable: the machine veered all over the road as the power exerted on the two wheels varied all the time, and it was very hard work to steer it in a straight line.

Starley's solution to this problem was a stroke of genius and a totally

James Starley's Coventry Lever Tricycle, patented in 1876, was the first tricycle successfully put into large-scale production. The lever-drive was later changed to a rotary chain-drive and was in use for many years in that form.

106 King of the Road

In an advertisement of 1884, Starley's sons continued to sell the machines invented by their father. In the machine at the top left, the chain wheel has made the important move from being attached to the end of a crank arm to being between the two cranks. The ultimate tricycle transmission was near. All seats have gone from these models, to be replaced by saddles.

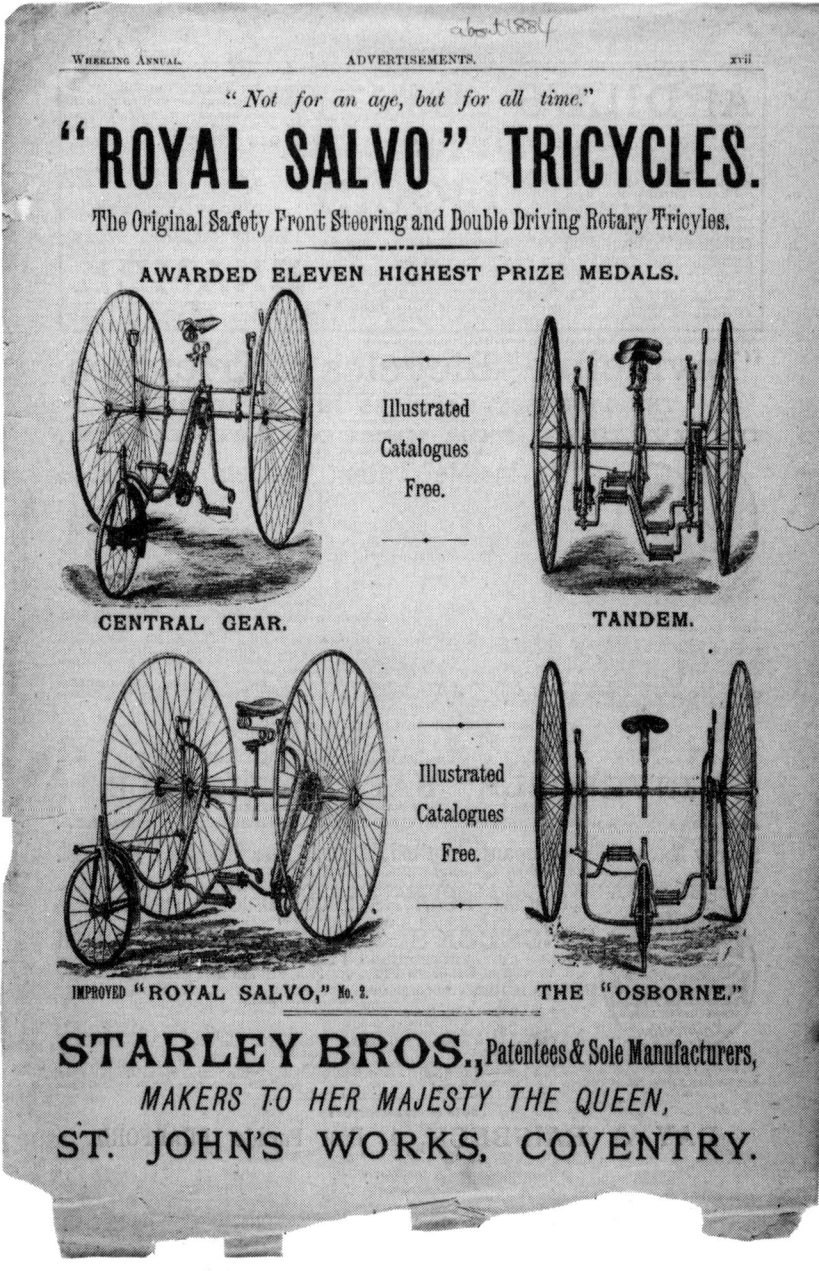

original application in cycle engineering, and was patented and embodied in the Salvoquadricycle in September 1877. It was called the 'balance gear' or the 'double-driving gear', and was later to be known almost universally as the differential.

Starley was not the inventor of the principle of the differential, since at least one French patent exists for it (taken out by Onesime Pecquer in 1828), and the idea had been in circulation in a number of forms in steam-engines and other machines. But Starley's 'discovery' and application of the principle in tricycle design showed his brilliant perception, his knack of reaching for just the right idea from the common fund of mechanical knowledge.

The 'balance gear' consisted fundamentally in breaking the main driving-axle with a system of bevel wheels and pinions, which allowed power to be transmitted equally to both wheels at the same time as though the axle were solid, and yet on turning a corner one wheel could rotate more quickly than the other. Starley's differential is the basis of the transmission of every car and truck made since.

The Salvoquadricycle was really a tricycle in spite of its name. The

George Moore's impression of a cycling club on the road in 1885. Almost every kind of machine, including a 'safety', is included.

'*En route* to the lake'; George Moore, 1885.

fourth wheel, at first at the front and then switched to the back, was really only a small emergency wheel to prevent the whole machine from capsizing. The Salvo was a major breakthrough in tricycle design, and the first really successful machine. The 'balance gear', which was used in almost every tricycle made, was driven by a chain from a chain-wheel connected to the end of the cranks. John Kemp Starley, James's nephew, claims in a lecture which he gave in 1898 that this was the first time that a continuous chain-drive was ever used in any kind of cycle: 'At the time Mr Starley introduced it he did not know where a chain could be procured; and he had to make the first few chains himself with his own hands. It was not long, however, before a Manchester firm began to supply them.'[8]

At least five types of chain were in fact available to Starley, but he did not seem to know where to find them.

The Salvoquadricycle was a catalogue of firsts; it was a remarkable machine, and one of the key machines in the history of cycle technology. It was driven by two large wheels, steered by a small front wheel with a very positive rack-and-pinion system; it had the 'balance

108 King of the Road

One of the tricycle's great advantages over the bicycle was that its greater stability gave a rider a better chance on steep hills. Once you had dismounted from an Ordinary on a hill, it was very hard to get under way again until you got to the top. This machine, optimistically advertised in 1882, was made by W. H. J. Grout, of London.

The New Inn, Ham Common, Surrey, taken some time in the early eighteen-eighties. By this time, the Ordinary bicycle was being challenged as a club machine by various kinds of tricycles. In this picture are, from left to right, a front-steering tandem tricycle, a rear-steering front-driven tricycle and a rotary tricycle, made either by the Coventry Machinists' Company or Rudge.

Tandem tricycles introduced a new element of companionship and adventure into cycling. They were not easy to master, but two people, economizing their effort, could go long distances. This picture was taken in the mid-eighteen-eighties, when the side-by-side 'sociable', never popular with men, had been challenged by this style. The aerodynamic advantages over the side-by-side were obvious.

gear' to distribute the work evenly to both wheels, and a rotary chain-driven transmission. It also had a hand-brake applied by a lever.

In December 1878 *Cycling* magazine paid a visit to the Starley factory in Coventry to see the production of the Salvo, more than 100 of which had by then been made: 'We went into the works with a preconceived idea that a tricycle or quadricycle was useful enough for slow-coaches, but for one who was in a hurry, it would not do. But after trying the Salvo, we were generally surprised at the ease with which it could be propelled.'[9]

The prejudice of bicyclists was hard to overcome, but most people were thrilled with the new tricycles. After Starley's pioneering epic they caught on rapidly. Some manufacturers more or less borrowed the Salvo design, while others, who had been making separate experiments had their own ideas about what a tricycle should look like.

By the end of 1879 there were twenty varieties of tricycle being manufactured in Coventry alone, and more in other cities. By 1884 Henry Sturmey writes in the *Indispensable Tricyclists' Handbook* of an industry 'employing many thousands of hands. One firm alone in Coventry employs nearly 500 hands, while three or four others employ between 200 and 400.' There are, he says, twenty tricycle-manufacturers in Coventry turning out about 120 different models, and another thirty models produced in London. He even mentions two makers in the United States, where tricycling was never especially popular.

The tricycle caused a minor social revolution:

Tricycling is much in vogue and even ladies find it an agreeable substitute for lawn tennis in the winter months. Where the roads are suitable, many fair riders may be seen making afternoon calls or shopping in the neighbouring village.

Doctors and clergymen have, in fact, greatly taken to these machines for their country rounds: the former, especially, use them for night work, instead of taking out the horses ...

What has mainly led to this revolution is the marvellous mechanical development in the construction of these machines.[10]

The first number of *The Tricyclist*, started in 1882 specially to cater for the tricycling public, tells how tricycles are rivalling bicycles in popularity:

Bicyclists of fair skill are astonished to find that tricyclists can hold their own upon the road, and even beat them at hill work ... When tricyclists can cover 150 or 180 miles within 24 hours; when many men, no longer young, can be found able to cover 70, 80, 90 and even 100 miles in a day; when members of the softer sex are able to cover similar distances, and surmount hills which are

Tricycling and 'Sociable' Cycling 109

110 King of the Road

The 'sociable' tricycle gave women the chance to ride out with their husbands or lovers, but a woman's dress was still hardly ideal for this kind of exercise. A picture taken in the early eighteen-eighties. The machine is a Cheylesmore 'sociable' made by the Coventry Machinists' Company.

considered a fair test for the bicyclist's skill, it cannot be denied that the tricycle can claim an equal place with its two-wheeled rival...[11]

Queen Victoria herself, seeing a Salvo on the road in the Isle of Wight, summoned first the rider, and then the maker, of the strange new machine into her presence. James Starley rounded off his career fittingly by receiving a request to deliver a Salvo in person to Her Majesty, and earned the Royal Patent thereby. The Salvo became the Royal Salvo.

Starley himself died of cancer in June 1881, leaving his sons and nephews to carry on building up their various firms in Coventry. The Queen's interest, widely publicized, gave the pastime the stamp of acceptability and respectability, and from then on it was considered quite the thing to do to own and ride a tricycle among the middle and upper middle classes, where tricycling found its home. The price of a machine always made it difficult for working-class people to own tricycles.

James Starley was one of those self-made Victorians who made a small fortune and earned a modest fame doing what they liked to do. He saw the possibilities of bicycles and tricycles and spent his life inventing and improving them. When he died in 1881 an industry existed where

Tricyclists on the road presented a varied appearance. In this picture, taken about 1882, the two sharply dressed clubmen are a contrast to the man in high bowler hat and long-cut jacket.

before there had been none.

Although Starley, and other manufacturers like him, dealt in a commodity that was mass-produced, he did not allow the manufacturing process to become a dull and repetitive one. There does not seem to have been a history of industrial unrest in the bicycle factories in the early years of the industry. A large amount of custom-building was still involved.

Starley shunned the role of manager and industrialist. He knew where he was happiest — in his machine-shop. He became the technical wizard of bicycles, designing new machines and components and then selling the manufacturing rights to other people.

He was not very rich when he died and seems to have been liked by everyone who knew him. His biographer says:

Unlike many inventive geniuses of whom we have read, he had no special peculiarities about him. He was a most unassuming man. His love for mechanics seemed to imbibe his whole nature ... He had a way of his for doing everything. After thinking briefly upon a matter, he would at once set to work to carry out an idea in a crude form, and if this answered his expectations, he would then make a complete machine, improving the details as he proceeded. We do not believe Starley ever had a personal enemy. He was familiar with his fellow workmen, a strong feeling of affection

112 King of the Road

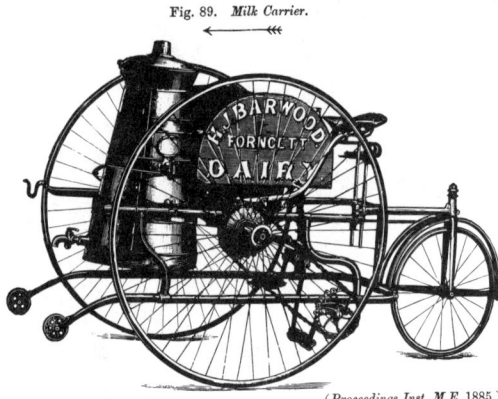

One practical and useful offshoot of the tricycle was the building of various kinds of carrier machines, two of which are pictured here.

existed toward him, and his name was always uttered with respect, and he was known as 'Old Man Starley' throughout the entire cycling trade of Coventry.[12]

The results of the tricycling fashion were not always happy for the cycling community as a whole. A miniature class war was waged between tricyclists and bicyclists, who were looked down on by some tricyclists as an inferior breed, definitely not to be associated with. More virulent, it seems, in the pages of the cycling journals than on the road, the conflict was nevertheless a very real manifestation of the kind of vehement and narrow-minded feelings that could still be aroused in a class society.

Feeling was so strong among some tricyclists that they wanted to form a whole new set of institutions. In 1878, right at the beginning of the popularity of tricycling, a 'Tricycler' writes to *Bicycling News*, suggesting the formation of a National Tricycle Association. 'Tricyclists will generally be of a better class than bicyclists,' he says haughtily, 'and will seldom consist of mere beardless youths, but men of position and experience, and above all, by the fair sex.' Women, he suggests, have to be shielded from the bad influence of the young working-class bicyclist. He protests against the new definition of an 'amateur', which allowed 'mechanics, artisans and labourers', formerly classed as professionals, to compete in the same races as the old-style 'gentleman amateur', a proximity which some 'gentlemen' found highly offensive,

"The wretch rides like the very demon — if we relax a minute we are lost!" muttered Fred.' A drawing by George Moore.

Tricycling and 'Sociable' Cycling

and which threatened to make it much harder for them to win. 'Mechanics, day-labourers, chimney-sweeps, costers etc,' rants 'Tricycler', 'who are now hailed as men and brothers in bicycle contests, shall never find a place in the Tricycle Association.'[13]

Such bigotry was not uncommon. A letter was sent out to tricyclist members of the Bicycle Touring Club about 1880, once again suggesting that tricyclists should break away and set up their own central organization:

It is desired by most Tricyclists to separate themselves entirely from the Bicyclists, who are a disgrace to the pastime, while Tricycling includes Princes, Princesses, Dukes, Earls etc. There are none of the upper circle who ride bicycles. This is easily seen, and it is plain that the Tricyclists are altogether a better class than the Bicyclists ...[14]

Bicyclists, not surprisingly, did not react very warmly to these unkind, though obviously accurate, references to their class origins. They treated them, in fact, with the contempt they deserved. Tricyclists, quips one bicyclist, 'should have a road specially made for them, where, before an audience of the fair sex, who seem to possess considerable attractions for them, they could disport themselves without fear of their serenity being disturbed by the obnoxious presence of the common herd of bicyclists'.[15]

The tricyclists had their way, and the Tricycle Union was founded in 1882. 'Although the bicycle and the tricycle are machines of the same

CARRIER TRICYCLE.

Humber advertisement of about 1885.

FIG. 15.—THE PREMIER TANDEM DWARF SAFETY ROADSTER.

The Premier Tandem Dwarf Safety Roadster was introduced by Hillman, Herbert & Cooper in 1887, using ideas from tricycles to create a two-wheeled tandem, which could be ridden on the front by a woman in long skirts. Its fault was certainly bad weight-distribution.

character to a large extent,' said the Chairman in his opening address to the Union, 'yet in the tastes and the individualities of their respective riders there is so wide a difference that it appeared impracticable to take any other course than to form an independent body consisting wholely [sic] of tricyclists ...'[16]

Tricycle design was a hotbed of technical ingenuity and sophistication. Each maker had his own particular preoccupations and whims. During the late eighteen-seventies and early 'eighties few changes were made in the Ordinary bicycle, the staple diet of the trade, but the tricycle was changing all the time, at a quite bewildering rate in fact.

The possibilities for technical improvement and experimenting seemed to be limitless. The perfect machine always loomed up in the distance as the goal to be aimed for. In ten years the tricycle changed from a mechanical oddity into its sophisticated final form, passing through many fascinating metamorphoses on the way.

'The heavy lumbering vehicle of yesterday,' says Henry Sturmey, 'has given place to dozens of varieties of light, airy, handsome structures, the outcome of the best mechanical skill in the country ... It is but a year or two since that rattling, creaking, clumsy contrivance, mounted on three or four wheels, and propelled laboriously in a tortuous and erratic fashion by some mechanic or labouring man, was the tout ensemble of tricycling.'[17]

The mechanical changes and varieties in tricycle development were

This machine, though only before the public or the last two years, has revolutionised the style of tricycles. It is much imitated, but as its vital principles are protected by patent rights, it continues still

THE FINEST ROADSTER IN THE WORLD.

MAKERS:
THE QUADRANT TRICYCLE CO.,
SHEEPCOTE STREET, BIRMINGHAM.

Advertisement for the Quadrant tricycle, 1884. Patented in 1882, it already looked forward to the final tricycle design. It had a central chain-drive, a much larger front wheel than had been usual up until then, and handlebar through indirect steering.

Advertisement of 1889.

ADVERTISEMENTS.

PARIS EXHIBITION, 1889.
The Gold Medal Awarded for Excellency of Workmanship and Design.

RUDGE CYCLE COMPANY
LIMITED.

YOUTHS' CYCLES for
Xmas & New Year's Presents

WORKS: COVENTRY.
LONDON DEPOT: 23, HOLBORN VIADUCT, E.C.

far from gratuitous, but were the results of a search for safety and efficiency. The only trouble was that almost no two makers could agree about what kind of a machine was safest and most efficient.

The front-steering Salvo was challenged early on by a model which had its steering wheel at the back. There was a lot of discussion about the relative merits of front- and rear-steerers. Rear-steerers tended to pitch forward going downhill. The arguments were finally settled in favour of the front-steerer; handlebars took over from rack-and-pinion steering, and were finally attached directly to the front wheel.

One objection to ownership of a tricycle was its width. People who did not have stables or outbuildings could not store them very easily as they would not go through the front doors of their flats or houses.

Between 1886 and 1887 the large front-wheeled direct-steerer gained a runaway victory. Bicycle and tricycle design coalesced. New models were all of this type. Hillman, Herbert & Cooper's Premier Racer sold for £25.

FIG. 7.—THE PREMIER RACER.

James Starley solved this problem by building the first of several collapsible or telescopic tricycles in 1879.

The growth of 'sociables' meant that a person who wanted to own one and also go out by himself had to have two machines. Rudge, and other manufacturers, brought out dividable 'sociables'. The Rudge machine simply reversed what Starley had done to create his first 'sociable'; he removed one large driving wheel from it, and a 'penny-two-farthings' Rotary was the result.

The 'sociable' itself took up a lot of space on the road and was hard to store. The answer was the tandem tricycle, on which the riders sat one behind the other, 'which is not quite so sociable as a proper sociable,' said Sturmey, but was faster and more efficient. Here again, one person was encouraged to own the tandem tricycle because it was nearly always made possible to remove either the back or front parts, making a single tricycle.

Experience showed that some tricycles worked better than others. The Humber 'Cripper', which got its name from a well-known rider, R. Cripps of Nottingham, who constantly won races on it, was introduced commercially in 1886, and by 1887 this design had become the most widely used, making many of the older designs redundant. Starley Brothers introduced a similar model called the 'Psycho'. The modern tricycle is recognizable in this design; it was driven by a chain drive to the rear axle and was steered with handlebars direct to a large front wheel. All that was needed over the next few years was for the rear wheels to be reduced in size and the front wheel to be made even bigger, and the final tricycle form had been arrived at.

The rise to popularity of tricycles and 'sociable' machines meant the end of the strict clannishness of the early Ordinary riders and of the bohemian image of cycling as a pastime. Some tricycle-riders went on proclaiming snobbishly that they as a class were better behaved and more of a credit to the sport than bicycle-riders, but they seem to have been in a small minority. In general, the growth of the tricycle gave a huge boost to the pastime and made it possible for those who would never have dreamt of riding an Ordinary to enjoy the freedom of the road.

Cycling became a family affair. Groups of all ages were seen out on the road together. What was especially different and new about the tricycle was the opportunity it gave for a new kind of relaxed informality in the way men and women related to each other. Some people found this very shocking, and saw it as a lowering of social standards, especially when men and women were seen riding together on Sundays. But the healthfulness of the tricycle gave women riders a marvellous explanation. 'Believe me ladies,' said one evangelist, 'if your health and strength leave something to be desired, if you feel the want of exercise in the open air; if you suffer from that terrible scourge which overcomes your sex, the sick headache, if you wish to strengthen yourself morally, ride a tricycle. Believe me, you will never regret it; from henceforth your existence will always be happy. You will laugh, eat and sleep.'

'Sociables' gave rise to a good deal of joking and ridicule, both inside and outside the cycling world, but there was no doubt at all that they were tremendous fun to ride. What was most convenient about a 'sociable' or a tandem was that it economized on effort, and gave a nervous woman confidence:

> The sociable possesses paramount charms, for not only can the stronger rider assist in increasing the pace, but there is increased pleasure in riding in such close proximity to one's companion as to overcome the necessity for raising the voice when conversing ...

> The novice can be taken aboard, and allowed to sit still and be carried along, the experienced rider doing all the propulsion and steering. Everything in fact is smoothed over for the learner who can blossom forth into a skilful and powerful rider by means of a sociable, without any of the trials which beset the nervous novice on a single machine ...

> No man is more popular in his set than he who owns a sociable

A "ROVER" TANDEM BICYCLE.

An experimental tandem made by A. J. Wilson in 1885, consisting of a 'Rover' 'safety' bicycle with a 'Kangaroo' fitting on the front wheel. It is ridden in this sketch by Wilson and Dan Albone, who the next year made and rode the first recognizable tandem bicycle.

F. T. Bidlake, debonair tricycle record-breaker, set a record which stood for sixty years when he covered 426 miles 440 yards in twenty-four hours at Herne Hill Track. He is pictured here in 1896, on a rationalized simplified tricycle, with pneumatic tyres and totally enclosed chain.

tricycle. His lady friends are always at home to him, and whether for a short evening ride, or for a more extended trip, he never need despair of finding a pleasant companion.[18]

Ten years later the editors of *Cycling* did not have such a rosy opinion of 'sociables', but of course by then times had changed considerably:

They were called double tricycles because they were double the weight of anything else of their kind, because they required double the exertion to propel them, double the time to clean, double the money to buy, and also for the less important reason that they carried two persons ... These engines were more generally known as sociables chiefly because after a few miles they made the two riders thoroughly unsociable.[19]

By 1885 cycling of all kinds no longer had such a bad reputation in the public eye. It had been through its birth-pangs. The cyclists' right to a share of the public highway had been affirmed again and again in the courts, although there were still occasional serious assaults by coach-drivers, one of which was reported in 1882:

War seems to have broken out upon that favourite highway, the Brighton Road, between tricyclists and the drivers of the Brighton coach. If any reliance is to be placed upon statements made by tricyclists, many deliberate attempts have been made by the driver of this coach to run down or otherwise injure riders of these machines encountered by him ...

Now that the right of a bicycle or a tricycle to the use of the highway is as undisputed as that of a coach, it is a matter for sincere regret that riders and drivers cannot exist harmoniously together; we had, indeed, hoped that all antagonisms between the two classes had practically disappeared.[20]

But people in general – and even most horses – had grown used to the fast and silent machines on the roads and had even begun to like them. Newspapers, instead of attacking cyclists, now often had a cyclists' column. An activity that had engaged the interest of Queen Victoria and other members of the aristocracy gained an official sanction and could not but be a smart and fashionable thing to do.

Tricycles were ridden over long distances by ordinary people. Although they were undoubtedly slower and heavier than bicycles, they were more stable, less nerve-racking and more comfortable. In 1886 the lightest racing tricycles weighed between forty and forty-five pounds, but an ordinary roadster weighed up to sixty pounds, and some of the 'sociables' and tandems even more; a 'Quadrant' tandem, for instance, weighed 112 pounds.

It was as touring machines that they were ideal. Here comfort was the most important consideration, and they were practical since it was much easier to carry a change of clothes and the tools and maps that were needed. English people began to tour Europe on tricycles, and some shockingly adventurous women asserted their independence by touring the mountains of Austria and Switzerland on 'sociables'.

Tricyclists attacked all the road and track records made by bicyclists, and sometimes over long distances came pretty near to beating them. Tricycles were acknowledged, even by bicycle enthusiasts, to have a special charm and excitement of their own.

In the whole history of cycling I doubt that there can have been a more extraordinary period than the mid-eighteen-eighties. It was a peak of cycling activity. There were still no other vehicles on the road to rival bicycles and tricycles for economy and convenience. For many people they were still the only form of independent transportation. A chain of friendly Cyclists' Touring Club hotels and restaurants catered for travellers at a fixed rate. There were hundreds of clubs waiting to welcome new members, and there were a dozen or so cycling newspapers, the most active press catering for any special-interest group in the country.

A wayside tricycling photo taken about 1887. On the left and right are two of the latest models, while between them are a 'sociable' and a rotary tricycle. The man in the hat is Sir Henry Kimber, but it is hard to say what they are doing.

Above all, the prospering bicycle and tricycle manufacturers, stimulated by the prospects of financial success, never lost touch for very long with the needs and criticisms of their customers. While the technical skill was something they alone possessed, they were continually receptive to the discussions about the relative merits of different machines that went on. There were no easy solutions to the problem of producing *the best* tricycle, and in the eighteen-eighties there were hundreds of different designs to choose between, covering a huge range of mechanical ingenuity. The variety, in fact, must have been quite bewildering for the general public. One of the problems for the makers, which cost many of them a lot of money, was that ideas were moving so fast that last year's favourite machine was liable to be this year's redundant stock.

In this clamour of invention, controversy and mechanical activity one problem had intermittently come to the fore ever since about 1876, and had increasingly attracted the attention of bicycle-makers. This was the invention of an efficient 'safety' bicycle. While they had actually engaged in solving all the practical problems of marketing the Ordinary bicycle and all the different kinds of tricycles, the search for the 'safety' had never been abandoned.

With the successful development of the 'safety', the tricycle would decline and virtually die out; it was not really needed any more. All the energy that had been invested in it was quickly redirected. Even an elderly person felt confident on the new low-down bicycle, and suddenly, almost overnight, the most fashionable thing a woman could do was to be seen out riding her bicycle.

120 King of the Road

CHAPTER 6
THE SEARCH FOR SAFETY

I have noticed with real and unfeigned pleasure the rapid growth of cycling in this country, for not only does it afford to many to whom it would otherwise be unattainable a healthy and pleasurable form of exercise, but it also enables them to derive all those advantages of travel which, previous to the advent of cycling, were out of their reach. It is far more profitable than the luxurious railway journey from the city to some definite point, along an unalterable route, over which the traveller is whirled with no time for observation, and no opportunity of examining the district through which he is carried. I can only emphasize the fact that I consider that physically, morally and socially, the benefits that cycling confers on men of the present day are almost unbounded. (W. E. Gladstone)

When Kirkpatrick Macmillan made his velocipede in about 1840, in a quiet corner of Scotland, he established certain mechanical principles which were, much later, to be generally accepted as the fundamentals of efficient bicycle construction. It had three prophetic aspects: two smallish wheels with the rider sitting between them, giving a low centre of gravity, a back wheel that was continuously driven by cranks and a front wheel that was steered and independent of the transmission. It was a hesitating, inventive, pioneering machine.

Through a long, and almost incredibly complex, process of trial and error, bicycle-makers were to arrive, forty years later, at the same conclusions as Macmillan, and with better materials and components, to perfect the principles which he had pioneered.

Macmillan's design did not receive much attention at the time. Four-wheeled velocipedes were the order of the day. Macmillan was perhaps at his most perceptive in understanding that a good, fast, man-powered machine could not hope to succeed with more than two wheels. Later, the old heavy velocipedes were forced out of business by the boneshaker, of which the front wheel was driven directly. Gradually

The mid-eighteen-eighties saw fierce rivalry between different kinds of 'safety' bicycle. On September 27th, 1884, George Smith established a record of 100 miles in 7 hours 11 minutes 10 seconds on a 'Kangaroo'. Just a year later, on September 25th, 1885, he broke his own record on a 'Rover' safety, in 7 hours 5 minutes 16 seconds. George Moore's drawing shows an imaginary sprint between the two bicycles.

122 King of the Road

One of the first 'safety' bicycles, designed by Thomas Wiseman, was illustrated and described in the *English Mechanic* for July 16th, 1869.

the front wheel grew bigger and bigger, immense improvements were made in its construction, and the result was the Ordinary bicycle, or the 'penny-farthing', which was dominant until about 1885.

The oddest thing about the Ordinary bicycle is that it succeeded at all, as it defied most of the elementary considerations of applied mechanics and the then unknown science of ergonomics. It was a kind of mechanical aberration, a freak. It nevertheless became hugely popular, and it did not die without a fierce struggle with its rivals.

Its faults were its instability and its danger, the insane difficulty of getting on and off it, and the fact that the large front wheel was driven and steered at the same time, which could be very tiring on the arms. Its defenders did not accept all these criticisms; they liked the position. The drive was direct, they said, and smooth, and you sat on top of your work and could bear down on the pedals with great efficiency and comfort. You were also high above the mud and dust of the road, and the big wheel did not cause a bad vibration on the terrible road surfaces.

Contributing to the strange success of the Ordinary was a restless desire to explore and to invent. Tricycles were one expression of the dissatisfaction with the Ordinary. Another was the interest in designing a 'safety' bicycle which existed in France and England even from the earliest days of the boneshaker.

Frederick W. Shearing's 'Norfolk' bicycle, the first design for a bicycle continuously driven to the back wheel by an endless strap and steered with the front wheel. Shearing does not appear to have actually made it.

The earliest claim of all for the design of a 'safety' is a bicycle reputed to have been built by M. Meyer, a Parisian engineer and velocipede-maker, after the design of André Guilmet, a watch-maker, in 1868. The outstanding feature of the machine was the chain-drive to the back wheel, which, if the date is right, would certainly be the very first bicycle of its type known to exist. But the date is suspect, and there is no proof at present, although in view of the precociousness of the French bicycle industry just before the outbreak of the 1870 War such an advanced idea as this might have been possible.

With the English pioneer 'safeties', we are on surer ground. In 1869 Thomas Wiseman sent a picture of his Safety Bicycle to the *English Mechanic*. It is driven by the front wheel, but steered by the back and, says Wiseman, has certain advantages over the 'French bicycle', by which he means the Michaux velocipede:

The front wheel having no lateral motion, there is no strain upon the arms, the legs having their full power while turning ... The seat is so placed that the rider can mount before starting, and therefore without risk. He can, without dismounting, stop and shake hands with a friend. The centre of gravity being so much lower, the danger of a cropper is not so great.¹

After a few days Frederick Shearing, who was still alive twenty years later to see the arrival of the commercially successful 'safety', sent a sketch of *his* bicycle, more advanced than Wiseman's. Shearing's is the first design ever published for a bicycle driven by the back wheel with a continuous rotary transmission, although this is not a chain, but 'a strap or a cord'. Although chains were made at the time, James Starley did not at first know where to find them and complained of having to make his own when he first started producing his Salvoquadricycle in 1877.

Shearing made not only this bicycle but two others similar to it. In 1887 he wrote to *Bicycling News* to rebut the claims that were being made at that time by H. J. Lawson, who had worked on 'safeties' in the 'seventies, as to who was the inventor of the 'safety' bicycle. 'I am surprised that Mr Lawson should claim to be the inventor of the safety bicycle,' he says. 'A half-score years before he dated his invention, I invented, made and rode three different safeties.'

Shearing's machines were not produced commercially; he was working for himself alone. But in Birmingham the firm of Peyton & Peyton in 1870 not only built, but manufactured and marketed, a crank-operated, rear-driven 'safety' bicycle. Based on Macmillan's ideas, the heavy iron machine does not appear to have enjoyed a big sale, but the company's advertising, even at this early stage, points out the disadvantages of the boneshaker and its danger.

Experimenting continued throughout the eighteen-seventies in the workshops of both amateur and professional bicycle-makers. While most of their energy went into the bread-and-butter business of improving and selling the Ordinary, the search went on for alternative systems of driving a bicycle. The exact sequence of the experiments is

H. J. Lawson's 'safety' bicycle of 1876 was in reality an Ordinary bicycle driven backwards. It was safer, in theory, because the rider was between the two wheels, and much nearer the ground, and therefore more stable.

hard to establish. In Coventry and London new ideas about mechanics cross-fertilized each other. Some ideas remained on paper, others were bought and sold.

In 1876 Henry Lawson, who claimed to have designed and made an earlier 'safety', patented his back-to-front Ordinary bicycle, an extraordinary machine, driven by long thin cranks. In the same year Thomas Shergold, living in Gloucester, made what is probably the earliest chain-driven 'safety' bicycle to survive. It was crudely put together and weighed eighty pounds, a late survival of the tradition of home-made machines established by the amateur mechanics, which was not marketed.

One London inventor, Henry Bate, experimented with and made two-speed Ordinary bicycles during 1876 and 1877. And then, on September 30th, 1879, Henry Lawson, the manager of the Tangent and Coventry Tricycle Company, took out a patent for 'Improvements in the construction of bicycles and other velocipedes, and in apparatus to be used in connection therewith'. He called his machine the 'Bicyclette', and other people called it the 'Crocodile'.

The 'Bicyclette' was a huge improvement on Lawson's previous design. The rider's weight was ideally distributed, and the transmission, a chain-drive to the back wheel, approximated to the final 'safety' bicycle design more closely than anything that had been built before. It was put into production, and attracted a lot of attention; it was exhibited at the beginning of 1880 at the Stanley Show, the big annual event for the bicycle trade, where rival makers could inspect each others' new inventions and new departures. An article about it appeared in the *Cyclist* on April 21st, 1880:

'Well, it's the queerest machine I ever set eyes on anyhow', remarked a bystander as we were gazing at the crocodilian form of the Bicyclette which was exposed to the admiring gaze of the cycle-knowing population of Coventry in the shop-window of a well-known bicycle agent in that city, and certainly the machine in question *is* a queer one. But its ungainly appearance is more than compensated for by its absolute and certain safety ... Here, indeed is safety guaranteed, and the cyclist may ride roughshod over hedges, ditches and other similar obstacles without the fear of going over the handles ...

Mr Lawson, late of Brighton, but now manager of the Tangent and Coventry Tricycle Co., habitually rides it in preference to his ordinary machine, especially in night work, and professes himself

This curiously amateur-looking 'safety' bicycle was made, it is claimed, by Thomas Shergold, of Gloucester, in 1876. It is a late survival of the tradition of home-made machines established by the amateur mechanics earlier in the century.

highly pleased with the results obtained …

The most serious challenge to the Ordinary bicycle came from designs that were closely related to it. The Singer 'Xtraordinary' Bicycle and the 'Facile' were both patented in 1878 and applied the same ergonomic principle. By throwing the rider's weight towards the back wheel, and making it possible to use a smaller front wheel by gearing it up, they were much safer to ride than the high, unstable Ordinary bicycle. Bicycling purists viewed both these new departures with scorn.

The 'Xtraordinary' was reviewed in *Cycling* in February 1879:
The principal advantages of the Xtraordinary are its great safety and comfort. On an ordinary machine the rider sits directly over the front wheel; consequently he feels all the bumps and vibrations produced by a rough road, and sitting as he does so nearly straight over the centre of gravity, very little suffices to overturn the machine … Here, the rider sitting midway between the two wheels feels scarcely any vibration from the rough roads, and is infinitely safer … Mounting and dismounting too are not only much easier, but safer.

Some riders did not like the odd way that the pedals prescribed an oval instead of a circle, but the 'Xtraordinary' was tenaciously popular for the next ten years. In 1885 one rider wrote to the *Cyclists' Touring Club Gazette*:
Its appearance is not altogether engaging, truly, and the levers, with their connecting links, involve friction and a terrifying rattle when running fast downhill, that are well-nigh abolished from the highest class of ordinary bicycle in all its glorious simplicity. Of its safety, however, there can be no two opinions.[2]

The 'Facile', patented by John Beale and Mr Straw, and manufactured by Ellis and Company of Fleet Street, was the principal rival to the 'Xtraordinary'. 'Easy to learn. Easy to ride. Easy to mount.

Lawson's 'Bicyclette', patented in 1879, was perhaps the first 'safety' machine in which the outlines of the present-day bicycle are perceptible. With its big front wheel and tiny back one, it has not escaped from the idea of the Ordinary bicycle, but the chain-wheel and continuous chain-drive is a new and progressive principle.

Singer's Xtraordinary 'safety' bicycle was a modified Ordinary, the strange-looking levers allowing the rider to sit further over the back wheel.

126 King of the Road

The 'Facile' allowed a smaller and safer driving-wheel to be used. Record-breaking provided the makers of the 'Facile' with invaluable publicity for their machine.

JUNE 4TH, 1884. THE CYCLIST. 585

THE "FACILE"
SAFETY BICYCLE.

LAND'S END TO JOHN-O'-GROAT'S

ALL PREVIOUS RECORDS BEATEN.

1880. Blackwell & Harman, 13 days.
1881. Jas. Lennox   12 „
1882. Keith-Falconer   13 „
1882. A. Nixon (Tricycle) 14 „
1883. Jas. Lennox   10 „
1884. J. H. ADAMS, 46in. 'Facile,'
      6 DAYS 23 Hours 45 Minutes.
1884. H. R. GOODWIN, 38in. 'Facile,'
      8 DAYS 15 Hours.

Total distance, 924 Miles. Average per day: Adams, 132 Miles; Goodwin, 108 Miles.

SOLE MANUFACTURERS:

ELLIS & CO., Ltd.,
165, FLEET STREET, LONDON, E.C.
(DESCRIPTIVE PAMPHLETS.)

Easy to dismount. Safe from side-falls. Safe from headers,' says an advertisement of 1883. 'All the claims made for this celebrated Machine have now been thoroughly established, and every season increases its popularity. The "Facile" is undoubtedly the BEST ROADSTER EVER INTRODUCED, and no one should purchase either a Bicycle or a Tricycle without first fully informing himself as to the merits of this Machine.'

As with the 'Xtraordinary', the pedals went up and down rather than round. Riders praised its hill-climbing powers; the leverage was good, though the 'Facile' was not fast for sprinting. The 'Facile' had its own club which was founded in 1880 and used to meet at a pub called the Green Man in Blackheath. And the exploits of 'Facile' racing men certainly left no doubt about its reliability as a long-distance road machine.

In September 1882 the makers, Ellis and Company, organized a twenty-four-hour race on the road and probably paid the riders to compete in it. It was won by W. Snook, who covered 214½ miles. The next year, over a different course, J. H. Adams won a similar race with

221¼ miles, and in 1884 Adams broke the record for the long ride from Land's End to John-o'-Groats, 924 miles, on a 'Facile', taking 6 days 23 hours 45 minutes to do it. An insatiable mile-eater, Adams went on later that same year to set a new twenty-four-hour record of 266½ miles on the 'Facile'. He did not however toil over all these miles on the 'Facile' for the love of it alone.

The third of a trio of strange modified Ordinary bicycles was called the 'Kangaroo'. It was designed by William Hillman, who had worked with James Starley on the 'Ariel' in the early 'seventies, and was one of the oldest craftsmen in the business. It was first introduced commercially by the firm of Hillman, Herbert & Cooper at the beginning of 1884. The 'Kangaroo' enjoyed a short and popular life during the two years before the 'Rover' 'safety' bicycle and the other rear-driven 'safeties' took the cycling world by storm. Like the 'Facile' and the 'Xtraordinary', the 'Kangaroo's' novelty was as much of an attraction as its practicality. The people who bought it were often Ordinary-riders who were intensely curious about its characteristics and its potential.

The *Cyclists' Touring Club Gazette* was flattering:

We regard the Kangaroo as being a thoroughly sound and reliable little mount, likely to win its way more and more into popular favour, particularly among those who value their necks too highly to risk them upon the ordinary bicycle, or who are occasionally apt to characterize the propulsion of a heavy three-wheeler — as Dickens' friend did the turning of the mangle — as 'a demm'd horrid grind'.[3]

The mechanics of the 'Kangaroo' were basically very simple, and the principle similar to the 'Facile'. The front wheel was geared up and

The 'Kangaroo'-type bicycle was a logical solution to the problem of designing a safe bicycle without sacrificing speed, and without challenging too much the traditional layout of the Ordinary bicycle.

The American 'Star' bicycle, patented in an improved version by W. S. Kelly in 1885, was an American attempt to construct a 'safety'. With a small wheel at the front, it would not pitch forwards.

could therefore be made a lot smaller. The rider was nearer the ground, his body better balanced between the two wheels than on an Ordinary, and he was therefore once again less likely to take a cropper forwards. The pedals were attached to an extension of the front forks, and the chain-wheels and chains were connected to cogs on either side of the front wheel.

'Faster than any bicycle. Safer than a tricycle. A perfect touring machine,' announced Hillman, Herbert & Cooper. Their claims were not unjustified. The machine took some time to get used to; the two chains gave a peculiar kind of kick to the rising pedals and were hard to adjust, it was tiring to steer, and there was more vibration than on an Ordinary. But the 'Kangaroo's' safety was undeniable:

> My opinion is most emphatically in favour of the 'Kangaroo'. I have ridden it since the end of January, often riding down hills at night in a most reckless manner, and I have not had one tumble. On Easter Monday, I gave the machine a very severe test. I rode from Birmingham to Bewdley and back, the whole of the return journey being made after dark. The road is one of the worst out of Birmingham, and was much worse than usual on account of frequent patches of loose stones, on which I think I should have quite come to grief on an ordinary machine.[4]

Once again, races proved how good the 'Kangaroo' was, and gave it wide publicity. Although not faster than the Ordinary bicycle over short distances, over longer distances its stability and security could be a big advantage. Hillman, Herbert & Cooper arranged a 100-mile race for 'Kangaroos' on the Bath Road, already a famous race-course. It was won by George Smith in 7 hours 11 minutes 10 seconds, beating the course record set in 1878 on an Ordinary by a Mr Appleyard by 7 minutes 45 seconds.

Other makers copied the 'Kangaroo', which became suddenly popular. But there were technical problems. The short chains stretched and there was an enormous strain on the bearings of each of the separately mounted chain-wheels. Mechanically, it was not at all an ideal solution to the problem of designing a safety bicycle.

The year 1885 was an extraordinary and momentous one in the history of cycling. Experiments and designs moved in dozens of different directions. All the ingenuity of the bicycle- and tricycle-makers was applied to the problems that cropped up in their many machines. There were so many different kinds of machines to choose between, so many conflicting claims by the manufacturers and so many passionate supporters of each model that a newcomer to cycling could be forgiven if he became totally confused. How could he decide which was the right machine for him when every advertisement claimed to have found the one and only perfect solution?

Bicycles and tricycles jostled each other for supremacy. The Ordinary bicycle was still King of the Road, but tricycles had challenged it, and the 'safeties' and 'dwarf' Ordinaries, the 'Facile', the 'Kangaroo' and the 'Xtraordinary' were the latest arrivals. And then there were tandem tricycles, 'sociable' tricycles, quadricycles — a range of machines never since equalled.

And then came the rear-driven 'safety' bicycle, intruding at first clumsily, then more and more competitively into the market. 'Many novelties are again introduced,' said the *CTC Gazette* about the Stanley Bicycle Show of February 1885 'but the most observable speciality is the safety bicycle, which every maker worthy of the name now considers it a religious duty to add to his stock.'

Many of the new rear-driven 'safeties' were exhibited in public in 1885 for the first time. The reaction to them ranged from laughter to intense interest and optimism. During 1884 there had been a great deal of experimental activity in the machine-shops of Coventry, Nottingham and Birmingham. H. McCammon patented a bicycle that was, in effect, the first women's 'safety'; Messrs Humber and Company introduced a 'safety' and so did the Birmingham Small Arms Company. And John Kemp Starley, the nephew of James Starley, with his partner William Sutton, produced the 'Rover' Safety Bicycle.

The first 'Rover's' main peculiarity was the indirect steering and the spiderlike complexity of its frame tubes, but with the second model, produced a few months later, the distant prospect of the bicycle as we know it today snaps suddenly into focus. It was absolutely necessary

The 'safety' bicycle produced by the Birmingham Small Arms Company in 1884.

Humber 'safety' bicycle, introduced in 1884.

The second 'Rover' 'safety', with direct steering, put on the market later in 1885.

Starley's and Sutton's first 'Rover', built in 1884, and first shown publicly at the beginning of 1885, was the earliest of the many successful 'Rover' safety bicycles.

that the new and untried 'Rover' should enter a cycle-race to establish it in the public eye as a serious rival to the 'Facile' and the 'Kangaroo'. Starley negotiated with the fastest 'amateurs', and on September 26th, 1885 a new 100-mile record of 7 hours 5 minutes 16 seconds was established by George Smith, who won a gold watch worth £50 for his efforts. Some of the competitors rode on new 'Rover' racers which weighed only thirty-three pounds. The record lasted less than a month however; William Hillman put up another candidate, and the 100-mile record fell to 6 hours 39 minutes 5 seconds.

Ordinary-riders found it hard to ride at first; one describes his unconventional way of learning to handle it:

> My first trial, I was hardly in the saddle when round flew the front wheel, and I was quickly on my feet. I then had assistance, and thought I would never master the machine, when the idea struck me that the best way of learning it would be to get it to a place some miles from home, and then ride it back by myself. Accordingly, I sent the Rover by rail to a place 54 miles from here, and from there started alone. After I had covered some 30 miles I could fly down the hills at full speed, so the learning did not really take very long.[5]

The 'safety' was tremendously boosted by the races and rivalry. The squat little 'dwarf' rear-drivers disappeared quickly. The 'Rover' proved that a long bicycle driven in this strange new way by a chain to the back wheel was not only safer than any other machine but also faster. It could not be ignored, and soon it was being widely copied. William Hillman introduced his 'Premier' Safety to rival his own 'Kangaroo', and the cross-frame 'safety', with a single heavy tube joining the back wheel to the steering socket, enjoyed wide popularity between 1886 and 1889.

One of the most popular cross-frame 'safeties', the 'Ivel', made by

The 1886 'Rover'; the bicycle as we know it today rapidly evolving.

Dan Albone, the landlord of a pub called the Olney Arms on the Great North Road as well as a bicycle-maker, was once again a record-breaker. On this bicycle G. P. Mills established two records in October 1886; 50 miles in 2 hours 4 minutes 45 seconds, and 295 miles in 24 hours. 'A remarkable record machine, although only on the market a few weeks,' said the advertisements. 'The "Ivel" Safety Bicycle, which can be ridden and steered without using the handles, has achieved the unique reputation of being incontestably the fastest bicycle ever made.' But this did not last for long. The astonishing succession of agonizing all-day rides continued, stimulated by the ambitions of the manufacturers. In 1889 M. A. Holbein did 324 miles on a Hillman, Herbert & Cooper cross-frame 'safety'. Rides like these were powerful publicity for the 'safety'.

By 1890 the structural deficiencies of the cross-frame had become apparent. The 'Rover' had led the way with its strong frame, and catalogues of 1890 show that nearly all the manufacturers had produced a bicycle resembling the 'Rover' to some degree.

Bicycle design had finally arrived at its ultimate form, although there were still big changes to come. Starley's 'Rover' was produced in about eight different models, and the Humber Company was selling eighteen different 'safety' models. Bicycles were costing less than £10 at the cheaper end of the market, and sales were increasing by leaps and bounds. Other designs fell behind in popularity; tricycles were less in demand. The modern bicycle had arrived.

Vibration was still a problem. The 'Whippet' was perhaps the most successful of the many bicycles with various arrangements of springs that were introduced to combat the ruts and pot-holes of the roads. Bicycles went faster and faster but the roads did not get any better or any smoother. By this time the CTC was making official complaints about the neglect of main roads, but conditions were, in general, much the same as they had been in the eighteen-seventies: mud and puddles in the winter and dust and dry stones in the summer.

The composition and fitting of the solid tyres which were used on every bicycle and tricycle had improved enormously since the first rubber strips had been tacked on to the metal rims of a boneshaker, but

132 King of the Road

A popular cyclists' rest, the Angel Inn, Ditton, taken about 1892. This picture is fascinating in the variety of machines being used. Four Ordinaries, three cross-frame 'safeties', five diamond-frame 'safeties' and a pneumatic-tyred tandem tricycle, including a lady with a dust-veil. There are also some chickens.

The first active cyclists' battalion was organized in the 26th Middlesex Regiment by Col. A. R. Savile, here standing in front of his men. In war, the bicycle became extremely important.

solid they remained. A slight improvement was made when 'cushion' tyres — rubber tyres with a hollow centre to absorb shock — were tried, and these were still being introduced after the first pneumatics were invented. But pneumatic tyres were a revolution.

John Boyd Dunlop was a Scot by birth, practising as a veterinary surgeon in Belfast. His son rode a tricycle, and Dunlop experimented with various ways of making it smoother for him. He fitted a crude rubber inner tube surrounded by a canvas bag and protected by a rubber tread. The tyre was patented on July 23rd, 1888, and Dunlop, in association with Booth's Cycle Agency, Dublin, began limited production. The tyre was tested and improved.

A pneumatic-tyred tricycle was ridden from Dublin to Coventry by a well-known Irish cycling journalist, R. J. Mecredy. It aroused huge interest there: 'The tyres were quite unknown, and when the tricycle was left outside a hotel (not in the centre of the city) for 10 minutes, a crowd of four or five hundred people were found pushing each other to obtain a sight of it.'[6]

Soon, everybody in the bicycle world knew about pneumatic tyres, although not all were equally confident about their future success. They were first used in a race in Belfast on May 18th, 1889, when W. Hume won all the four races in which he competed on them. Soon races were regularly won on pneumatic-tyred bicycles.

The fat, bulging tyres caused a great deal of merriment, and even some derision. But their speed and comfort could not be laughed at. It was obvious that they had come to stay. When Hume's pneumatic-tyred bicycle was displayed in a shop window in Liverpool, the crowd that collected there had to be dispersed by the police.

'Within a year of the commencement of the serious manufacture of pneumatic tyres,' says Grew, 'no racing man of any pretensions troubled to compete on anything else.' Belfast was too far from where bicycles were produced, and the Dunlop factory soon moved to Coventry. The first tyres had to be fitted to the wheels at the factory itself, and 'the Dunlop carts were soon careering about Coventry collecting the tyreless wheels and delivering them, fitted, to the various factories'.

By 1890 the death of the solid tyre was imminent. By the end of 1892 there were still a few solid-tyred bicycles to be found in the makers' lists, but the second-hand market was overflowing with them for a few pounds each. The revolution was complete and Dunlop already a millionaire.

The pneumatic-tyred safety bicycle which emerged from the

The Biggar Cycling Club, Lanark, in about 1890. The cross-frame 'safety' bicycle reigns supreme, and the Ordinaries are in the background.

The Search for Safety 133

A group of Catford Cycling Club members taken in 1887. They are still uniformed, but not exactly immaculately dressed as were some of the earlier club members.

Robert Jefferson set new standards in the mid-'nineties with some astonishing rides on a pneumatic-tyred 'safety' bicycle.

experiments of the eighteen-eighties brought about a social revolution. Its impact was far bigger and affected many more people than any previous development in bicycle technology. It made possible a huge increase in the number of people who were initially willing to ride bicycles, and enthusiastically propagate them. Now, for the first time, the excuses about danger and discomfort were no longer valid. Before 1890 cycling had been the pastime of a small minority; after 1895 it was open to almost everyone.

The reason for its success was that it was ergonomically efficient. As a machine which had to relate to the human body, it was carefully considered. The distance at which the rider sat from the ground, the ability to gear up or down, so that riders of different heights and strength could choose a suitable gear, the relative position of the seat to the pedals, its adjustability in a vertical or horizontal direction, and the position of the handlebars relative to both the seat and the pedals with a similar adjustment were all taken into account.

In 1882, according to one estimate, there had been 200,000 bicycle- and tricycle-riders in England. By 1893 this had increased to 500,000, and within ten years the number had more than doubled again. In 1926, said *Cycling*, there were six million cyclists in Great Britain.

The number of people – the keenest cyclists – who joined the Cyclists' Touring Club declined surprisingly between 1886 and 1894, but after that increased dramatically. In 1895 there were 16,343 members, in 1896 34,655, in 1897 44,491, in 1898 54,332, and in 1899, the highest total ever in the club's existence, 60,449 members. At the Stanley Bicycle Show in 1895 about 3,000 different models were displayed by about 200 firms.

The expansion of the industry meant a change of style in its organization. Bicycles were big business, and were mass-produced on an assembly line. The early struggles of the pioneers, who had had to make all their components and tools themselves, making almost every nut and bolt that went into their bicycles, were over. Manufacturers of components in Birmingham and Wolverhampton now supplied standardized fittings to the Coventry makers. The design process was separated from production.

Bicycle-manufacture was soon a ripe area for investment. The growing companies were in need of capital and were soon approached by speculators who offered to buy control for handsome and seemingly irresistible sums. The king of these operators was Terah Hooley, a stock-broker from Nottingham, who during the mid-'nineties dabbled in and profited from the finances of almost all the largest cycle companies. The Raleigh Cycle Company was his first speculation; he bought it for £180,000 and floated it for £200,000. Then came the Humber concern, and others quickly followed. Hooley's greatest *coup* was to buy the Dunlop Company for £3 million, and to float it soon after for £5 million. 'Money poured into the coffers of men who had done nothing to build the businesses,' says Grew of the bicycle boom of 1895-6. 'They had only been astute enough to see that the market was ripe for flotation, and as the public cried for cycle shares, they got them.'

The huge demand for machines caused every dealer to order three times as many as he expected to sell. The boom gathered momentum, share prices rose and a few speculators became very rich. In 1896 *The Cycle* reported that in the previous year 800,000 bicycles were produced in England. But the manufacturers soon found that the demand was a bubble; there were many cases of over-capitalization, and many bankruptcies. A slump was the inevitable result, and by 1897 the bubble had burst, leaving behind it chaos in the bicycle industry.

As cycling became more and more popular in the eighteen-nineties, and the boom of 1895 approached, it became almost a crusade. For the working class the bicycle was an obvious advantage, and there was a growing demand for cheaper machines. But changes were also taking place in the attitude of the upper classes to what they had for a long time considered a 'common' pastime.

In 1894 *Cycling* published an article called 'Breaking through the Upper Crust':

> Slowly, but surely, and with lately a slight perceptible quickening of the pace, the sport of cycling is gaining a foothold in the upper ranks of society ... In England, where the cycle chanced in the first instance to take the taste of the middle classes, and where the upper class have strong 'horsey' instincts and prejudices, the work of popularizing the bicycle is difficult. It is the 'horsey' instinct, we take it, that has been the largest factor in practically barring the use of the cycle in the upper ranks of society. [7]

Perhaps not just the 'horsey' instinct but also the behaviour of cyclists kept them away:

> If cycle riders wish to secure the consideration and respect of others who have an equal right to the use of the highways, they must see that they do not grossly abuse the privileges they already possess ... It is no uncommon sight to see crowds of men racing through crowded towns on the hollow-shod mounts, straggling all over the roadway, utterly regardless of aught but their own progress through space, incessantly whooping, tootling their cyclorns and generally bringing the sport in disrepute. [8]

'Scorchers ... whose only ideas of enjoyment consist in tearing along as fast as possible and back' were hated by gentle cyclists and anti-cyclists alike:

> Many a time have I looked at these idiots tearing along and perspiring in the scorching sun, with faces rivalling the expression of an Indian warrior at the stake, and looking like enormous monkeys as they sat doubled up ... These hump-backed, tearing and sweltering scorchers are no credit to cycledom, and are a positive desecration to the charms and loveliness of the country. [9]

But suddenly, in 1895, society ladies decided that cycling was just what they needed. They paraded in the London parks, and everybody

The result of the boom was that family cycling was all the rage. It is interesting that only the woman here has a brake. Taken about 1895.

The cycling club of the firm of Rabbits & Sons in south-east London, in the early eighteen-nineties. A works club was not very common. The swaggering rider in the centre is holding a spring-frame 'Whippet', introduced before pneumatics to fight the roughness of the roads.

138 King of the Road

was talking about cycling for a month or two. The aristocracy took up this middle-class sport, an almost unheard-of thing, and gave it a respectability it had never had before. They were not well known for the strenuousness of their cycling exertions, but their flirtation with the bicycle generated interest and enthusiasm for it.

People who had previously sworn they would never be seen dead in as undignified a position as astride a saddle took to the road. Old men and dainty ladies alike could plead that it was good for their health; fat people took to cycling to get thinner, while thin people were equally keen on it as a way of putting on weight.

The old social and class barriers did not of course disappear, but the bicycle at least levelled them a little. Upper and lower classes could not maintain their aloofness as they struggled over an awkward hill, or perhaps stopped on the road to help each other out of a spot of mechanical trouble. The growing cycling press mostly adopted a rather conservative attitude towards behaviour and dress on the road, and were always concerned about the effect the bad behaviour of a few cyclists would have on the reputation of the sport, but they admired none the less the adventurousness and pluck of the 'scorcher' and the record-breaker.

The cycling craze had an unfortunate and serious effect on the lives of people who worked with horses. The *Hub* maintained that the horse-trade lost £5 million in 1896, and printed an article called 'Servants who deplore the cycle':

> 'Since the mistress took to riding, the staff of servants has been reduced' deplored an undergardener to the writer. 'You see, there are four young ladies, and they are all devotees of the wheel. The young men of the family are ardent cyclists, some of the horses have been sold, the grooms have been dismissed, and the work of the stables has fallen to the coachmen and a stable-boy.'
>
> So frequently do the girls go away, that it has been deemed advisable to dispense with the services of a housemaid, the cook bemoaning the loss, as many extra duties fall to her lot in consequence.[10]

The absolute superiority of pneumatic tyres was convincingly demonstrated by the dramatic new times established for long-distance records.

In 1896, at the height of the bicycle craze, H. G. Wells published his novel *The Wheels of Chance*. It was well timed. Its hero, Hoopdriver, is a working-class draper's assistant, accustomed to bowing and scraping to the wealthy behind the counter of a shop. He takes his annual holiday on a bicycle, and finds a new kind of freedom as he rides towards an adventure in the Sussex countryside with a 'New Woman' from a class distinctly higher than his own.

Hoopdriver lives on his fantasies: 'Like many of those who do the fetching and carrying of life, his real life was absolutely uninteresting, and if he had faced it realistically, he would probably have come by way of drink to suicide in the course of a year.'

He becomes infatuated with the upper-class girl he meets on the road. He rescues her from her pursuer, a male chauvinist suitor, who thinks that because she has left home with him on a bicycle she has hopelessly damaged her reputation and must therefore marry him. Her relatives are equally shocked about her 'flaunting her freedom — on a bicycle, in country places. In this country, where everyone is so particular — Fancy *sleeping* away from home. It's dreadful. If it gets about it spells ruin for her.'

This kind of adventure could only happen because all the characters are away from their homes, in the limbo created by the bicycle. On the road, Hoopdriver is almost Jessie's equal. In the end, of course, he loses his heroine, and is mercilessly put down by her relatives. The story is a light but illuminating account of a class society during a time of change, and a marvellous evocation of the pleasures of cycling on empty, unspoiled country roads:

> It was fine, full of promise of glorious days, a deep blue sky, with dazzling piles of white cloud here and there, as though celestial

'One of the oldest, largest and wealthiest cycling clubs in existence is the St Helens Cycling Club, although little is heard of it outside Lancashire, nevertheless the club enjoys a healthy existence.'

By 1896 the battle between the 'safety' bicycle and all other models had been won. In this picture, taken outside the Old Salisbury Arms, Barnet, record-breakers Bidlake and Shorland are conspicuous with white carnations in their buttonholes.

140 King of the Road

The Anchor, Ripley, 'the Mecca of all good cyclists'. A remarkable picture taken in 1896, at the height of the bicycle boom. The woman in the centre is Miss Harriet Dibble, the proprietress of the pub; she died a few months after the picture was taken. Her mother made this pub popular in the early days when many pubs treated cyclists with great suspicion. The woman on the front of the tandem is wearing 'rational' dress, while the man on the left wearing the cap is undoubtedly a 'scorcher'.

haymakers had been piling the swaths of last night's clouds into cocks for a coming cartage. There were thrushes in the Richmond Road, and a lark on Putney Heath. The freshness of dew was in the air; dew or the relics of an overnight shower glittered on the leaves and grass. Hoopdriver wheeled his machine up Putney Hill and his heart sang within him ... All the big red-brick houses behind the variegated shrubs and trees had their blinds down still, and he would not have changed places with a soul in any one of them for a hundred pounds.

The typical bicycle of the eighteen-nineties had a fixed wheel, and the rider had to keep pedalling all the time, though he might occasionally put his feet up on the foot-rests if his bicycle had them. It had slightly dropped bars and a leather saddle, sometimes it had a plunger brake, but often no brake at all. Since it was rarely necessary to stop suddenly, the rider simply eased back on the pedals to slow down. The cycle had pneumatic tyres, of course, probably a thirty-inch front wheel and a twenty-eight-inch back one, and perhaps a completely encased chain. If it was a racer, it might have toe-clips, but no straps, and weigh as little as twenty pounds, though a roadster with rubber pedals would weigh up to thirty-five pounds.

It is not hard to understand why so many people were drawn into cycling in the eighteen-nineties. To have remained outside it or resolutely opposed to it would have been rather like refusing in the nineteen-seventies to have anything to do with travelling in cars. Bicycles were so pervasive that they could hardly be ignored. People went to work on them, for long holidays, out into the country in the evenings, and of course they 'scorched' and raced just for the pleasure of riding hard and fast.

Once cycling had thrown off the last vestiges of the bad reputation it had had for so long, it became everybody's transport. Only those daring

Rotten Row, in Hyde Park, was crowded out with week-end cyclists during the short-lived society boom of 1895 and 1896.

young women who insisted on wearing trousers to ride in and the 'scorchers' with their heads down could still prick moral and sexual prejudices, bringing out the anger and indignation in respectable people.

Gwen Raverat in *Period Piece*, her account of her Cambridge childhood, tells of the coming of the safety bicycle:

> The Bicycling craze came in when we were just about at the right age to enjoy it. At first even 'safety' bicycles were too dangerous and improper for ladies to ride, and they had to have tricycles ...
>
> Then one day, at lunch, my father said he had just seen a new kind of tyre, filled up with air, and he thought it might be a success. And soon after that everyone had bicycles, ladies and all, and bicycling became the smart thing in Society, and the lords and ladies had their pictures in the papers, riding along in the park in straw boater hats. We were then promoted to wearing baggy knickerbockers under our frocks, and over our white frilly drawers. We thought this horridly improper, but rather grand ... I only once saw a woman (not, of course, a lady) in real bloomers.
>
> My mother must have fallen off her bicycle pretty often for I remember seeing, several times, the most appalling cuts and bruises on her legs. But she never complained, and always kept these mishaps to herself ...
>
> How my father did adore those bicycles! Such beautiful machines! They were as carefully tended as if they had been alive; every speck of dust or wet was wiped from them as soon as we came back from a ride, and at night they were all brought into the house and slung up to the ceiling of the kitchen passage by a series of ingenious pulleys for fear that the night air in the covered backyard might rust them.[11]

Cycling was above all an active pastime. You did not watch someone else perform, you performed yourself to the best of your ability. And cycling mixed ideally with other activities, photography, sketching and painting, visiting historical sights and simply visiting new places. On their long touring holidays, people lived for weeks at a time on the road, and began to understand the rhythms of the countryside.

On the new pneumatic 'safety', astonishing journeys were undertaken, and the road and track records that had been bettered almost year by year since the early eighteen-eighties were slashed by huge margins. The beating of records played a very important part in demonstrating the superiority of the 'safety'.

By 1893 100 miles on the road had been covered in 5 hours 27 minutes 38 seconds; $366\frac{1}{2}$ miles covered in twenty-four hours. The Land's End – John-o'-Groats ride, the ultimate English endurance-test, was lowered to 3 days 23 hours 55 minutes in 1892, and then to 3 days 5 hours 49 minutes in 1894. London to Brighton and back was done in 6 hours 49 minutes 1 second, which compared with a previous coach record established by James Selby, who had done 108 miles in 7 hours 50 minutes, with sixteen changes of horses! By 1898 the records were still lower; 100 miles in 4 hours 16 minutes 35 seconds, and 428 miles in twenty-four hours.

In 1895 and 1896 Robert Jefferson wrote two books about the grand tours he had made, stripped of everything except absolutely essential luggage, to Moscow and back (4,281 miles in 49 days), and then across Siberia (6,574 miles). His record journeys were subsidized heavily by bicycle-manufacturers and widely advertised on his return. Dunlop tyres, Perry's chains, the Signal Fork Cyclometer, Wood's Wire Saddles and Grose's gearcase were all fitted to an Imperial Rover frame made by J. K. Starley in Coventry, not forgetting 'a plentiful supply of Bovril'.

At about the same time, John Foster Frazer and two friends were outdoing Jefferson by riding 19,237 miles round the world in 774 days. Even these trips pale a little in daring, however, compared with the great eccentric bicycle explorer Thomas Stevens, who rode an Ordinary bicycle in the mid-eighteen-eighties across America from San Francisco to New York, and then from Europe to Japan, surely one of the most foolhardy journeys ever undertaken by a human being.

Everybody learned something from cycling. It took the city worker out into the country and brought him into contact with country people, while the middle- and upper-class riders came down to earth and benefited from the exercise.

The bicycle was used on a massive scale. Between 1890 and 1920 people probably travelled more miles on bicycles than on any other kind of transport. It was an extraordinary period of almost universal,

Danger-boards, erected by the Cyclists' Touring Club, were a familiar sight all over the country.

A professional pacing triplet on Herne Hill Track during the heyday of big-time racing.

pollution-free mobility. The roads were not yet improved in many places, but they were still almost free of other traffic. It was possible to ride all day and hardly see a soul.

Only the spreading city suburbs and the dirty, noisy, unhealthy factories from which the bicycles themselves came, and the motorcars which gradually increased in speed and number, gave some idea of a rapidly changing society, in which the relaxed and economical bicycle would soon have a less important place.

Ironically, the independence and mobility which bicycles gave people whetted their appetite for even easier travelling. Many of the first English car-manufacturers were originally bicycle-makers — Humber, Morris, Singer, Austin, Hillman — and the technology that had been developed in making bicycles was to be the foundation of the car industry. By 1908, when H. G. Wells wrote his novel *The War in the Air*, things had changed a good deal since the relaxed days of *The Wheels of Chance*. Old Smallways sits over the fire grumbling about motorcycles and the present, but nobody takes any notice:

> The world had thrown up a new type of gentleman altogether, a gentleman of most ungentlemanly energy, a gentleman in dusty oilskins and motor goggles and a wonderful cap, a stink-making gentleman, a swift, high-class badger, who fled perpetually along high roads from the dust and stink he perpetually made.
>
> 'Orf to Brighton' said Old Smallways, regarding his youngest son from the sitting-room window over the greengrocer's shop with something between pride and reprobation. 'When I was 'is age, I'd never bin to London, never bin south of Crawley, never bin anywhere on my own where I couldn't walk. And nobody didn't go. Not unless they was gentry. Now everybody's orf everywhere; the whole dratted country sims flying to pieces. Wonder they all get back. Orf to Brighton indeed! Anybody want to buy 'orses?' [12]

CHAPTER 7
WOMEN'S LIBERATION

If the race of women could be got into a good, sound, physical condition, the world would inevitably become physically regenerated. If the New Woman is one who claims that outdoor exercise is as beneficial for her as it is for her brother; who insists upon designing her clothing so that every muscle and limb shall be as free and capable as God intended it to be; who claims health to be hers and her children's by birthright and counts it a sin to be ill; who demands the right to think for herself ... then I will do my best to swell her ranks.

Nothing short of death seems to make the apathetic woman of fashion recognize that her life is one long suicide. Hers is a living death; fainting, hysteria, indigestion, anaemia, lassitude, diminished vitality and a host of other sufferings arise from interference with the circulation of the blood and the prevention of the full play of the breathing organs.

Such is the woman of old, now happily dying out. Dress reform is one of the great factors in this result, and the cycle is an aid to this reform. Therefore, the cycle is to be gratefully welcomed, and its use promoted by all thinking women.[1]

There are times when the subject of cycling seems a very slight affair, a private matter for a few enthusiasts. Bicycling and tricycling are not matters of great importance compared with the hard business of national and international politics, conflicts between capital and labour and the common struggle to keep alive and find work and money.

Yet momentous social changes sometimes grow out of small beginnings, and comparatively small social conflicts can be very significant.

Of all the controversies which surrounded the growth of cycling as a popular activity, probably none was more bitterly debated or aroused more passionate feelings than the subject of women and cycling. For more than thirty years, the topic was continually discussed from almost every angle under the sun.

The 'New Woman' rides towards freedom with the man of her choice. An advertisement for Elliman's embrocation from the late eighteen-nineties.

146 King of the Road

A Pilentum, or Lady's Accelerator: the lady might perhaps make a few circuits of the grounds of her country mansion, but her dainty arms would hardly be strong enough to take it far along a rough road. The most interesting thing about this machine is that it is one of the very earliest machines which could be continuously driven.

It was not just a question of whether women should have the right to ride or not (and this was always the main issue until about 1895), but what they should wear when they rode, how they should ride, when they should ride, who they should ride with, whether they should race, whether it was good for their health, their morals, their families, their complexions, their hair and their reputations.

The discussion was really a much bigger one than women and bicycles and tricycles; what was really being talked about was women and men, and by implication women's position in a society that was organized and dominated by men. The debate that went on between about 1870 and 1890 about women and cycling was in fact a continual battle fought by an increasingly large number of women for the right to do what they pleased, when they pleased, in the face of a vast army of mostly unwritten laws about how they were to live their lives. And older women as well as men were the guardians of these laws.

The story of women and the bicycle is an extraordinary one. Men, of course, designed and manufactured the velocipedes and bicycles which enabled them to liberate themselves from the confines of their homes and their jobs and to taste a new kind of freedom and adventure. The only barriers to their success were their own inventive limitations.

As cycling became more and more popular, and women kissed their husbands and sons goodbye on Saturdays and Sundays and waited for them to come home in the evenings with their exciting stories of the road, some of them began to grow resentful. Working-class and middle-class women alike found themselves in the often disagreeable position of being isolated from these new experiences which the men enjoyed so cheaply. Most quite easily added bicycling to the long list of things which were 'not quite done' for a woman, and would not have been seen dead on a bicycle. But others were quite justifiably envious; they knew that they were missing something.

Women's Liberation 147

And so the right to ride a bicycle or a tricycle became one of the many things that a woman had to struggle for. And there were a lot of people who opposed her for all sorts of reasons. The most minute aspects of an activity that men had an unquestioned right to take part in were put under a questioning microscope.

For most women the question of their right to ride a bicycle was not of any importance until the mid-eighteen-eighties. But a few did take a very early interest. Denis Johnson made some ladies' hobby-horses, especially adapted to accommodate long skirts, in 1819, and at about the same time the delicate ladies' 'Pilentum' was put on show in London, and probably used in the gardens of country houses. A few women certainly rode Sawyer's velocipedes, and there were ladies' tricycle velocipedes.

But it must have been a very rare woman indeed who, between 1820 and about 1865, would have been willing to expose herself to the ridicule that velocipedes encouraged. Machinery and athletic activity were parts of a man's world, and most people saw a man's world and a woman's as being quite distinct and separate. Working-class women might go down the mines and work in factories, but respectable and upper-class women were the 'fair sex', or the 'gentle sex', and there was seen to be no contradiction in the belief that they should be protected from the dangers of sweating and over-exertion.

Velocipedomania, the sudden popularity of the fast two-wheeled

French women velocipede-riders in 1868 threw aside their qualms and appeared in public wearing this attractive and *risqué* costume. This daring display of leg was probably unprecedented outside the music-hall.

148 King of the Road

boneshaker, saw the first women riders staking their claims to the bicycle, and the first strong reactions against their doing so. 'The pleasures of the new mode of locomotion were confined exclusively to the sterner sex,' says J. F. Bottomley-Firth in 1869, 'and the fairer and frailer portion of creation were bound to stand quietly by whilst husbands and lovers revelled in the new sensation.'

Pickering, the New York maker, invented a ladies' model, and J. T. Goddard in *The Velocipede* was enthusiastic about women riding:

While young men have been dashing about on velocipedes, many young women have looked on with envy. They have not been satisfied with the tricycle designed for their especial use, and have felt it hard that they should be denied the exercise, amusement, risk, dash and delightful independence which the bicycle so abundantly affords ...

It would be a bright and beautiful day for our land should a laudable and reasonable ambition once fairly get possession of our young women, to cultivate and develop their physical natures and to become strong, healthy, robust and enduring.[2]

Velocipede schools for women were opened in Boston and New York, and even a rather respectable paper, the *Scientific American*, did not complain about their wearing bloomers, or something similar:

The bicycle has been introduced into gymnasiums for ladies exercise, who use the dress commonly used by them in calisthenic exercise. The fair ones who have learned to manage the beast are in transports, and a rush is the consequence of the new attraction. Gentlemen are excluded while the ladies practice the art, but a few Benedicts who have been permitted to look behind the scenes while their better halves were performing on their firey [sic] untamed steeds say that they make a very pretty and graceful

Some French women did actually race as early as 1868, and this picture shows the final sprint in a race at Bordeaux. 'At the starting gun,' wrote a woman velocipedist to *Le Monde Illustré* 'they all went off quickly, and almost at once Mademoiselle Louise took the lead and held it for a long time. About 50 metres from the finish Mademoiselle Julie, who had been riding behind her, caught her up, and with a superhuman effort won by about half a wheel.'

appearance. We can see no valid objection why ladies should not adopt a special dress for this sport, and enjoy it in the open air, instead of in closed and confined rooms.[3]

American women were less inhibited than their European counterparts. Already in America, there was a tradition of women's rights campaigning. Amelia Bloomer and Elizabeth Cody Stanton had been active in pressing for women's suffrage, and in their temperance paper, the *Lily*, first published in 1849, the world's first women's emancipation journal, they had attacked the fantastic weight and length of women's skirts, which, they said, deformed and restricted women's bodies, and hindered them in their attempts to prove that they were men's equals.

In 1851 Amelia Bloomer and Elizabeth Stanton had been visited at their home in Seneca Falls, New York State by Mrs Libby Miller, who had arrived in pantaloons and caused a local scandal. Mrs Miller's pantaloons, inspired by the dress of Eastern women, soon came to be known as 'Bloomers', and the name stuck, despite Mrs Bloomer's frequent assertions that Mrs Miller had been the originator of this kind of rational dress and the first person to wear it in public. Mrs Bloomer, from a distance, was to be an influential figure in the women's cycling movement in England.

'American ladies are many of them so strong-minded and independent,' wrote J. F. Bottomley-Firth, 'that they do not believe in looking for guidance and support to the other vessel. They have fought for equality on the platform and the pulpit and they are not intending to allow the velocipede to remain a standing token of the subjection of women.'

In France too, women did not allow prejudice to deny them access to the velocipede. Much of their riding was done indoors, and the scantily dressed *vélocipédestrienne* entertaining men at the music-hall was hardly a symbol of emancipation. But the four women on bicycles crossing the finishing-line in a picture of a race at Bordeaux (on page 148) have obviously no qualms about exposing their legs in what must have been a quite unprecedented display of public athletic vigour. There was no question of long skirts being an obstacle to *their* riding bicycles.

Bicycle-riding in public streets in Paris was an opportunity for a flippant display of fashion:

> The velocipede is suited for displaying to admiration the dainty boots, faultless ankles and smoothly-drawn stockings for which Parisian belles are so justly renowned, and indeed, to see tiny 'tootsicums' encased in pale fawn-coloured or gleaming bronze leather, urging the wheeled machine on its swift career, whilst the little gloved hands on the bar guide it deftly through all the intricacies of a crowded thoroughfare, is a sight seriously calculated to affect the interior economy of the spectator.[4]

English women were more bashful. There is not very much evidence of their having ridden boneshakers at all. *Punch* reacted with horror at even the idea of a woman on a bicycle. Our friend J. F. Bottomley-Firth, in his discussion of women and velocipeding, comes down firmly against it, and thinks women should stick to the tricycle:

> Of course the Bloomers and Mary Walkers of the States cannot rest content with such a machine, but we in Europe are still so old-fashioned as to prefer propriety to sensation.
>
> It would no doubt be mighty pleasant, to go out velocipeding with your fair friends, each mounted on her own bicycle, but custom and nature revolt against it, and there can be no doubt but that it is in the 'external fitness of things' that it should be so. At least half the interest of one sex in the other arises from their respective dependent and protective positions. When a lady velocipedes she destroys all this kind of subtle interest, and thereby loosens one of the sweetest and firmest bonds of existence. Every velocipedestrienne ought to be compelled to wear blue stockings.[5]

Women's Liberation 149

Caricaturists made the most of the women velocipede-riders in France and mocked them mercilessly.

150 King of the Road

The suggestion of an American paper in 1869 that women might share men's enthusiasm for the velocipede was immediately answered by *Punch* with this light-hearted, though acid, cartoon.

"With a proper teacher of their own sex, and with suitable dresses for the preliminary practice, ladies can obtain such a command over the velocipedes in one week's practice, of an hour daily, that they can ride side-saddle-wise with the utmost ease." — *New York Sun*.

OH! THEN, THIS IS WHAT WE MAY EXPECT TO SEE THIS SEASON.

Some women rode horses side-saddle, so why not the velocipede? This curious machine, with both cranks on the same side of the front wheel, and an extra balancing wheel hanging to one side, was Samuel Webb Thomas's impractical idea of how to overcome the difficulties caused by a woman's skirts.

The nature of opposition to women riding bicycles is quite plainly laid out here: there are some things women do and some they are ordained by nature not to do. Bicycle-riding is one of the latter, and to insist on doing it would be somehow to upset the natural order of things, and to become an anarchist.

Women's velocipeding did not become popular in England, and as mentioned earlier, even in France and America the craze was short-lived. Most women did not want to ride, and even if they did they could not. Their long skirts were an insuperable obstacle. The design of the machine, with its high backbone and pedals on either side of the front wheel, was not suitable for them; fashion stood in the way of mechanical efficiency. As we have seen, one maker, Samuel Webb Thomas, made an attempt to overcome the problem of skirts by building a curious side-saddle velocipede in 1870, but there is no record of it having been successful.

The Ordinary bicycle was a nail in the coffin of women's hopes for a rideable machine. James Starley created another version of Samuel Thomas's idea when he built his ladies' 'Ariel', but that too was a failure.

For nearly twenty years to ride the Ordinary bicycle was out of the question for women. There are hardly any accounts of women riding it, and it was unsuitable for them in almost every possible way. It was dangerous, it was difficult to mount and dismount and, above all, it demanded a pair of legs absolutely unhampered by anything except skin-tight trousers. Rather than encouraging women to press for acceptance of bloomers for riding, the Ordinary drove them away from bicycles altogether, and towards tricycles.

The cult of the Ordinary was a total male preserve. I can find hardly a mention of women riding the high bicycle. One account that does give a little insight dwells quite predictably not on how good it is that women are riding, but on how they expose their bodies in doing so:

> The young ladies, and also some who are no longer young, at Detroit, U.S. have taken to bicycling. The costume, a sort of Bloomer, is very becoming to a really good figure and leaves little of the fair wearers' proportions to the imagination of the beholder.[6]

Tricycles at last gave women the possibility of riding. It was partly the realization that they were so totally excluded from bicycle-riding that encouraged the manufacturers in Coventry to provide them with a machine. Profit, the search for an expanding market, ironically always helped the cause of women's cycling. 'Sociables' ovecame the extreme pressure that was initially put on a woman who ventured out alone. With a man at her side, she was no longer exposed to the many dangers, mostly imaginary, which were supposed to await her at every turn of the road.

Tricycling chaperones came into vogue for those ladies who did not have a male protector, and a number of Chaperones' Associations guaranteed to provide a suitably responsible lady cyclist companion for individuals or groups when she was needed. 'A nimble chaperone might form a series of engagements to last all summer, or even, by a judicious choice of foreign countries with a genial climate, the whole year,' commented *Wheeling* (October 5th, 1884). Tricycling ladies, evidently, were certainly not be found among the poor.

But there were still people who thought that any kind of tricycling was completely unsuitable, even degrading, for a woman. Even Queen Victoria's early interest, in 1881, could not shake the opposition of the most determined.

Women could not and mostly would not change their style of dress; the machine could on the other hand be arranged around their skirts. It is curious that social conventions could be so strong that manufacturers had to go to the extreme lengths of designing tricycles which allowed a woman to pedal as freely as possible in a skirt, and with a bit of room too for the skirt to flap around. The open-fronted front-steering type of tricycle was best. But skirts would still blow up in the wind, and got caught up in the complicated machinery, sometimes causing nasty accidents.

The sight of a woman struggling along on a tricycle encumbered by all those yards of useless material, and suffocating herself with a tight waist and neckband, was too much for Mrs King, the secretary of the Rational Dress Society and an ardent emancipationist. She launched a campaign in the cycling press for the liberation of women from what she saw as the prison of fashion and convention. She sent a description of her 'rational' tricycling dress, consisting of a long jacket and baggy trousers, to the *Tricyclist,* and a woman reader replied:

> It must surely be known that the great objection to tricycling entertained by the upper classes of society is not so much to the sport, but the idea that it is conducive to the horrid fashion of 'aping men' so prevalent at the present time. The adoption of this masculine habit would most certainly retard the adoption of the

As the front wheel of the bicycle got bigger, it presented an insuperable obstacle to women's skirts and their modesty. James Starley was aware of the problem, and in 1872 made this lever-driven side-saddle bicycle. A nice gesture to women, but impractical. The photo shows F. J. Warman, who worked for the Coventry Machinists' Company, and Miss Ellen Parvin, posing on 'Ariels'.

Wheeling on Riverside Drive, 1886; a beautiful, evocative engraving from the more relaxed days of New York City.

tricycle among ladies. They have even now, as I can testify, no small annoyances to put up with from boys and very proper ladies. The result of the adoption of such an outré dress would be that *no lady* either could or would ride and subject herself to the insults such a novel costume would entail.[7]

Mrs King wasted no time in replying:

I am truly sorry that my rational tricycle dress has shocked the lady-like feelings of your correspondent. She must have been on the mountain tops for a long time not to know that in the practical world which lies below her, the accusation of 'aping men' no more prevents women from doing what they think it right to do, than the epithet 'shrieking sisterhood' ever prevented them from saying what they thought it right to say ...

Bye and bye, no lady will think of mounting a tricycle without wearing tricycle trousers.[8]

Mrs King did have a little success, but it was uphill work. The Rational Dress Society held several shows and a lot of support was expressed for its ideas. The *Tricyclist* even reported that it had seen two 'rational'-dress-wearers on the road, one at Barnes and the other on the Ripley Road. In July 1883 a Miss Jessie Choice rode 113 miles in a day on a tricycle. But still the vast majority of women refused to see the light, at a time when the number of women tricyclists was increasing every month.

Mrs King persisted. Later in 1883 she wrote impatiently to the *Cyclists' Touring Club Gazette*:

Sir — When women were sensible enough to accept the advantage which tricycle riding could offer them, it was in their power either to adopt for a new and rational dress, or to

The necessity to accommodate a woman's skirts gave rise to some very odd tricycle designs.

perpetuate and increase the follies and the irrationalities of their old style of garments ...

With the usual folly of our sex, women tricycle riders are on the way towards adopting the inconvenient long skirt and unhealthy tight bodice, and of rejecting decent and convenient riding trousers.

I have not the time nor indeed the patience to again attempt to combat this folly. I have quite given up all hope of influencing these riders by any arguments I could adduce. One reason for this is that, for the most part, the ladies and gentlemen who at present ride cycles are of that class who are so dreadfully afraid of not being thought ladies and gentlemen, that they cannot venture on any novelty in dress, or appear to countenance it until it has received the cachet of a superior class.[9]

Women, it seemed, were their own worst enemies. The way was open for them if they wanted to take it, but they were all afraid of what everybody else would think.

If women did not immediately all start wearing 'rational' dress, it was perhaps understandable. It was hard enough for many of them to tolerate the jibes and jokes of their friends and relatives as they left the house on their tricycle, let alone expose themselves to the ridicule that wearing trousers would be sure to bring. Most tricyclists did not consider their pastime important enough to want to make a political platform out of it, and they were happy enough to have their new freedom and exercise. To be able to ride at all was a huge victory for women in general. The mixed parties of tricyclists who went picknicking in the country at week-ends were made up of people who were enjoying a new kind of independence and mobility.

'He stoops to conquer ... !' a drawing by George Moore

Tricycle-riding gave most women riders their first taste of the pleasures of the road, but the kind of clothes which this woman is wearing were not only impractical but dangerous.

Most women tricyclists opposed 'rational' dress and women's racing because they saw them as a threat to public acceptance of their pastime. The cycling press came out strongly against racing, which was being pioneered in the mid-eighteen-eighties on the road and track by a few brave women:

> The novelty of seeing a lady on the track is so great, that at present the wheeling world hardly appreciates the disastrous results which must accrue from what is now a rarity becoming in the future a general thing. To the cause of wheeling, the results would be dire; but not so much as to the whole female sex. Scandal is always more ready to fasten its poisoned fangs upon woman's reputation than man's, and once let the sport of wheeling become branded with the iron of adverse public opinion, and it will indubitably suffer in prestige and popularity.[10]

A 'Lady' writes back to the same paper in even stronger terms:
> When we consider and reflect upon the question, the first idea that arises is one of utter surprise at the bare notion of any woman so far forgetting her innate modesty and dignity, as to be seen tearing along in a most inelegant fashion, to say the least of it, before hundreds of spectators of all sorts and conditions ...

One hears a great deal about the advanced state of civilization and culture we have arrived at in the present day. I think if we look back at what we are pleased to call the dark ages, we shall find it difficult to discover any woman with the least pretence to refinement, setting such an example of unwomanly conduct as I consider tricycle racing to be ... [11]

And if there was still any room for doubt about what the ladies themselves thought about such excesses, Miss T. R. Coombs added her somewhat irrational objections:

Racing does violence to a woman's natural and proper wish to look as nice as possible. Even the ugliest girl has some desire to make herself not actually unpleasant to those about her; but how can we admire a girl, however beautiful she may be, whose face is as red as a boiled lobster, and streaming with perspiration, whose hair is hanging in a mop about her ears, whose hairpins are strewed along the race-course, and whose general appearance is dusty, untidy and unwomanly ... [12]

During the eighteen-eighties women gradually established their right to ride when and where they pleased (except that Sunday riding always gave some people good reason to complain), and this was in itself a huge advance for those who could afford to buy tricycles, or could borrow them. But it was still rather daring and unconventional to go riding and there were not yet many women who did so.

Women had not tried the experimental 'safeties', the 'Kangaroo', the 'Xtraordinary' or the 'Facile'. The two events which made possible the huge, unprecedented expansion of cycling in the early eighteen-nineties, the development of the diamond-framed 'safety' bicycle and the invention and production of efficient pneumatic tyres, brought with them new possibilities for women and a huge growth of interest in cycling.

The Starleys were quick, as usual, in feeling out the needs of the market. Among the models produced for 1889 by Starley Brothers, the sons of James Starley, at St John's Works, Coventry, were the Psycho Ladies' bicycle, with a drop frame and no shadow of a cross-bar of any kind, and a 'lady-front' tandem. And shortly after, John Kemp Starley brought out his ladies' 'Rover'. 'The Rover has set a fashion to the World,' says his advertisement: it cost £20 with solid tyres at first and a dress-guard over the back wheel, but it was soon available with pneumatics. A grateful lady writes them a testimonial in 1890:

Dear Sirs — My husband purchased for me one of your Ladies Rover Safeties in July last, and I should like to tell you how delighted I am with it. I had been used to tandem riding, but had never been on a safety before ... I should be pleased to see the Lady's Rover become more general, for the more popular they get the less will be the remarks passed on them ...

The demand for ladies' bicycles was increasing rapidly, and catalogues for 1892 show several more in production. But the real boom did not come until 1893 and 1894, by which time no self-respecting maker was without a ladies' drop-frame bicycle in his range.

With the 'safety' bicycle, women took another step forward. It became obvious that it was ridiculous for them to go riding tricycles, which were much heavier, or to have to be always in the company of another man or woman on a 'sociable' or a tandem. Why shouldn't women ride the lightest and most versatile machine available? Why should they be slaves to public opinion and convention? Why should they not do exactly what they felt like doing?

'Woman has taken her stand, and her seat in the saddle,' wrote the *Northern Wheeler* on February 22nd, 1893, 'and like the author of the historic phrase, we men can only say — This is not a revolt, it is a revolution. I am tolerably certain that the net result will be that woman

An early ladies' bicycle, made by R. S. Lovelace for his wife in the early eighteen-nineties.

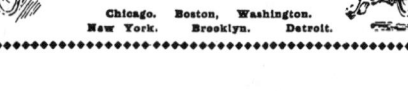

An advertisement from the *Lady Cyclist* in 1895.

will take her true position as man's equal.'

The first ladies' club, the Coventry Lady Cyclists, was founded in 1892, the same year as the Lady Cyclists' Association. Clubs for women were a startling innovation. Where was a precedent for an organization of any kind organized by women for the benefit of women?

It was over the 'safety' bicycle that women came up against the fiercest opposition, even from other women. An independent machine gave her a freedom and mobility which most respectable people thought utterly unacceptable, even immoral. For many people, this kind of independence was just too shocking to contemplate.

Cycling women were regarded with a kind of pious horror by society and by the public at large. It was openly said that a woman who mounted a bicycle hopelessly unsexed herself; she was stared at and remarked upon in town. It was supposed that no woman would take so masculine an amusement unless she was fast, unwomanly, and desirous of making herself conspicuous, and accordingly all cycling women had to suffer from the supposition.[13]

But gradually, almost surreptitiously, more and more women fought their battles and won, appearing on the roads more and more frequently. And yet, what a battle it was, what a lot of discussion was necessary to establish quite elementary truths about the nature of women's position in society, and what a lot of emotional energy was invested in trying to persuade women that a little gentle cycling was really all they should contemplate.

At the end of 1892 *Cycling* issued its first broadside against a new danger to the sport of cycling, women 'scorchers', some of whom had recently been doing a spot of record-breaking:

This is a go-ahead age, an age when woman is as characteristically go-ahead as man, when she is prepared to uphold her 'rights' against all comers, and when she even wants a voice in the government of her country. In such an age we venture, daringly perhaps, to raise our voices in protest against female record-breakers ...

When a record-breaking craze takes hold of wheel women, we fear the end of the tether is within reach, and female cycling is doomed ... There is a prescribed limit beyond which her modesty and deportment should absolutely forbid her to step: and moreover beyond which she becomes an exhibition that excites neither envy in her compeers or admiration in the opposite sex.

The record-breaking woman cannot be graceful; the peculiar action of cycle propulsion at high speed will not permit it in her case, and as she poses in scorching attitude, twists her pedals as rapidly as she is able, and in fact centres all her attention and energy towards the attainment of speed, she cannot fail to be other than an object of ridicule.[14]

In September 1893 a shocking event occurred which filled the pages of the cycling press with heated discussion for about a month. Sixteen-year-old Miss Tessie Reynolds, from Brighton, rode a *man's* bicycle from Brighton to London and back, wearing 'rational' dress and paced by some men friends of hers. She did about 120 miles in $8\frac{1}{2}$ hours, and became a *cause célèbre,* and a martyr to the cause of 'rational' dress, and, perhaps inadvertently, to the cause of women's emancipation.

After the advances that had been made by women in the few years before 1893, an event like this might have been expected to pass almost unnoticed. But *Cycling* once again took a very hard line on the whole affair, in spite of the fact that it was generally in favour of women riding bicycles:

Every cyclist who truly loves the sport, every lady rider who has striven, in the face of many difficulties, to spread the gospel of the wheel amongst her sisters, every wheelman who has managed to retain a belief in the innate modesty and sense of becomingness in the opposite sex, will hear with real pain, not unmixed with disgust, of what it would be moderate to call a lamentable incident that took place on the Brighton Road early last Sunday ...

We were just spared seeing her, but we heard from various sources along the road that her attire was of a most unnecessary masculine nature and scantiness ...

It is not, however, so much the dress we take exception to, as to the fact of women racing in public. We object, because we want to see every woman a cyclist, yes, even in breeches if they will, for we know such costumes can be designed so as to rob the fair wearer of none of her grace, or the respect that is her privilege; and we also know that nothing is more calculated to give cycling for women a setback than this racing ...[15]

The response to the editorial was a polarization of opinion. 'My only feelings were of admiration for a girl with sufficient courage to break through the stupid and conventional rules governing female attire, and of hope that very soon my wife, my sisters, my cousins and even my aunts might go about in similar sensible costumes,' writes one broadminded reader. But other readers were just as scandalized as the Editors had been. 'Does not the picture strike one with disgust and abhorrence', writes one, 'and is it not a sight likely to deter many of the

Miss Reynolds, of Brighton, a 'pioneer' of 'rational' dress, wearing the kind of costume which was considered by many people in 1893 to be quite scandalous.

The 'New Woman', riding on the front of a tandem wearing 'rational' dress, issued a challenge to the established order of society.

A male cyclist salutes the newly emancipated women of the mid-eighteen-nineties.

The convertible skirt and knickerbocker was the answer to the problem of designing an outfit that would be suitable for both riding and walking.

fair sex from learning the rudiments of a pastime which, taken in moderation, brings health and happiness?' And another goes so far as to see the whole issue as almost a religious one:

> As a cyclist and an occasional racer, I am extremely glad to notice your leading article ... Such an exhibition is, as you say, totally immodest and degrading to both sexes, and would soon harm the feminine side of the sport, apart from the moral question.
>
> Be assured, sir, as citizens, sportsmen and Christians, we shall support you in your denunciation of wrong.[16]

But the voice of reason is also allowed to speak:

> The young lady, to whom you allude as the Brighton Female Scorcher, is known to several Londoners, as well as to Brighton cyclists, and has probably done more than anyone else of her age to encourage the adoption of our pastime among her sex in Brighton ... Her dress, which I have seen, and regard as remarkable for its fitness, modesty and good taste, was so inconspicuous that many wheelmen were unconscious of her sex.[17]

Evidently there was to be no agreement about Miss Reynolds, and the controversy was only increased when yet another reader of *Cycling*, a man, asked the question 'What is the effect of prolonged fast riding upon a young girl's health?' The answers were glowing testimonials to the ignorance of the male sex and its prejudice and patronizing attitudes towards women: 'Such prolonged and unnatural exertion is a deplorable example to young girls just budding into womanhood,' writes one doctor, and an American doctor in a different paper made some even more spurious and ridiculous claims about women's bodies and minds:

> In young girls, the bones of the pelvis are not able to resist the tension required to ride a bicycle, and so may become more or less distorted in shape, with perhaps, in after life, resulting distress.
>
> Then again, with characteristic perseverance, females of all ages may be so anxious to excel in learning quickly, or after learning to be able to ride long and far, that they may overdo that which otherwise might not hurt them.[18]

Cycling's editors once again showed their strangely confused attitude towards women; on the one hand they want to support them riding bicycles, but on the other hand they put them down terribly: 'A woman can best show what little exertion is required in propelling her cycle by riding with modest ease and moderate pace. For feats of speed and protracted endurance, she is by nature physically unfit, and bound morally, if she respects her sex, to avoid anything in the nature of deleterious excess of exertion.'[19]

But not everybody who rushed into print with their opinions about women's cycling was so prejudiced. G. Lacy Hillier, a respected and perceptive cycling journalist, expressed ideas which were probably more typical of the cycling community as a whole, and of many women:

> Miss Reynolds, I am well assured, is but the forerunner of a movement, the stormy petrel heralding the storm of revolt against the petticoat.
>
> Why should the weaker sex be handicapped with the skirt? Not only does it catch the wind like a sail, but it necessitates a weakening of the bicycle frame to accommodate it.
>
> Miss Reynolds sets us an example. If practical female dress reform originates with cyclists, I for one shall be delighted.[20]

Cycling, in fact, soon saw the light of day and withdrew its opposition to 'rational' dress. Its sudden turnabout showed how quickly public opinion was changing.

The Rational Dress Society had been escalating its propaganda between 1887 and 1895. In 1887 they launched a new crusade from Westminster Town Hall. Their objects were 'to protest against the

introduction of any fashion in dress that either deforms the figure, impedes the movement of the body, or in any way tends to injure the health'.

Lady Harberton, the founder of the Society, wanted to see women of all ages dressed so that they could participate in energetic games and sports, and irrational cycling dress was her biggest enemy:

> What can be the true state of intelligence of a creature which deliberately loads itself with quantities of useless material round its legs, in spite of discomfort and danger, without any object in view beyond the abject copying of one another. And then, in order to correct the ugliness of such a dress, squeezes in its body until the vital functions can only be carried on imperfectly ... [21]

Irrational and dangerous dress, argued the Society's *Gazette*, stopped women from doing many jobs that would otherwise be open to them, made them look ridiculous and ruined their health: 'Not till our women have learned how far more important than anything else in the world is the cultivation of health, will they have fully seized the meaning of that great problem of women's rights.' [22]

Quite suddenly, in the spring of 1895, cycling was all the rage. The boom burst over England, and men and women on bicycles were everywhere. More and more women had been riding in the early eighteen-nineties, but always against the tide of public opinion. But an increasing number of the upper middle class decided that there was not really anything so objectionable in the bicycle after all; this seems to have swung the pendulum in favour of the new pastime.

The best names from the best families discovered the bicycle, and the social stigma attached to bicycle riding was lifted. 'It would be hardly too much to say that in April of 1895, one was considered eccentric for riding a bicycle, whilst by the end of June, eccentricity rested with those who did not ride.' [23]

The critical voices were nearly all silenced; 'those people who protested so vigorously against the first advancing steps of cycling woman, and who foretold with such frankness the dire disasters that would follow in her wake, have gasped and withered and shrivelled up, like air-balloons pierced by a pin.'

'Distinguished lady cyclists', nearly all with titles, and often without bicycles, had their photographs on the front pages of the heavy and glossy magazines that were hastily produced. Bicycles took pride of place in the houses of the rich in London and the country.

The sport which had been denounced as injurious to the health and dangerous for delicate women became suddenly the very best way for idle, sensitive women to improve their health:

> What enjoyment to a cramped and warped women's life is the whirl of the wheel, bringing back as it does God's gift of health, and the memory of childhood's delight in out of door activity. With a sense also of rest to the brain, and by raising the thoughts in gratitude above the household cares and drudgery, it gives a woman for one brief while the chance to rejoice in the feeling of liberty and delight in her own strength. [24]

The bicycle was patronized by nearly every royal family in Europe, and little boys in uniform were to be seen waiting on the steps of smart houses in Mayfair and Belgravia, to clean the bicycles as they came in from the street. Ladies took their bicycles in cabs to the parks, where they displayed themselves in their latest cycling dresses before taking the cab back home again.

But the society craze, like the bicycle boom which was happening at the same time, was short-lived. Almost as soon as the smart society ladies had acquired their expensive hand-painted bicycles from the showrooms of the well-known manufacturers in the street of the bicycle in London, Holborn Viaduct, they grew tired of them.

The gymkhanas, the country picnics, the week-end house-parties

Keeping up with the aristocracy – 1895.

'It is really quite a sight on any sunny morning to watch the crowds of prettily dressed cyclists taking their morning spins. Cycling in Battersea Park has indeed become an institution.'

with the obligatory 'Bring your bicycle' printed on the bottom of the invitation cards were gradually abandoned, and the fire went out of the bicycling fervour. The upper class had, after all, a lot of other things on its mind. 'Bicycling has not ceased to be a fashionable rage,' said the society magazine *The Cycling World Illustrated* in the summer of 1896, 'but the mornings are hot, and dancing all night does not make people anxious for violent exercise.'

The crowds which had gathered in Hyde Park and Battersea Park to gaze at the aristocracy awheel thinned and became less obsessed, and the craze faded out in high society almost simultaneously with the end of the general bicycle boom. Quite suddenly all the animated discussion among high-society ladies, and their imitators, about what was the best style of cycling dress and hat, and what they were wearing this month in Paris, and how dainty Lady Cyclecharmer looked when she was good enough to put in an appearance in the Park, ceased to matter very much.

Magazines that had been floated on the crest of the wave of public enthusiasm collapsed and disappeared quietly; those that had been introduced specifically for lady cyclists suffered especially badly. Some of the upper-class bicycle enthusiasts switched their attentions to the motorcycle or the car, and the rich became the first patrons of the new pastime of motoring.

Serious cyclists watched with amusement, and some of them with a good deal of sarcasm, the flight of the aristocracy from the bicycle. They had predicted that the craze would be short-lived. They knew that riding a bicycle was hard work. Lillias Campbell Davidson, the President of the Lady Cyclists' Association, founded in 1892, was annoyed that fashionable cyclists had completely ignored 'rational' dress, but was optimistic for the future:

> Women who only ride because everybody else does, or whose one object is to attract admiration and attention, are naturally not inclined to sacrifice any picturesque adornment to the demands of health, safety and common sense. It is extraordinary how foolish a fashionable woman can be when she sets herself to work ...
>
> A vast number of them, by this time next year, will have gone back to golf and croquet, or have forgotten, in some new craze not yet born into the world, what cycling was like. But by far the greater proportion will have sobered down into cyclists with discretion. They will love their bicycles no less, but they will adore them more rationally; they will have caught the real spirit of the pastime, not merely trifled with it like painted butterflies.[25]

The craze was not a bad thing ultimately for the future of women's cycling in England. It had given cycling respectability and had stimulated production of women's bicycles. Really fine, light and cheap machines were now available. By 1900 a huge market existed where ten years before there had been none. The size of the potential bicycle-buying public had doubled within a few years. The manufacturers in this sense were definitely on the side of the emancipationists.

If Her Ladyship rode to the village to do her shopping and made her calls in London on her bicycle, how could fathers and mothers stop their daughters from owning and riding one? Her Ladyship set an example to women everywhere. Every servant-girl could now claim that it was a very fashionable thing to do, and probably some of them began to ride just because it was what everybody else was doing.

Polite society had rejected 'rational' dress as far too unconventional and unladylike. Whereas in Paris it was considered very chic and modern, most real English ladies, as well as those who thought of themselves as real ladies, still thought it monstrous and unmentionable. It was more or less tolerated in London, but outside London a woman who wore trousers in public was always thought to be making an exhibition of herself. By sticking to their skirts, most women had thus accepted cycling without at the same time allowing themselves to be thought of as feminist radicals.

The Rational Dress Society had to content itself with winning a few small skirmishes here and there, but in the eighteen-nineties, it failed to win much sympathy from the vast majority of women. 'Rational' dress had, however, come to stay, and would always be worn by keen women cyclists in the future.

In October 1898 Lady Harberton, the founder and President of the Rational Dress Society, and the wife of a Viscount, went to a pub at Ockham, Surrey, called the Hautboy Hotel, wearing rational dress. The landlady refused to serve her in the coffee-room, but showed her into the public bar, a dirty room where men usually drank alone. Lady Harberton thought this an insult and left. As a traveller, she argued, she had a legal right to be served where she chose to be served and, backed by the Cyclists' Touring Club, she took the landlady to court.

The defence pleaded that Lady Harberton had chosen not to stay in the public bar which had been open to her, and they produced a rather flattering photo of the bar in court. There had been no discrimination on the grounds of her being improperly dressed, they claimed. The judge upheld the defence and Lady Harberton lost her case.

'Rational' dress thus suffered a symbolic defeat, but the struggle had not been in vain. The bicycle had given women a new freedom and independence, and it had played a vital part in their fight for recognition of their rights and in their emancipation: 'The tens of thousands of wheel women of this country who have demonstrated that their sex are not an inferior portion of the human family in this wonderful form of outdoor sport, have rendered untold aid to the cause of equal suffrage, by dispelling the mistaken idea of women's dependence and helplessness.[26]

The society craze saw many titled and influential names putting in a brief appearance in cycling history. But their commitment was short-lived.

CHAPTER 8
A FACT OF EVERYDAY LIFE

Socialism can only come riding on a bicycle. (José Antonio Viera-Gallo, Assistant Secretary of Justice in government of ex-President Allende of Chile)

The velocipede is one of the finest inventions of the 19th century. (J. T. Goddard, 1869)

The invention of the pneumatic-tyred 'safety' bicycle was a decisive event. Soon it was being mass-produced. Within ten years of J. K. Starley's first 'Rover', the 'safety' easily outnumbered all other designs. Within twenty years tricycles and Ordinaries were ridden only by racers and eccentrics, and today it is very rare to see a tandem or a tricycle at all. By 1895 the bicycle as we know it had arrived and come to stay.

The story of the bicycle between 1900 and the present could fill another book. It is the story of the expansion and consolidation of a huge industry, the spread of cycling from Western Europe and America all over the world; of the rise of a sport and the development of a uniquely harrowing ordeal like the Tour de France; of the growth of touring, a wonderful way of travelling; of the continual experimenting and improvement in the design and manufacture of components. It is the story of the growth of cycling clubs all over the country, and the story of the acceptance of the bicycle as a fact of everyday life, a functional object that is used every day by millions of people who do not stop to think about where it came from.

There have been immense changes in the 'safety' bicycle since 1895. The freewheel soon became popular, introduced mainly so that a pedal would always be at the top of a stroke for starting off, and to make swift descent less dangerous. Good brakes became an absolute necessity. Rod-operated brakes gave way to the Bowden cable-operated brake. Two- and three-speed hub gears were developed and perfected soon after the turn of the century by the Sturmey-Archer Company and then multiple-speed *dérailleur* gearing gave cyclists a

166 King of the Road

Mlle Dutrieux, one of the first professional woman cyclists, rode for the Simpson Lever Chain Company in the late 'nineties.

A beautiful costume, but hardly ideal for riding a bicycle. The actress Mabel Love, interviewed in 1896, claimed that she was a keen cyclist, but admitted that she could not find much time to ride. She learned in Battersea Park in the summer of 1895, and managed to ride at the third lesson. Her spick-and-span Elswick bicycle is typical of the period, with a plunger brake, chain guard and dress protector around the back wheel.

versatility undreamt of in the 'nineties. Gradually, aluminium alloys were introduced to make bicycles lighter, until today only frames, bearings, chains and load-bearing parts must still be made of steel. Racing bicycles have become gradually lighter, and the use of titanium is now making a ten-pound bicycle possible.

There have been many experiments in basic design. Alternative projects continued to rival the 'safety' strongly for some years after 1895, and have always been hovering in the background. The Crypto 'Bantam' was a geared-up front-wheel-driven bicycle intended to appeal to older riders who had a strong prejudice against the nasty long, low 'safety'. The Dursley Pedersen, one of the most successful of the Edwardian luxury bicycles, with its so-called cantilevered forks and scientifically designed triangulated frame, was the lightest cycle at the time. The shaft-driven bicycle did away with the necessity to clean and protect the chain since it did not have one, and streamlined or recumbent bicycles, which put the rider almost on his back with his feet forwards, were faster over short distances, but were found to be less efficient for general, everyday use, and no good at all uphill. They were put on the market in the nineteen-twenties and 'thirties, but never caught on. Almost any idea that could possibly be applied to a bicycle has at some stage probably been tried.

But one notable fact stands out like a shining light. The basic design of a good, strong, efficient bicycle has not been improved on since the eighteen-nineties. The ergonomic principles which were worked out

after so much effort and such persistence by a few pioneering manufacturers like the Starleys, William Hillman, Thomas Humber, Dan Rudge and others have been proved to be fundamentally satisfactory. After a twenty-year struggle they built a machine based on the human body which was right for that body in almost every respect. It is certainly not impossible that improvements will be made to bicycle design, or that some dramatic new machine could be invented, but it seems unlikely. A racing bicycle is an almost perfect machine; it is very hard to see how it can be improved. The little small-wheeled bicycles invented by Alex Moulton and introduced in large numbers in the last few years have several advantages — they allow more room for carrying baggage, accelerate quickly and are more easily folded than a conventional bicycle — but in almost every other ergonomic sense they are less efficient, and do not represent any advance.

Except for walking, there is no cheaper way of travelling than on a bicycle. Its convenience for city living is so obvious that it has become almost a cliché. For the last eighty years people have used them every day of their lives. Bicycles have been absolutely essential to them in getting to work, giving them pleasure and health, and allowing them to maintain contacts and friendships at distances which would be impossible to walk.

In the country, the bicycle speeded up crucial services like the post and the doctor, and made contact between neighbouring villages and towns far easier. Before there were cheap cars, the roads were crowded

Cyclists on the Epping Road in April 1914, shortly before the outbreak of war. Not a car in sight.

It is understandable why some women were apprehensive about riding on main roads. The George and Dragon, York Road, Battersea, London, was photographed in the mid-eighteen-nineties.

168 King of the Road

A bicycle outing of the International Labour Party at Yarmouth in 1906.

Edwardian cycling picture, taken about 1900. The woman has a Dursley Pedersen, and a rather unusual hat.

A touring party of the North London Cycling Club in 1897. There are still only five women among all those men.

with cyclists at the week-ends. Many of them would probably never have gone out of the cities without a bicycle: 'The factory lad comes out of the hot stuffy factory choked up with dust and dirt. There is only one cure for it, and that's a cycle and a burst on the open road. There is more joy, more of the true feeling of freedom in a cycling holiday than in any form of holiday-making.'[1]

Before there were cheap cars, the fact that a man and his wife had children did not inevitably tie them to their homes. They could put a trailer or a sidecar on their tandem, and set off for the country.

As an almost universally popular pastime, and an absolutely necessary part of everyday life, cycling has been killed by the car. Its gradual murder was perpetrated in the nineteen-forties and 'fifties in England, and probably twenty years earlier in the United States. Speed, comfort and power took precedence over convenience, economy, health, strength and the natural rhythms of the human body. The values that the car represents won a massive victory over the humbler but more profound virtues of the bicycle. Times had changed. A bicycle could no longer be sold on the old-fashioned basis that it was cheap and good for the health and gave pleasure and fresh air. The bicycle's simplicity and efficiency were forgotten.

How efficient is a bicycle? What kind of advantages does it offer?

By the nineteen-thirties the barriers of convention had become much less restrictive. The argument over 'rationals' was now irrelevant.

What is so special about it?

When bicyclists first started to ride 100 miles in a day, such feats provoked articles in newspapers expressing astonishment and sometimes even disbelief. What was most incredible was that a horse could not do it, and yet a man on a new-fangled machine could. The dreams of the amateur mechanics had come true.

A lot of work has been done quite recently to establish in scientific terms what every cyclist understands and demonstrates in a practical way, that cycling is more efficient than walking. The bicycle's efficiency may be summarized briefly in the following way. The amount of power output which is necessary for an average non-athletic person to walk at three miles an hour is about 1/10 horsepower, while on a bicycle the same person may easily ride at ten miles an hour for the same expenditure of power. Moreover, while riding at this speed, producing his 1/10 horsepower, the rider is still consuming less than half the maximum amount of oxygen which most non-athletic people are capable of consuming ($2\frac{1}{2}$ litres per minute); he still has a lot in hand.

Expressed in another way, this means that the amount of energy which the rider uses in propelling the weight of his machine and himself over a given distance is much less than the amount of energy he would need to expend in walking the same distance.

Obviously, then, the more he reduces the weight and the friction of his machine, and the more he increases the efficiency of his own body, the more he will conserve his energy, and the easier it will be to propel his bicycle over the given distance. But why is a bicycle more efficient than walking? In an article in the *Scientific American* in 1973 Stuart

170 King of the Road

Wilson explained it very well:

The reason for the high energy efficiency of cycling compared with walking appears to lie mainly in the mode of action of the muscles. Whereas a machine only performs mechanical work when a force moves through a distance, muscles consume energy when they are in tension but not moving. A man standing still maintains his upright posture by means of a complicated system of bones in compression and muscles in tension. Hence merely standing consumes energy. Similarly, in performing movements with no external forces, as in shadowboxing, muscular energy is consumed because of the alternative acceleration and deceleration of the hands and arms, although no mechanical work is done against any outside agency.

In walking the leg muscles must not only support the rest of the body in an erect posture but also raise and lower the entire body as well as accelerate and decelerate the lower limbs. All these actions consume energy without doing any useful work. Walking uphill requires that additional work be done against gravity.

Contrast this with the cyclist, who first of all saves energy by sitting, thus relieving his leg muscles of their supporting function and accompanying energy consumption, The only reciprocating parts of his body are his knees and thighs; his feet rotate smoothly at a constant speed and the rest of his body is still. Even the acceleration and deceleration of his legs are achieved efficiently, since the strongest muscles are used almost exclusively; the rising leg does not have to be lifted but is raised by the downward thrust of the other leg, The back muscles must be used to support the

The Dursley Pedersen bicycles produced at about the turn of the centruy were a radical departure in design. This model weighed twenty-three pounds, and cost sixteen guineas.

Ingenuity and ambition outran practicality in 1895. The bamboo bicycle could not have the resilience and strength of steel.

trunk, but the arms can also help to do this, resulting in a little residual strain on the hands and arms.[2]

Also, the cyclist, as rolling weight, seems to earn a bonus. Although in fact he must himself generate the momentum to freewheel, and climb up the hill that he so easily descends, in freewheeling and descending he is in fact travelling with no expenditure of energy during that time.

A racing cyclist, who trains himself to make full use of all the advantages outlined here, travels more efficiently, with less waste of power for each mile covered, than any other kind of man-machine. On a bicycle, he also has some subtle advantages. To minimize wind resistance, when he wants to go as fast as possible he must crouch as low as possible. But when he tires, or is just touring, he may sit with his hands on the top of the handlebars. But the cyclist's master-stroke is that his whole body is always free to move about: when he needs to produce a lot of extra power, to go up a steep hill, or to put on a sudden spurt, he may stand up and allow the whole weight of his body to fall on each pedal stroke, with the kick of the unflexing leg as an additional force. He is thus not only efficient, but he has several different variations of his efficiency to use for different conditions.

This excursion into human physiology and ergonomics is not intended to be merely of objective interest. The facts are not just the product of a whimsical and academic interest in bicycles. They are immensely important in a very down-to-earth and practical way.

One of the most pressing needs of the developed world, we are continually being told, is for energy, to drive machinery, to make steel, to light and heat our homes and for transport. Our demand for energy is

172 King of the Road

Once upon a time, married couples managed to combine having a family and riding a tandem ...

... and this was still true even in 1948.

all the time increasing, and because supplies of coal, oil and petrol are barely sufficient to supply our expanding needs it has become fashionable to talk of an 'energy crisis'. The sense of crisis is increased because the centre of oil production, in the Middle East, is politically volatile, and political conflict brings with it economic instability.

Yet the real nature of this 'energy crisis' is only just beginning to be seriously examined. And what is becoming increasingly obvious to most thoughtful people is that the 'crisis' is a self-imposed one, a crisis created by the life-style that the majority of people in the developed world have chosen, and which is continually sold as the best and only way to live by those who profit from it. The expression energy crisis', says Ivan Illich, an outspoken critic of our chosen life-style, 'canonizes the illusion that machine-power can indefinitely substitute manpower — an illusion which is equally fatal for the affluent and the disowned.'[3] We do not need electric toothbrushes, but somehow they manage to sell; we do not need to drive a twenty-horsepower car half a mile to the shops, but somehow it seems to be easier to do it than to think about another way. It is our transport habits that are hit hardest by shortages of the fuels to drive our chosen machines, and a real crisis will occur when there is no more petrol unless alternative systems are developed.

People choose to drive cars because they offer comfort, convenience and instant mobility. And they also choose to pay very heavily for these advantages. When there were only a few cars and petrol was cheap, they were a blessing, but those days are over. Now that there are billions of cars and they are all competing with each other, the blessing

Tommy Simpson, probably England's greatest-ever bicycle-rider.

Alf Engers, record-breaker.

has turned into a curse.

Cars bring with them pollution, accidents, stench, massive individual expenditure and an even more massive public expenditure. They discriminate against very young people, against old people, against pedestrians, against the people who live beside the roads that they drive along, and against cyclists. They consume vast quantities of raw materials, steel, rubber and oil, and equally vast quantities of power are needed in their manufacture.

Cars in cities are the most uneconomical and the most inequitable. The average speed that a car achieves in a city like London or Paris is between five and ten miles an hour. Yet the almost untapped reserves of human energy would enable the majority of the population to achieve almost the same speed on bicycles at a fraction of the individual and social cost. There is enough stored up fat walking the streets of our cities to drive whole armies of bicycles.

According to a London Traffic Survey published in 1964, the average distance travelled by just over four million people in their daily journey

174 King of the Road

Cycling in Wisley Woods, on the Ripley Road, in 1915.

'The factory lad comes out of the hot stuffy factory choked up with dust and dirt ... there is only one cure for it, and that's a cycle and a burst on the open road.' Picture taken in 1911, on one of the roads out of London.

to work and back was 3.7 miles each way, an absolutely ideal distance for cycling, easily within the physical capabilities of even quite elderly people.

The advantages of the bicycle stare any observant planner full in the face. There are already millions of bicycles in this country, many of them never used. There are about five million bicycles in regular use in Holland among the total population of thirteen million people, and there is probably a similar volume of bicycle-use in Denmark. Peterborough, Stevenage New Town, Berkeley, Davis and San Francisco, California and New York City, Copenhagen, Amsterdam and other places have thriving bicycle pathways. And the bicycle industry, in the middle of a boom unprecendented since 1895, reports record sales each year. In June 1974 nearly 9,000 Danes set out from the Klampenborg Wood in Copenhagen, to ride fifty kilometres through the countryside just for the pleasure of doing it.

In spite of all these facts, our Ministry of Transport remains blind to the existence of bicycles. For all the publicity and discussion recently, there is not one indication that anybody in central government is interested in them. There is hardly any recognition of bicycle-riders in traffic surveys, road schemes or street planning. Whereas in Holland there is barely a main road without segregated bicycle paths, in England there are almost none. There is not one bicycle path in central London, except Herne Hill and Paddington Tracks. There are no facilities for bicycle storage at London's main-line railway stations. Taking a bicycle on trains is exorbitantly expensive. Far from being accepted as a valuable contribution to economy, safety and tranquillity on the roads, bicycle-riders are the most disadvantaged group of road-users. Where there should be initiative and action on the part of the authorities there is only ignorance and inertia. Cyclists go on being killed, and nearly all of them are killed by cars.

Bicycle-manufacturers, who should be militantly in the forefront of a campaign to remedy this neglect, have not used the environmental and ecological arguments very wisely in promoting their product. In fact, one suspects that they are as inert as the politicians. While they are still making the old-style functional roadster, the emphasis is now on novel designs and on 'fun' machines, on leisure rather than on utility. The manufacturers seem to have capitulated to the car along with everybody else.

The Chopper is the worst example of this collapse of confidence in the real value of bicycles. Raleigh's Chopper advertisements encourage

A small bicycle-manufacturer's workshop; taken in East Anglia some time in the eighteen-nineties.

A Fact of Everyday Life 175

King of the Road

Bicycling and tricycling in Peking, China.

a very strange kind of cycling:

> Chopper. The Hot One. Ride the bike with burn-up potential. Straddle the hottest number Raleigh have ever produced. Chopper. A machine inspired by the screaming rubber and roaring fantails of the dragster racing slick. Chopper, designed on lean, tough, taut, tear-away-and-love-it lines. For guys and gals who want a bike built for action. With the lid off! ... This is a machine with a mind of its own; a machine that's got the sort of power and dash normally encountered only on a dragster circuit.

This rubbish was not written by a cyclist, neither was it sanctioned at an executive level by a cyclist. The Raleigh Company's message to its young customers and their parents seems to be: 'We really want to sell you a racing car, but of course you're too young, so until you're a bit older, you can buy our fantasy substitute to pretend with.'

It is an alarming revelation of the corporation mind. Cycling is forgotten; the special qualities of a bicycle, its silence, its grace, its convenience and its gentle effect on the human body are brushed aside. The company has failed completely to understand that a good bicycle is its own best salesman, and that people merely need to be reminded honestly of its advantages. And Raleigh are the biggest bicycle-manufacturers in the world.

The machine in the Chopper advertisement is not really a bicycle any longer. It is a luxury consumer toy. James Starley would be horrified. Design-wise, it goes backwards. As a trainer for trick cyclists it might be fine, but as a bicycle for children it is unsafe and needlessly heavy.

The need to put bicycles back on the roads of our cities is urgent. Equally urgent is the need of people in the Third World, the less developed countries, for some kind of basic short-distance transportation. In India, Africa, South America and the Far East bicycles are already widely used and absolutely essential tools to many people. But there are still millions of people who cannot afford a bicycle, and many places where there are none at all and no paths to ride them on. But it is in these places, where there is almost no other form of transport, that bicycles could be most useful and least disruptive. 'Eighty-four per cent of the world's land surface is completely roadless terrain,' says Victor Papanek:

> Often epidemics sweep through an area: nurses, doctors and medicine may be only 100 kilometres away, but there is no way of getting through. Regional disasters, starvation and water shortages also develop frequently; again there seems to be no good way of getting through. Helicopters work, but are far beyond the monies and expertise available in many regions of the Third World.[4]

We in England have a choice between many different kinds of transport. It is something we take for granted. Bicycles were able to become popular and useful in the eighteen-seventies because an excellent road system already existed. Without it, they would have stayed in the cities. Countries like Brazil or India, which do not have good main roads, could best improve everybody's mobility by building urban and rural bicycle tracks, instead of investing millions of pounds of mostly foreign money in prestigious super-highway systems. Ivan Illich has rightly pointed out that a super-highway serves only the needs of those people who possess the money and expertise to plug into it, and leaves the rest out, and is therefore fundamentally undemocratic. A bicycle path also is only available for those people who can plug into it, but there is a huge difference between the price of a bicycle and the price of a car. A railway is open to anyone who has the money to buy a ticket; a road only to people who can afford cars.

The Chinese are already making intensive use of bicycles. The streets of Peking are full of bicycles and empty of cars; it is illegal to own a private car. Tricycle carriers are used for carrying incredibly heavy loads and as taxis, school buses and road sweepers. In 1949 only 14,000 bicycles were produced in China; in 1958, 1,174,000. There are now more than 2 million bicycles in Peking alone.

At the Canton bicycle factory, producer of the 28" Kapok model, so popular with Chinese workers, many methods need further mechanization, and what changes have been made, such as painting and electroplating, came from the shop floor, rather than from outside advisers. An output of 14,000 cycles daily is not regarded as satisfactory and the revolutionary committee is preoccupied with raising productivity by its own efforts.[5]

The Chinese evidently will not and could not start to consume energy at the same wasteful and polluting rate as America. Chinese politicians have made it quite clear that it is not in the people's or the country's interest for them to do so.

It is not just bicycles themselves that could be more and more useful in coming to terms economically and equitably with some of the problems of the developing countries, but also bicycle-based machines. The bush ambulance in the illustration on this page was developed for the Intermediate Technology Development Group. Bicycles can be used to drive generators and grinding and milling machinery. An idea borrowed from the bicycle, the application of the strength and efficiency of legs in driving cranks, can be used for other purposes, for driving water-pumps, corn-grinders, winnowing-fans and rice-threshers. There are many processes which are quite simple and repetitive that could be made much easier and quicker by linking simple machines to a man-powered, bicycle-based energy source.

The development of new bicycle-based machines should not be confined to Third World countries. We are also in need of simple alternatives. The versatile range of bicycles and tricycles that once existed catered for many different kinds of people. There is a desperate need for a really good city pedal-car, which would overcome one of the most fundamental criticisms of the bicycle, that in wet weather you get wet and in cold weather you freeze. It is incredible that governments can put rockets into outer space, but will not bother to sponsor a proper study of man-powered vehicles for our cities and towns.

Machines and tools which are used by people are never in themselves either evil or benevolent. It depends what they are used for. But machines do have certain tendencies built into them. A gun is designed to kill, a bomb to explode. Cars are not intended to kill, but, quite predictably, they do. Aeroplanes are not intended to crash, but inevitably they do.

The bicycle is a humane machine, 'one of the finest inventions of the 19th century', which achieves its intended purpose without accidental

A bicycle bush ambulance designed by the Intermediate Technology Development Group.

Pedalcar, 1974 style.

negative side-effects. It is a machine which is absolutely under the control of the rider, but which allows him to travel faster and farther than he can walk.

There is a tendency in the world at the moment to believe in complicated, highly sophisticated solutions to every problem. Simple, elegant and suitable solutions also exist. The principles that 'soft' technology or alternative technology stands by are that small is good, and simplicity is cheap. It attempts to economize in energy and materials, and to find simple human ways of achieving results that are related in scale to people's real needs.

The bicycle will not solve all our transport problems overnight, but it is an ideal solution for certain kinds of people in certain situations, that is for short journeys of up to twenty or thirty miles. That fact has to be recognized. The bicycle points a direction. It allows people, in a simple but radical way, to gain control of their own lives.

We take the bicycle too much for granted but at the same time, we in England do not use it enough. It is a simple machine. But it *could* have a far-reaching and revolutionary effect on the world in the next century.

Bicycles are only a hundred years old. But that hundred years may one day turn out to have been merely the bicycle's childhood.

The obvious economy of the bicycle; sixteen bicycles in the same space as one car.

NOTES

Introduction

1. Ivan Illich, **Energy and Equity** (Calder & Boyars, London, 1974).

1 Bicycle Archaeology

1. From **Journal de voyages de M. de Monconys** (Lyon, 1665).
2. J. Ozanam, **Récréations Mathématiques et Physiques** (Paris, 1696).
3. William Hooper, **Rational Recreations** (London, 1774).
4. **Universal Magazine** (London, 1761).
5. Quoted in J. T. Lightwood, **The Romance of the Cyclists' Touring Club** (C.T.C., London, 1928).
6. Quoted in 'Velox', **Velocipedes, Bicycles and Tricycles: How to Make and How to Use Them** (Routledge, London, 1869).
7. Quoted in L. Baudry de Saugnier, **Histoire de la Locomotion Terrestre** (Paris, 1935).
8. Quoted in H. O. Duncan, **The World on Wheels** (Paris 1928).
9. **La Petite Chronique de Paris** (April 7th, 1818), quoted in Duncan, op. cit.
10. **Liverpool Mercury** (April 24th, 1818), quoted in Duncan, op. cit.
11. **Ackermann's Magazine** (London, February 1st, 1819).
12. Quoted in Duncan, op. cit.
13. Ernest Lacon, **Moniteur de la Photographie** (Paris, October 1st, 1868). 1868).
14. Patent no. 4321 (June 21st, 1818).
15. **London Magazine** (1819).
16. R. Ackermann, **Repository of Arts, Literature, Commerce, Manufactures, Fashions and Politics** (London, February 1st, 1819).
17. **English Mechanic** (London, May 28th, 1869).
18. J. F. Bottomley-Firth, **The Velocipede: Its Past, Present and Its Future** (London, 1869).
19. **Gentleman's Magazine** (London, May 15th, 1819).
20. Bottomley-Firth, op. cit.
21. **Journal de la Côte d'Or** (August 24th, 1828).
22. **Mechanics' Magazine, Museum, Register, Journal and Gazette** (London, September 29th, 1832).

2. Amateur Mechanics

1. **Monthly Magazine** (London, November 1st, 1819).
2. **Repertory of Arts, Manufactures and Agriculture** (London, vol. XXXIX, June 1821).

3. Quoted in the **Boneshaker** (No. 7).
4. **Imperial Magazine** (London, 1819).
5. **Mechanic's Weekly Journal** (London, December 27th, 1823).
6. ibid. (December 20th, 1823).
7. **Mechanics' Magazine** (April 17th, 1824).
8. ibid. (March 6th, 1830).
9. ibid. (April 21st, 1832).
10. ibid. (May 3rd, 1832).
11. ibid. (November 28th, 1829).
12. J. F. Bottomley-Firth, **The Velocipede: Its Past, Present and Its Future** (London, 1869).
13. **Mirror of Literature, Amusement and Instruction** (London, March 23rd, 1839).
14. **Mechanics' Magazine** (April 13th, 1839).
15. ibid. (May 18th, 1839).
16. ibid. (April 13th and May 18th, 1839).
17. ibid. (December 2nd, 1843).
18. Quoted in J. Gordon Irving, **Devil on Wheels** (1946).
19. **English Mechanic** (June 11th, 1869).
20. Sawyer catalogue, 1858 (Science Museum, London)
21. ibid.
22. ibid.
23. ibid.
24. From a copy of a diary in the possession of Derek Roberts.
25. Sawyer catalogue, 1863 (Bartleet Collection, Coventry City Library).
26. **English Mechanic** (November 24th, 1865).
27. ibid. (August 10th, 1866).
28. ibid. (February 1st, 1867).
29. ibid.
30. ibid.
31. **English Mechanic** (December 11th, 1868).

3 Velocipedomania

1. **The Velocipedist** (New York, February 1st, 1869).
2. **London Society** (November 1868).
3. J. T. Goddard, **The Velocipede: Its History, Varieties and Practice** (Cambridge, Mass., 1869).
4. ibid.
5. **Harper's Weekly** (New York, December 19th, 1868).
6. **Scientific American** (New York, January 9th, 1869).
7. Goddard, op. cit.
8. **Scientific American** (January 9th, 1869).
9. Goddard, op. cit.
10. ibid.
11. ibid.
12. **The Velocipedist** (New York, February 1st, 1869).
13. ibid.
14. **Scientific American** (April 17th, 1869).
15. ibid. (February 20th, 1869).
16. **English Mechanic** (March 5th, 1869).
17. W. Starley, **The Life and Inventions of James Starley** (Coventry, 1902).
18. **Wheeling** (London, March 11th, 1891).
19. **Ixion – A Journal of Velocipeding** (London, 1875).
20. **The Times** (London, March 31st, 1869).
21. Starley, op. cit.
22. Charles Spencer, **The Bicycle: Its Use and Action** (Frederick Warne, London, 1870).
23. **The Sphinx** (April, 1869); quoted in J. T. Lightwood, **The Romance of the Cyclists' Touring Club** (C.T.C., London, 1928).
24. **English Mechanic** (September 17th, 1869).

4 The Cult of the Ordinary

1. Flora Thompson, **Lark Rise to Candleford** (Oxford University Press, London 1945).
2. G. H. Smith **Some Notes about the Anerley Bicycle Club.**
3. ibid.
4. A. W. Rumney, **Fifty Years a Cyclist** (London, 1927).
5. G. H. Smith, op. cit.
6. **Bicycle Journal** (January 19th, 1877).
7. **Bicycle Journal** (September 8th and 15th, 1876).
8. **The Times** (September 5th, 1878).
9. **Bicycle Journal** (October 20th, 1876).
10. **Bicycling News** (April 14th, 1876).
11. **Bicycling Times** (June 6th, 1878).
12. **Wheel World** (May 1880).
13. **Bicycling News** (August 2nd, 1878).
14. Catalogue of the 'Ariel' Bicycle, issued by Smith & Starley (Coventry, 1872).
15. **Ixion – A Journal of Velocipeding** (January 1875).
16. **Bicycling News** (April 18th, 1876).
17. W. Starley, **The Life and Inventions of James Starley** (Coventry, 1902).
18. **Bicycling Times** (July 25th, 1878).
19. **Daily News** (August 23rd, 1876).

5 Tricycling and 'Sociable' Cycling

1. **Wheel World** (August 1882).
2. **Cycling** (Newcastle upon Tyne, April 1879).
3. **English Mechanic** (January 29th, 1869).
4. ibid. (July 30th, 1869).

5. J. F. Bottomley-Firth, **The Velocipede: Its Past, Present and Its Future** (London, 1869).
6. W. Starley, **The Life and Inventions of James Starley** (Coventry, 1902).
7. ibid.
8. J. K. Starley, 'The Evolution of the Cycle' **Journal of the Society of Arts** (May 20th, 1898).
9. **Cycling** (Newcastle upon Tyne, December 1878).
10. **Wheel World** (February 1881).
11. **The Tricyclist** (London and Coventry, June 30th, 1882).
12. W. Starley, op. cit.
13. **Bicycling News** (May 31st, 1878).
14. Quoted in the **Boneshaker,** no. 8.
15. **Bicycling News** (June 14th, 1878).
16. **Cycling Annual,** (ed. J. C. Fox), 1884.
17. H. Sturmey, **Indispensable Tricyclists' Handbook** (London, 1881).
18. **The Tricyclist** (June 30th, 1882).
19. **Cycling** (February 20th, 1892).
20. **The Tricyclist** (August 4th, 1882).

6 The Search for Safety

1. **English Mechanic** (July 16th, 1869).
2. **Cyclists' Touring Club Gazette** (April 1885).
3. ibid. (November 1884).
4. ibid. (May 1885).
5. ibid. (September 1885).
6. W. Grew **The Cycle Industry** (London, 1921).
7. **Cycling** (April 14th, 1894).
8. ibid. (March 7th, 1891).
9. ibid. (March 5th, 1892).
10. **Hub** (June 5th, 1897).
11. Gwen Raverat, **Period Piece** (London, 1952).
12. H. G. Wells, **The War in the Air** (1st edn, 1908).

7 Women's Liberation

1. C. Leigh Hunt Wallace, the **Lady Cyclist** (March 1895).
2. J. T. Goddard, **The Velocipede: Its History, Varieties and Practice** (Cambridge, Mass., 1869).
3. **Scientific American** (March 20th, 1869).
4. **Girl of the Period Miscellany** (London, March 1869).
5. J. F. Bottomley-Firth, **The Velocipede: Its Past, Present and Its Future** (London, 1869).
6. **Bicycling Times** (May 22nd, 1879).
7. **Tricyclist** (December 8th, 1882).
8. ibid. (December 15th, 1882).
9. **Cyclists' Touring Club Gazette** (1883); quoted in the **Boneshaker,** no. 50.
10. **Wheeling** (August 20th, 1884).
11. ibid. (October 1st, 1884).
12. ibid. (October 8th, 1884).
13. Miss L. C. Davidson, **Handbook for Lady Cyclists** (London, 1896).
14. **Cycling** (October 8th, 1892).
15. ibid (September 16th, 1893).
16. ibid. (September 23rd, 1893).
17. ibid. (September 30th, 1893).
18. **Northern Wheeler** (Bolton, August 17th, 1892).
19. **Cycling** (October 7th, 1893).
20. **Bicycling News** (September 3rd, 1893).
21. **Rational Dress Society's Gazette** (July 1888).
22. ibid.
23. **Hub** (April 9th, 1898).
24. **Wheelwoman** (May 23rd, 1896).
25. **Cycle Magazine** (November 1895).
26. **Lady Cyclist** (London, August 22nd, 1896).

8 A Fact of Everyday Life

1. The **Clarion** (London, June 21st, 1912).
2. S. S. Wilson, 'Bicycle Technology' **Scientific American** (March 1973).
3. **Guardian** (June 15th, 1973).
4. V. Papanek, **Design for the Real World** (Thames & Hudson, London, 1972).
5. **The Times** (March 21st, 1973).

BOOKS ABOUT CYCLING

Old bicycle books are very hard to find, and you will not be able to get the rarest of them however much you are prepared to pay. They are highly valued by collectors. Sometimes, just by chance, you may come across something in a second-hand-bookshop, but it is usually only compulsive hunters who find them. Good libraries do have a few, though it is surprising how many are not even in the catalogue of the British Library. Of those that are in the catalogue, many were burnt when an incendiary bomb fell in the war.

I have listed here most of the interesting old books and periodicals. The list itself is fascinating since it shows what a large number of books about velocipeding and cycling were being published, and what a wide range of subjects the authors were interested in.

Dozens of cycling magazines were published in England and the United States in the eighteen-eighties and 'nineties. There was a great deal of publishing speculation at the time. The best of them, such as **Cycling**, set a new standard in popularizing specialist subjects and were very successful. But many only lasted a few issues and died, and some were only of local interest. The **Cyclists' Touring Club Gazette,** founded in 1878, the oldest surviving cycling journal in the world, is always a rich source of information. The ones I have listed here are of more general cycling interest, dealing not only with current events but with historical and social aspects of cycling.

There are a number of reprints of old books, which are very useful, and I hope publishers will bring out more. I have listed the titles and the names and addresses of the publishers of these reprints.

Books about cycling in print at the moment are really a mixed bag, and there are not many. Most of them are slick, hastily produced, directionless and inaccurate. A few have nice illustrations but bad texts; others are good as far as they go but leave out a great deal and take too much for granted. The ones I have listed here are all useful in one way or another, though I would advise readers to treat them all with suspicion, since there are a great many wrong facts, wrong deductions and misinterpretations in all of them.

Cycling history is hard to write, and a lot more research needs to be done. You cannot learn about bicycles from one book alone. The **Boneshaker**, the excellent quarterly magazine of the Southern Veteran-Cycle Club, is the only place, as far as I know, where a continuing critical discussion is carried on, while the **Cyclists' Touring Club Gazette** concerns itself with the problems of cyclists today but is rather traditional and old-fashioned in its approach.

Adams, W. C., 'The influence of age, sex and body weight on the energy expenditure in bicycle riding', **Journal of Applied Psychology** (London, 1967)

Alderson, F., **Bicycling, A History** (London, 1974)

Anon., **Bicycling, Its Rise and Development: A Text Book for Riders** (Tinsley Bros., London, 1874; reprinted by David & Charles, Newton Abbot)

Bartleet, H. W., **Bartleet's Bicycle Book** (London, 1931)

'Early Cycles and Cycling: The Beginning of the Bicycle Trade in England', **Cycling** (February 27, 1919)

Baudry de Saugnier, L., **Histoire de la Locomotion Terrestre** (Paris, 1935)

Histoire Générale de la Vélocipèdie (Paris, 1891)

Bottomley-Firth, J. F., **The Velocipede: Its Past, Present and Its Future** (London, 1869)

Bowden, F., **Cycling for Health** (Criterion Press, London, 1890)

An Experienced Velocipedist', **The Velocipede: Its History and Practical Hints on How to Use It** (J. Bruton, London, 1869; reprinted by C.T.C., 69 Meadrow, Godalming, Surrey)

Caunter, C. F., **The History and Development of Cycles** (Science Museum, London, 1972)

Claxton, E. C., 'The Future of the Bicycle in a Modern Society', **Journal of the Royal Society of Arts** (January 1968)

Cortis, H. L., **Principles of Training for Amateur Athletics, with Special Regard to Bicyclists** (London, 1882)

Davidson, Miss L. C., **Handbook for Lady Cyclists** (London, 1896)

Duncan, H. O., **The World on Wheels** (Paris, 1928)

Erskine, Miss F. J., **Tricycling for Ladies** (Iliffe, Coventry, 1884)

Lady Cycling (Iliffe, Coventry, 1897)

Frazer, J. Foster, **Round the World on a Wheel** (London, 1899)

Garry, R. G., and Wishart, G. M., 'On the existence of a most efficient speed in bicycle pedalling, and the problem of determining human muscular efficiency', **Journal of Physiology** (London, 1931)

Gattey, G. N., **The Bloomer Girls** (London, 1967)

Goddard, J. T., **The Velocipede: Its History, Varieties and Practice** (Cambridge, Mass., 1869)

Grand Jacques, Le (Richard Lesclide), **Manuel du Vélocipède** (Paris, 1869)

Grew, W., **The Cycle Industry** (Coventry, 1921)

Griffin, H. H., **Bicycles of the Year** and **Bicycles and Tricycles of the Year** (Upcott & Gill, London, various issues between 1877 and 1887; reprint of **Bicycles and Tricycles of the Year,** 1886, by Olicana Books, 25 The Oval, Otley, Yorks.)

Cycling (George Bell, London, 1890 and 1903)

Hoffmann, Professor, **Tips for Tricyclists** (London, 1887)

Howard, A., **The Bicycle** for 1874, also for 1876, 1877, 1878 (Bicycle Journal Office, London)

Herschell, Dr G., **Cycling as a Cause of Heart Disease** (London, 1896)

Hillier, G. Lacy, **Amateur Cycling, with Hints on Training** (London, 1893)

The Art of Ease in Cycling (London, 1899)

Hillier, G. Lacy, and the Earl of Albemarle, Badminton **Cycling** (Longmans, Green & Co., London, 1st edn, 1887)

Illich, Ivan, **Energy and Equity** (Calder & Boyars, London, 1974)

'Recycling the World', **Guardian** (June 15, 1973)

Irving, J. Gordon, **Devil on Wheels**

'He builded better than he knew; the story of Kirkpatrick Macmillan', **Gallovidian Annual** (Glasgow, 1940)

Jefferson, R. L., **Across Siberia on a Bicycle** (Cycle Press, London, 1896)

Awheel to Moscow and Back (London, 1895)

Jennings, Oscar, **Cycling and Health** (London, 1893)

Jerome, J. K., **Three Men on the Bummel** (London, 1900)

Jones, F. Warner, **Treatise on the Theoretical and Practical Construction of the Tricycle** (London, 1884)

Kron, Karl, **Ten Thousand Miles on a Bicycle** (Karl Kron, New York, 1887)

Leechman, G. D., **Safety Cycling** (London, 1895)

Lightwood, J. T., **The Romance of the Cyclists' Touring Club** (C.T.C., London, 1928)

Mecredy, R. J., and Wilson, A. J., **The Art and Pastime of Cycling** (Iliffe, London, 1895)

'Member of the O.B.C.', **Bicycle Riding, Its Theory and Practice** (Ward, Lock & Co., London, 1878)

Nauticus, **Nauticus in Scotland** (London, 1888)

Nauticus on his Hobby Horse (London, 1880)

Palmer, A. J., **Riding High** (London, 1958)

Papanek, V., **Design for the Real World** (Thames & Hudson, London, 1972)

Pemberton, A. C., and others, **The Complete Cyclist** (London, 1897)

Pennell, J. and E., **A Canterbury Pilgrimage** (London, 1885)
Peterborough Development Corporation, **Cycleways** (Peterborough, 1973)
Pratt, C., **The American Bicycler** (Cambridge, Mass. 1879)
Ray, Alan J., **Cycling: Land's End to John-o'-Groats** (Pelham Books, London, 1971)
Rennert, J., **100 Years of Bicycle Posters** (Hart-Davis, MacGibbon, London, 1973)
Richardson, Sir B. W., **The Tricycle in Relation to Health** (London, 1885)
Scott, Robert P., **Cycling Art, Energy and Locomotion** (Philadelphia, 1889)
Sharp, A., **Bicycles and Tricycles. An elementary treatise on their design and construction** (London, 1896)
Spencer, Charles, **The Bicycle: Its Use and Action** (Frederick Warne, London, 1870) **The Modern Bicycle** (London, 1876)
Stables, Dr G. W., **Health upon Wheels** (London, 1887)
Starley, W. **The Life and Inventions of James Starley** (Coventry, 1902)
Stevens, T., **Around the World on a Bicycle** (London, 1887)
Sturmey, H., **Indispensable Bicyclists' Handbook** (Coventry, 1878 et seq.) **Indispensable Tricyclists' Handbook** (London, 1881 et seq.)
Swann, R., **Days of Davies** (U.S.A., 1968) **The Life and Times of Charlie Barden** (Wynlap Publications, London, 1965)
'Velox', **Velocipedes, Bicycles and Tricycles: How to Make and How to Use Them** (Routledge, London, 1869; reprinted by S. R. Publishers Ltd, East Ardley, Wakefield, Yorks.)
Wagenvoord, J., **Bikes and Riders** (Van Nostrand, Reinhold Co., New York, 1973)
Wallis-Taylor A. J., **Modern Cycles, Their Repair and Construction** (London, 1897)
Wells, H. G., **The Wheels of Chance** (London, 1st edn, 1896)
Whitt, F. R., 'A note on the Estimation of the Energy Expenditure of Sporting Cyclists' **Ergonomics,** vol. XIV (London, 1971), no. 3
Wilson, A. J., **The Pleasures, Objects and Advantages of Cycling** (London, 1887)
Wilson, S. S., 'Bicycle Technology', **Scientific American** (March 1973)
'Working Mechanic, A', **The Modern Velocipede: Its History, and Construction** (George Maddick, London, 1869)
Woodforde, J., **The Story of the Bicycle** (Routledge & Kegan Paul, London, 1970)

Periodicals

Bicycle Journal (London, 1876–8)
Bicycling News (Birmingham, 1876–1900)
Bicycling Times (London, 1877–83)
Cycling (Newcastle upon Tyne, 1876–80)
Cycling (London, 1891–1974)
Cyclist (London, 1879–1902)
Cyclist Annual and Year Book, ed. H. Sturmey (London, 1882–1900)
Cyclists' Touring Club Gazette (London, 1880–1974)
Engineer (London, 1868–70, for velocipedes)
English Mechanic and Mirror of Science, Engineering, Buildings, Inventions, Electricity, Photography, Chemistry etc. (London, 1865–70, for velocipedes)
Hub (London, 1896–9)
Ixion – A Journal of Velocipeding, Athletics and Aerostatics (London, 1875)
Lady Cyclist and Wheelwoman (London, 1895–9)
Mechanics' Magazine, Museum, Register, Journal and Gazette (London, 1823–72)
Rational Dress Society's Gazette
Tricyclist (London and Coventry, 1882–5)
Vélocipède Illustré (Paris, 1869)
Velocipedist (New York, February 1st, 1869)
Wheel World (London, 1880–86)
Wheeling (London, 1884–1901)

INDEX

ADAMS, J. H., 126-7
'Aellopodes', 28 illus, 33, 40
Albert, Prince, velocipede built for, 44 illus
Albone, Dan, 117 illus, 130-31
America:
    bicycle boom in, 10
    velocipede in, 46 & illus, 60 illus, 61-6, 101 illus, 102-3
Appleyard, Mr, 129
'Ariel' bicycle, 82 illus, 95, 96, 104-5, 151 & illus
'Arrow' tricycle, 108 illus
Artamonov, E. M., 54

BADDELEY, WILLIAM, 33 & illus, 34
Bamboo bicycle, 171 illus
Bate, Henry, 124
Beale, John, 125
Bicycle-based machines, use for, 178
Bicycle bush ambulance, 178 & illus
Bicycle clubs, 81 illus, 86-9, 90, 91, 107 illus
    Biggar, 132 illus
    Boston (U.S.A.), 82
    Cambridge University, 89, 98
    Catford, 134-5
    Coventry Lady Cyclists', 156
    'Facile', 126
    Liverpool Velocipede, 72
    Middlesex, 72, 96
    North London, 168 illus
    Pickwick, 86, 87
    Rabbits & Sons, 137 illus
    St Helens, 138
    San Francisco, 82, 83
    Trafalgar, 85
Bicycle Touring Club, 86-7, 98, 113 See also Cyclists' Touring Club
Bicycle Union, 86
'Bicyclette', 124, 125 illus
Bidlake, F. T., 117 illus, 138
Birmingham Small Arms Company, 129 & illus
Blanchard, M., 17
Blood, William, 104
Boneshaker:
    American, 102
    English, 46, 102
    French, 46, 47, 102
    mechanical difficulties, 46, 61 illus, 94, 123
    tricycle, 100, 102, 104
    upper-class interest in, 75 illus
    velocipede, competition with, 46, 121
    wheels, 61 illus, 77 illus, 94, 95, 131
Booth's Cycle Agency, Dublin, 132
Bottomley-Firth, J. F., 20 illus, 76, 104, 148, 149
Bowden cable-operated brake, 165
Bown, William, 97 illus
'British Facilitator, or Travelling Car', 31 & illus

CAREY BROTHERS, 104
Carrier machine, 112 illus, 113 illus
Carroll, J., 56
Cartwright, Dr Edmund, 31
Castera, André, 59 illus
'Celeremane', 47 illus
Céléripède, 16 illus, 18 See also Vélocifère
Cheylesmore 'sociable' tricycle, 110 illus
China, cycling & tricycling in, 176, 177 illus, 178
Choice, Jessie, 152
'Chopper' bicycle, 174, 177
City Bicycle School, 86 illus
Cobb, Mr, 98
Collapsible tricycle, 116
Cooper, Fred, 94, 97
Cortis, H. L., 97-8
Coventry Lever Tricycle, 105 & illus
Coventry Machinists' Company:
    'Gentleman's' bicycle, 90
    largest cycle maker, 98
    Ordinary bicycle, 151 illus
    tricycle, 109, 110 illus
    velocipede, 70, 72, 74
'Cripper' tricycle, 116
Cripps, R., 116
'Crocodile', 124 See also 'Bicyclette'
Crypto 'Bantam' bicycle, 166
Cyclists' battalion, 133
Cyclists' Touring Club:
    change of name, 86
    club uniform recommended by, 87

complaints about roads, 131
danger boards erected by, 142 illus
Gazette, 125, 127
hotels & restaurants, 118
'Kangaroo' recommended by, 127
legal aid by, 162
membership increase, 136

DALZELL, GAVIN, 37
Dana, Charles, 66
Dandy-horse, 21, 23 *See also* Hobby-horse
Davidson, Lillias Campbell, 161-2
Dean, Josiah, 83 illus
Denmark, popularity of cycle in, 174
Devey, J. & Company, 90
Dineur, Louis-Joseph, 18
Dodgson, Wilfred, 52 illus, 53
Drais, Baron Karl von:
   Draisienne, inventor of, 18 & illus, 19 & illus, 20, 26
   'Improved Velocipede', 27 & illus
   Niepce as rival, 20
Dreuze, M., 32-3
Dunlop Company, 132, 136, 142
Dursley Pedersen bicycle, 166, 168 illus, 170 illus
Dutrieux, Mlle, 166 illus

ELLIS & COMPANY, 125, 126 & illus
Elswick bicycle, 166 illus
Engers, Alf, 173 illus
England, velocipede in 31-4, 39-46, 66-77

'FACILE' SAFETY BICYCLE, 125, 126 & illus, 127, 129, 130
Fairfield, Geoffrey, 83 illus
Findlater, John, 35
Fischer, Philipp, 54
France, velocipede in, 16-20, 46, 47, 48, 53-61, 102
'Frank's Mechanical Horse', 34 illus
Frazer, John Foster, 142

GEE, MR, 85
'Gentleman's' bicycle, 90
Germany, velocipede in, 54
Goddard, J. T., 61, 62, 63, 66, 148
Goddard, Mr, 48
Gompertz, Louis, 29, 30 & illus
Gormully & Jeffery Mfg. Co., 156 illus
Grew, W., 132, 136
Griffin, H. H., 98
Grose gearcase, 142
Grout, W. H. J., 78, 94, 108 illus
Guilmet, André, 122

HANLON BROTHERS, 62, 64 illus, 65
Hautsch, Jean, 16
Haynes & Jefferis, 95, 105
Hedges, K. W., 69 illus
Hemming, Richard, 49 illus
Hillier, G. Lacy, 158

Hillman, Herbert & Cooper, 114 illus, 116 illus, 127, 128, 131
Hillman, William, 72, 94, 95, 127, 130
Hobby-horse, 14, 20-26, 29, 62, 147
Hodgson, Henry Hill, 42 illus, 43
Holbein. M. A., 131
Hooley, Terah, 136
Hooper, William, 16, 17 illus
Howard, Alfred, 53
Humber Company:
   Hooley, bought by, 136
   racer bicycle, 97 illus
   safety bicycle, 129 & illus, 131
   tandem, 113 illus
   tricycle ('Cripper'), 116
Hume, W., 132
Hutchings, Mr, 98

INTERNATIONAL VELOCIPEDE & LOCO-MACHINE CONFERENCE, 75
'Ivel' safety bicycle, 130-31

JACKSON, W., 102 illus, 103
Jefferson, Robert L., 136 illus, 142
Johnson, Denis, 14, 20, 21 & illus, 22, 147
Johnson, L. H., 83 illus

'KANGAROO' BICYCLE, 117 illus, 120, 127-9, 130
'Kapok' bicycle, 178
Kech, Karl, 54
Keen, John, 97
Keen, William, 88
Kelly, W. S., 128 illus
Kimball Brothers, 62
Kimber, Sir Henry, 119 illus
Kron, Karl, 66

LADIES' BICYCLES, 42, 104-51, 151 illus, 155 & illus, 166 illus, 168 illus; tricycles, 45 illus, 147
Lady Cyclists' Association, 156, 161
Lady's Accelerator, 146 illus *See also* Pilentum
Lady's Carriage, 42
Lagrange, M., 26-7
Lallement, Pierre, 55, 56, 57, 62
Lawson, Henry J., 103 illus, 123 & illus, 124, 125 illus
Leicester Cycle Company, 139 illus
Leopold, Prince, rides boneshaker, 74, 75 illus
Lesclide, Richard, 61
Locomotive carriage, passenger-propelled, 34 & illus
Love, Mabel, 166 illus
Lovelace, R. S., 155 illus, 157 illus

McCALL, THOMAS, 35 illus, 36, 37-8
McCammon, H., 129
MacDonald's Adjustable Bicycle, 61 illus, 62
Macmillan, Kirkpatrick, 34, 35 & illus, 36-9,

Manumotive Exercising Carriage, 33 & illus
Markham, Arthur, 72
Marriott, Thomas, 94
Mayall, John, 70, 71, 72
Mecredy, R. J., 132
Meldrum, Mr, 48
Mercer & Monod, 62
Merryweather, Richard, 33 & illus
Meyer, M., 122
Michaux, Ernest, 54 & illus, 59, 60
Michaux, Pierre:
    decline & death, 61
    Draisienne, modifies, 54
    Lallement, dispute with, 55, 56
    velocipede pioneer, 54 illus, 56-7, 62, 67-8, 122
Mills, G. P., 131
Monocycle, 60, 99 illus
Moore, George, 94 illus, 107 illus, 112 illus, 120, 153 illus
Moore, James, 59 & illus, 60, 97
Moulton, Alex, 167

'NEEDHAM' SAFETY TRICYCLE, 100
'New World' Pleasure Velocipede, 67 illus
Niepce, Claude, 20
Niepce, Joseph-Nicéphore, 20
'Norfolk' bicycle, 122 illus, 123

OLIVIER FRERES, 57, 61
Ordinary bicycle:
    America, in, 82-3, 83 illus, 84 illus, 102-3
    clubs, 86-9, 90
    France, in, 87 illus
    legal & statutory pressures on, 84-5, 98
    mechanical drawbacks, 92-3, 99, 102, 122, 125, 150-1
    prices, 90
    racing & record-breaking with, 87 illus, 94 illus, 96-8
    technical improvement, 94-6, 99, 124, 125-9
    tricycles & safeties, challenge from, 95 illus, 99, 108 illus, 129
    two-speed, 124
'Osborne' tricycle, 106 illus
Ovenden, Mr, 16
Ozanam, J., 16

PARVIN, ELLEN, 151 illus
Patence, Mr, 17
Pearce, Mr, 99 illus
Pecquer, Onesime, 106
Pedalcar, 179 illus
Pedestrian curricle, 21, 32 *See also* Hobby-horse
Pedomotive carriage, 31, 32 & illus, 33 & illus
'Peregrine' bicycle, 139 illus
Perry (chainmaker), 142
Peyton & Peyton, 123

'Phantom' bicycle, 75, 76 & illus, 94
Pickering's American velocipede, 60 illus, 61, 62, 68, 72; ladies' model, 148
Pilentum, 146 illus, 147
Pneumatic tyre, 117 illus, 132, 133, 136 illus, 139 illus
Pope Manufacturing Company, 82, 83 illus
Pratt, Charles, 83 illus
'Premier' bicycle, 114 illus, 116 illus, 130
'Psycho' ladies' bicycle, 155; tricycle, 116

'QUADRANT' TRICYCLE, 114 illus, 118
Quadricycle, 60, 105, 106-8, 129

RACING & RECORD-BREAKING:
    England, in, 86 illus, 96-8, 126-7, 143 illus, 173 illus
    France, in, 59 & illus, 60-1, 87 illus, 148 illus, 149
    hobby-horse, 22-4
    Kangaroo-type bicycle, 128-9
    Ordinary bicycle, 87 illus, 94 illus, 97-8, 126-7
    Safety bicycle, 120, 130, 131, 142
    tricycle, 117 illus
    women, by, 59, 148 illus, 149, 154, 156-8, 166 illus
Racing bicycle 40, 90, 97 illus, 116 illus, 130; velocipede 40, 41
Raleigh (Cycle) Company, 136, 174, 177
Revis, Mr, 28 illus, 33
Reynolds & Mays, 75, 94
Reynolds, Tessie, 156, 157 & illus, 158
Richard, Dr Elie, 16, 17 illus
Riding-schools:
    hobby-horse, 21 illus, 22
    velocipede, 57 & illus, 58, 63-4, 69, 74
Rogers, Mr, 31
Rotary tricycle, 109, 116, 119 illus
Rousseau (velocipede-maker), 57
'Rover' safety bicycle, 117 illus, 120, 127, 129-30, 131 & illus; ladies' model, 155
Rudge (also Rudge-Whitworth) Company, 94, 109, 115 illus, 116, 160 illus
Russian velocipede, 54

SAFETY BICYCLE, 120-43, 155, 156, 165-6
    alternative designs to, 166
    American, 128 illus
    chain-driven, 129 & illus, 130
    cross-framed, 130-31, 132 illus
    diamond-framed, 132 illus, 155
    early models, 103 illus, 122 & illus, 123 & illus, 124 & illus, 125 & illus
    French claim on, 122
    pneumatic-tyred, 132, 136 & illus, 139 illus, 142, 165
    racing & record-breaking with, 120, 126-7, 130, 131, 142
    rear-driven, 129, 130
    women's, 129, 166 illus
Salamon, Mr, 98

Salisbury, Mr, 68
'Salvo' (later 'Royal Salvo') cycles, 102 illus, 106-8, 110, 115, 123
Samuel & Peace, 61, 68, 72
Sargent, William P. & Company, 62
Sawyer, Willard, 38 illus, 39-46
Shearing, Frederick W., 122 illus, 123
Shergold, Thomas, 124 & illus
Shorland, Frank (record-breaker), 138
Side-saddle machines, 150 & illus, 151 illus
Signal Fork Cyclometer, 142
Simpson Lever Chain Company, 166 illus
Simpson, Tommy, 173 illus
Singer 'Xtraordinary' bicycle, 125 & illus, 126, 127, 129; tricycle, 103 illus
Sivrac, M. de, 17
Skeffington, Hon. J. C., 42-3
Small-wheeled bicycle, 167
Smith, George, 120, 128, 130
Smith, Stephen W., 62
Smythe, B., 31 & illus
Smythe, F., 97
Snook, W., 126
Snoxell & Spencer, 70, 72, 73
'Sociable':
   dividable, 116
   quadricycle, 105
   tricycle, 110 illus, 116, 117-8, 119 illus, 151
   velocipede, 40
   women riding, 117, 151, 152 illus
Sparrow, Thomas, 96
Spencer, Charles, 70, 71, 72, 85 illus, 96
Stanley Bicycle Show, 124, 129, 136
Stanton, David, 97
'Star' bicycle, 128 illus
Starley Brothers, 106 illus, 155
Starley, James:
   'Ariel', introduction of, 82 illus, 95, 96, 104-5, 151 & illus
   business dealings, 68, 69
   inventive genius, 70, 111
   pioneer rider, 72, 94, 102 illus
   tricycles, production of, 104, 105-8, 116, 123
   wheel development by, 95-6, 104
Starley, John Kemp, 129-30, 131, 142, 155, 165
Starley & Smith, 82 illus, 95
Stevens, Thomas, 142
Straw, Mr, 125
Sturmey, Henry, 108, 114, 116
Sturmey-Archer Company, 165
Sutton, William, 129, 130

TANDEM:
   bicycle, 117 illus, 140 illus, 159, 172 illus
   'lady-front', 155
   roadster, 114 illus
   sidecar, with, 172 illus
   tricycle, 106 illus, 109, 113 illus, 116, 133, 159

Tangent & Coventry Tricycle Company, 124
Tangent wheel system, 95-6
'Tension' Bicycle & 'Arrow' Tricycle Company, 108 illus
'Tension' wheel, 82 illus, 95
Théson, Jean, 16
Thévenon, M., 60-61
Thomas, Samuel Webb, 150 & illus, 151
Tribout & Meyer, 57
Tricycle, 100-19, 132, 151-4
   America, in, 101 illus, 102, 108, 152 illus
   boneshaker, 100, 102, 104
   carrier, 112 illus, 113 illus
   collapsible, 116
   pneumatic-tyred, 117 illus, 132
   racing & record-breaking with, 117 illus, 118
   rotary, 109, 119 illus
   'sociable', 110 illus
   tandem, 109, 113 illus, 116, 133
   velocipede, 45 illus, 101 illus, 147
   women riding, 108, 147, 151-4
Truffault, Jules, 57
Turner, Josiah, 68, 69
Turner, Rowley, 68-9, 70-71, 72, 74

Vélocifère, 17 & illus, 18
Velocipede, 31-77
   advertising, 73
   books about, 72 & illus, 76
   clubs, 58
   early invention, 16-20, 29-34
   Macmillan, development by, 34-9, 121
   racing with, 58-61, 65-6, 72
   riding-schools, 57 & illus, 58, 63 & illus, 64
   Russian, 54
   tricycle, 45 illus, 101-4
   women riding, 42, 45 illus, 51 illus, 147-9, 150 & illus
'Velox', 103, 104
Victoria, Queen, interest in tricycling, 110, 151

WARD, J., COACHBUILDER, 44 illus
Warman, F. J., 151 illus
Weed Sewing Machine Company, 83 illus
Weston, Frank, 83 illus
'Whippet' bicycle, 131, 137 illus
Whitty, Calvin, 62
Wilcox, H. F., 43-6
Williams, Mr, 34 & illus
Wilson, A. J., 117 illus
Wilson, Stuart, 169-71
Wiseman, Thomas, 122 & illus, 123
Women and the bicycle, 144-63, 166 illus, 167 illus, 168 illus
Wood Brothers, 62
Wood's Wire Saddles, 142
'Working Man's Friend' (bicycle), 90

'XTRAORDINARY' BICYCLE, 125, 126, 127, 129
   See also Singer